THE TORCH

OF THE

TESTIMONY

THE TORCH
OF THE
TESTIMONY

John Kennedy

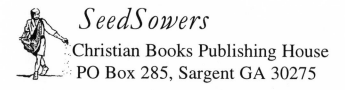

SeedSowers

Christian Books Publishing House
PO Box 285, Sargent GA 30275

© GOSPEL LITERATURE SERVICE

First published October 1965

Reprinted
by
Christian Books
by permission
of the author

Printed in the United States of America.

CONTENTS

PREFACE

In these days, particularly in the West, there is a fervid urge towards what is called 'communication'. "We must communicate," is the cry of the would-be dispenser of learning. Not so long ago I was interested to read an article on this subject in a well-known journal. At the end of the article, the writer asked the simple question, "Why?" That familiar monosyllable seems to leave not an inconsiderable number of 'communicationists' stammering for words. There is a grave danger that knowledge should be an end in itself, practically divorced from the art of living.

"For whatsoever things were written aforetime were written for our learning, that through patience and through comfort of the Scriptures we might have hope." These are the words of the apostle Paul to the Romans (Rom. 15:4). The history of the Old Testament was not written for us only that we might know, but that we might learn from the experience of those who have gone on before, lessons which will vitally affect our daily living and order the progress of our spiritual walk. The great need of the present day is not for more knowledge, theological or historical, but that what knowledge we have should be practically related to life.

The writer of a book of this nature owes a tremendous debt to others, for it inevitably contains so little that is truly original, and so much that is the fruit of others' research. The following chapters, therefore, do not profess to contain any fresh light on the details of historical events. They contain little with which anyone acquainted with the general course of Church history will not already be familiar. The purpose of this book is to set down, as far as possible, the implications for us, in the circumstances of the late twentieth century, of what God has been doing over the past two thousand years. If we agree that we can legitimately learn anything from the spiritual experience of others, surely we have much to learn from the triumphs and defeats of the past.

It is the reader's prerogative to judge whether or not the conclusions which have been drawn in the forthcoming pages are justified. Some may disagree, and disagree strongly, with the writer's deductions, but this book will have served its purpose if it stimulates honest thought on a very important subject, and encourages a desire to learn and obey what God has to say from the pages of history.

In seeking to trace the course of the spiritual movement of the church, it is evident that, within the limited compass of this present work, it has been possible to give but a selection of the ways in which the Spirit of God has sought to accomplish His purpose down through the ages. It is hoped, however, that this brief survey will be a sufficient indication of divine principles which are as important today as they were in the days of the church's infancy.

Any study which sets out to draw theological lessons from historical facts is bound to run into difficulties over terminology. Terms which, used in a purely Scriptural context, mean one thing, often, in a historical context, mean something quite different. The word 'church', which largely indicates the subject of this book, is a case in point. Its use, therefore, has not been confined to its strict, Biblical sense. An attempt has been made to obviate the confusion which might result from the broad use of the word by using Church, with a capital 'C', to indicate highly organized, historic Christianity, while church, with a small 'c' has generally been used in other places. But even this is by no means a complete answer to the difficulty. If the reader is sometimes perplexed why one form is used in preference to the other, it may be indicative of little more than the same perplexity in the mind of the writer. The context, together with whatever form of the word is used in a particular place should, however, always make the meaning clear.

The short bibliography at the end has the particular aim of seeking to encourage a start on further reading by those whose desire might be stimulated by the following chapters to know more. The books in the list are, therefore, in the main, easily available and readable.

Scripture quotations are given throughout in the Revised Version unless otherwise stated.

The history of the church is an account of man's reaction to the Word of God. It shows the result both of obedience and disobedience. It is the prayer of the writer that, above all else, this book may be the means of some entering a walk of closer obedience to the Living and Eternal Word.

Guntur   JOHN KENNEDY
March 1964

CHAPTER ONE

THE FOUNDATION

"THINK not that I came to destroy the law or the prophets : I came not to destroy, but to fulfil" (Matt. 5 : 17). "God, having of old time spoken unto the fathers in the prophets by divers portions and in divers manners, hath at the end of these days spoken unto us in his Son" (Heb. 1 : 1-2). Thus Scripture establishes the relationship between the work of Christ and the Old Testament. The revelation of the New Testament is but the fulfilment of the Old. Any account of the emergence and growth of the church, therefore, must begin with the nation Israel through which the church was born.

For generations the Temple and the priestly ministrations had been the centre of Jewish life, but with the coming of the One in whom all these things were to find their fulfilment, the old Temple order lost its significance. There existed, however, alongside the Temple, an institution which, in the time of our Lord, exercised a vital influence among the Jews, and which was to become increasingly the centre of national life. This institution was the synagogue. From the destruction of the Temple by the Romans in A.D. 70, the preservation of the Jews as a distinct race is probably due more to the power of the synagogue than to any other single factor, and it was the synagogue that pre-eminently formed the link between the church and Judaism in the early days of the church's life.

The exact origin of the synagogue is unknown, but it probably dates back to the Babylonian exile when it provided the Jews with a partial substitute for the Temple worship. On the return from captivity the ministry of the synagogue seems to have been perpetuated by Ezra, a man raised up of God to meet the need of the hour in bringing the law back into its place of rightful prominence among the people. "Ezra had set his heart to seek the law of the Lord, and to do it, and to teach in Israel statutes and judgments" (Ezra 7 : 10). Nehemiah ch. 8 gives a clear account of how this was actually carried out. "They read in the book, in the law of God, distinctly; and they gave the sense, so that they understood the reading" (Neh. 8 : 8). Here

1

then was the basic ministry of the synagogue, the exposition of the Word of God, and from this stemmed the functions of which the synagogue was later to be the centre, the spread of learning among the people, and the administration of justice in the Jewish community. The centrality of God's Word in the life of the synagogue was, and still is symbolized in the ark containing the Scriptures which is placed in the centre of each synagogue, and the desk beside it from which the Scriptures are read and expounded.

Ezra was also the founder of the order of the Scribes, that sect of Judaism which was so virulently opposed to our Lord and earned His withering condemnation. In fact the interpretation of the law was the purpose of the Scribes' existence, and although, as a party, they did not occupy a place of particular authority in the synagogue, their ministry was that upon the life of the synagogue was based. It is obvious that the Scribes often occupied leading positions in the synagogue administration as individuals. Our Lord remarked how they loved the 'chief seats', referring to the places which were set apart for the synagogue elders (Matt. 23 : 6). It is important, therefore, to understand Christ's attitude to the function of the Scribes in order to understand His attitude towards the function of the synagogue, whether He recognised it as an institution divinely established, or simply as a human expedient outside the order of God. His summing up of the Scribes is unequivocal. " The Scribes and the Pharisees sit on Moses' seat : All things therefore whatsoever they bid you, these do and observe : but do not ye after their works; for they say, and do not " (Matt. 23 : 2-3). He recognised the function with which they had been commissioned as from God, but also recognised that, over the years, they had forsaken the spirit for the letter. Ideally, they were the mediators of God's Word to the people as was Moses in an earlier age, and this function as enshrined in the institution of the synagogue was one upon which the Lord set His seal.

Both Christ and the apostles made it their practice to frequent the synagogue wherever they went, and they enjoyed the customary liberty of ministry. In Nazareth, we read of our Lord that, " He entered, as His custom was, into the synagogue on the sabbath day, and stood up to read " (Luke 4 : 16). Of Paul and Barnabas in the synagogue at Antioch of Pisidia it is recorded that the rulers sent unto them with the invitation, " Brethren, if ye have any word of exhortation, say on " (Acts 13 : 15). The apostles took full advantage of the opportunity

2

to present Christ as He was, the fulfilment of the Old Testament Scriptures.

When it is considered how widespread the synagogues were, and their influence among the Gentiles as well as among the Jews, it is very evident how well the Spirit had prepared the ground for the preaching of the Gospel in the initial stages of the establishing of the churches. The Jews of the dispersion were possessed of a profound sense of their unique mission in *Is. 66* the world, and assiduously proclaimed the true God among the heathen. As a result, great numbers of Gentiles were brought into the light of Old Testament revelation. An important factor in this work was the translation, in the third century B.C. of the Hebrew Scriptures into the Greek of what we now know as the Septuagint. Greek was the lingua franca of the known world, and even among the Jews in the time of Christ had largely replaced Hebrew in common life. The centres of this propagation of the Word of God were the synagogues which sprung up wherever Jewish communities existed. In Jerusalem alone there were well over four hundred. James aptly remarked, " Moses from generations hath in every city them that preach him, being read in the synagogues every sabbath " (Acts 15 : 21).

In the heyday of Greek and Roman culture the Jewish way of life had a definite appeal to many. The Greeks and the Romans were polytheists and idolaters. Their god was amoral, and many of their religious practices were, therefore, immoral. This sensuous worship of sensuous divinities found its expression in the great heathen temples which were centres of profligacy, the temple of Aphrodite at Corinth, for example, and the temple of Artemis at Ephesus. The Jewish communities provided a stark contrast to the religious debauchery which was the order of the day, and many who were sick at heart with this mixture of high sounding, philosophic confusion and heathen squalor turned to the one source which seemed to provide something different. Surely the least that truth can do is to encourage a decent way of life, and this decent way of life they found among the Jews. There they learned that God was One and holy, and that He expected holiness to be a mark of those who followed Him. True, this revelation had been particularly confided to the Jewish race, but others might also share its benefits by entering the community as proselytes.

Proselytes were of two orders, " Proselytes of Righteousness," and " Proselytes of the Gate." The former were obliged to undergo the rites of circumcision and baptism, undertook to

3

obey all the observations of Jewish law, and received all the privileges of a born Jew (cf. Ex. 13 : 43-49. Num. 15 : 14-16). The latter had a much looser, yet none the less vital attachment to the Jewish community. They were not circumcised, and probably not baptized, neither were they bound by the ceremonial observances of the law, but they worshipped regularly in the synagogue, and were bound by the moral precepts of the law which the Jews regarded as binding on all mankind. Some other markedly Jewish practices they also observed in varying degrees, such as abstinence from eating certain kinds of flesh and from work on the sabbath day. In the Acts of the Apostles these people are referred to as ' devout men ' or those ' that fear God ' (Acts 8 : 2; 10 : 2, 35; 13 : 16, 26; 17 : 4, 17 22 : 12). The centurion who came to see Jesus, asking healing for his servant was, in all probability, one of these ' devout men ' (Luke 7 : 5).

The important point to notice for the purpose of the present discussion is that here was a large community both of Jews and Gentiles, possessed of the light that God's revelation had then given to men, prepared of the Spirit for the proclamation of the Gospel as it was fulfilled in Christ. It was almost entirely from these that the believers in the early churches were drawn.

We must now turn our attention briefly to the pattern of the synagogue. If the institution of the synagogue itself was of God, it follows that the basic pattern given for its development was also dictated by divine wisdom. It has already been shown how the spread of the synagogues was probably due, under God, to Ezra. At the commencement of Ezra's public ministry on the return from captivity he is found in company together with thirteen other men amongst whom it would appear he was first among equals (Nehemiah 8 : 4). This may well be the first Scriptural indication of the synagogue eldership. In the New Testament they are variously called ' elders ' and ' rulers ' (cf. Matt. 16 : 21 Acts 13 : 15 Mark 5 : 22 Acts 4 : 5). All were equal, but one was recognised as spokesman of the group. Jairus, for example, whose daughter our Lord raised to life, may have functioned in this capacity (Mark 5 : 22, 35, 38). There appears to have been no precise rule as to their number, but, at least at a later period, no synagogue was instituted in any place unless there were ten such men who could exercise the oversight. This group was responsible for choosing someone, either from among themselves or elsewhere, competent to read and expound the Scriptures during the sabbath worship, the duty in which our Lord was engaged on the notable occasion recorded in Luke

4 : 16-22. Verse twenty of this passage also mentions 'the attendant' whose chief office was the custody of the sacred rolls of Scripture and who also not infrequently acted as school-master. The elders of the synagogue also formed a local san-hedrin, the counterpart on a much more restricted level of the Great Sanhedrin at Jerusalem which was the final court of appeal throughout Jewry and had jurisdiction in matters both civil and spiritual. Qualifications for eldership were high and strictly adhered to. All were required to be married, beyond the age of thirty, instructed in the Scriptures, and bearing a godly testimony. These qualifications quite possibly form the basis of the conditions laid down for eldership in the church as recorded by Paul in his letter to Timothy (1 Timothy 3 : 1-7).

The significance of the synagogue to the emergence of the church is obvious. It did, in fact, bridge the gap between the Temple and the church in the transition from the pure symbol ism of the former to the spiritual reality of the latter. There are four respects in which the likeness of the church to the synagogue is of particular note.

1. As in the life of the synagogue the Scriptures were central, so our Lord, the Word incarnate, is the centre of the church. "Where two or three are gathered together in my name," He said, "there am I in the midst of them" (Matt. 18 : 20). In these words our Lord established for all time the principle of His Headship in the assembly.

2. The relationship of 'devout men' and Jews in the syna-gogue brought to the fore much more vividly than it had ever been possible in the old Temple order the fact that God's purpose was not confined to one race, but extended to all men. The essence of the church is that Christ dwells in the midst as Head over a new, spiritual race in which every earthly barrier has been completely and once for all shattered (cf. Eph. 2 : 13-22).

3. Both synagogue and church were governed by a plurality of elders. The existence of the synagogue eldership is not, of itself, conclusive proof of the pattern that found place in the churches, but it is a significant indication of God's mind, and this indication is well substantiated from Scrip-ture and the practice which pertained in the churches of apostolic times.

4. The synagogue was a centre of worship and instruction, and its life was a powerful testimony to the Gentile world, the means of bringing many non-Jews into the light of

5

B

divine revelation. Thus also the fellowship of the church is basic both to the building up of God's people and to their witness in the world. The New Testament gives a place of prime importance to the assembly in the fulfilment of God's purposes. It is no doubt for this reason that the church has been the focus of satanic stratagem and attack down through the centuries.

Against this background of the Jewish synagogue we must look at the beginnings of the church itself.

The day of Pentecost saw Jerusalem crowded with visitors, Jews and proselytes from both within and without the boundaries of the Roman Empire to offer the traditional thanksgiving to God for the bounties of a full harvest. Luke, in his account of the day in Acts 2 describes how, according to the promise of the Lord to His disciples, the Spirit was revealed establishing the presence of Christ in the midst of His people, and founding that divine community upon the earth, the church. On the declaration of Christ as the fulfilment of all the law and the prophets there were immediately added unto the church some three thousand who 'continued steadfastly in the apostles' teaching and fellowship, in the breaking of bread and the prayers' (Acts 2 : 42). That those who believed at once became witnesses for Christ is attested by the fact that God continued to add unto the church daily (Acts 2 : 47), and there can be no doubt, as many returned to the far-flung corners of the Roman Empire and beyond, they carried with them the testimony of a new life and boldness from their encounter with the Christ. Subsequent persecution, in further scattering the disciples abroad, also helped forward the rapid dissemination of the Word of Life. "They therefore that were scattered abroad went about preaching the word" (Acts 8 : 4).

Most of what is known of the early expansion of the Gospel is confined to its spread within the Roman Empire. This is the chief concern of Luke's history in the Acts as he traces the workings of the Spirit from its Palestine beginning Romeward from Jerusalem. There are, of course, suggestions of a much wider movement, in the constitution of the Pentecost crowd for example, some of whom, as we have already noticed, came from beyond the jurisdiction of Rome, "Parthians and Medes and Elamites, and the dwellers in Mesopotamia" (Acts 2 : 9), all of whom were subjects of the Parthian Empire on the other side of the river Euphrates. Then there was the Ethiopian official of the court of Candace who, returning home from Jerusalem

6

was met by Philip and baptized on his confession of faith, Philip having preached Christ to him from the Scripture on which he had been meditating, Isaiah 53 (Acts 8 : 26-39). It cannot be doubted that such people were the means, to some extent, of the Gospel's wider penetration both East and South.

And what of the apostles themselves? It is, in some ways, surprising how little is known of the career of the twelve after Pentecost. The lives of Peter, and of the brothers James and John can be reconstructed from historical evidence with a fair degree of certainty, but of the others practically nothing is known apart from the multitudinous legends which have grown up around their names. There is no reason to believe that they remained inactive and unknown in Jerusalem, so it is to be presumed that they travelled abroad in the preaching of the Gospel. There is strong tradition associating both Thomas and Bartholomew with India, and it may well be that, under God, India owes its first contact with the Gospel to them. The Christian community in South-West India, the State known today as Kerala, is of undoubted antiquity. When Pantaenus, the head of the great catachumens' school at Alexandria, visited this part of India about A.D. 180 he found Christianity there already established and possessing what was supposed to be a Gospel of Matthew in the Hebrew script. The message of the cross, therefore, must have penetrated to India at a very early date, and it is no more difficult to associate the two apostles with this ministry than it is to suppose that the preaching of Christ was brought by others.

But what of those who remained in Jerusalem after the revelation of the Spirit, the first church? On the one hand, they maintained their association with the traditional Jewish community while, on the other, they met in their own homes to remember the Lord Jesus in the breaking of bread as He had commanded them, for mutual exhortation, fellowship and united prayer (Acts 2 : 42, 46; 4 : 23-24, etc.). This two-fold relationship, however, was soon to suffer a severe jolt and a shaking which was ultimately destined to sever the connection of the church with orthodox Judaism entirely. As it was, the relationship was precarious enough with the apostles' insistence on continuing to preach Christ, one whom the Jews had officially condemned, but they were not without their sympathisers, and a most influential voice of wisdom and caution was raised in their favour by Gamaliel, a Pharisee and highly honoured doctor of the law (Acts 5 : 34-40). But this counsel of restraint and

7

open-mindedness to God's working was to be over-ruled by an event shortly to take place.

One of the believers in Jerusalem was a Greek speaking Jew named Stephen. We first meet Stephen as one of the seven deacons appointed to look after the needs of a section of the church which, it was alleged, was being unfairly neglected. It is soon apparent, however, that Stephen was also a gifted teacher and preacher with a particularly sharp, God-given insight into some of the implications of the Gospel as touching Jewish tradition (Acts 6 : 10). In one of the Jewish synagogues he preached a sermon which so stirred up the hot-head champions of Jewish orthodoxy, that he was seized and arraigned before the Sanhedrin on a charge of blasphemy.

The outline of Stephen's sermon is preserved for us in Acts 7. What was the main burden of his message? It was simply this, that the old, Jewish sacrificial order was destined from the beginning to pass away, and the time had now come for its departure. With the revelation of Christ, all the traditional trappings of the Temple had become obsolete, and there could be no reconciliation of the two orders. Life and tradition could not carry on side by side. Judaism as it was could not contain Christ; it would have to give way to Christ or die a spiritual death in isolation. Stephen points out that the transitory nature of the traditional, sacrificial system was symbolized in the impermanence of the tabernacle, and that the building of a permanent structure in the Temple was out of accord with God's ideal (Acts 7 : 44-50). It is true that God honoured the devotion with which the Temple was built, but it was, nevertheless, man's idea (1 Chron. 17 : 1), while the tabernacle was erected on the specific command of God Himself (Ex. 25 : 8).

It is noteworthy that there was one eminent disciple of Gamaliel whose devotion to his master did not extend to accepting his master's advice of moderation in dealing with the followers of Christ. That disciple's name was Saul. The sentence passed upon Stephen met with his full approval. "And Saul was consenting unto his death" (Acts 8 : 1). Saul, or Paul, as he was afterwards to be called, totally rejected Stephen's claim that Jesus was the Christ in whom all the law and the offerings were fulfilled, but he plainly recognised that, if Stephen's claim were fact, it would mean an end to all the tradition in which he had been nurtured, and for which he was so zealous. In the light of Saul of Tarsus' future ministry, it is of interest to see how, in his tacit compliance with the condemnation of Stephen, there was an awareness, probably shared at that time by few if any of the disciples themselves, that this new movement, the church, could not be confined within the limits of Judaism. Separation was inevitable.

Theoretically, it might be maintained that the synagogue could have become the church, but practically this was never the case. No doubt, as has already been shown, the synagogue, being free from the sacrificial ritual of the Temple and with the Scriptures as central to its life, was in a position to accept Christ as the fulfilment of the Word of God without having to undergo quite such a radical upheaval as such an acceptance would have occasioned in the life of the Temple, but it was never likely that a ruling majority of the synagogue adherents would accept this. Loyalty to the orthodox, Jewish tradition was too strong and too deep-seated to be thus rooted out. The Spirit of God had to move elsewhere to start on fresh and more free ground. We see here but the beginning of a pattern of events which is repeated over and over again through the history of the church. When that which is revealed of God is crystallized into a tradition, rigidly held and propagated with purely human energy, it becomes an impenetrable barrier to the truth. The life of the Spirit can never be confined within the framework of religious tradition. God is much greater than man's thoughts concerning Him, and the plant of the church grows best in a soil uncluttered by the pretty hedgerows of man's limited understanding.

Wow.

9

CHAPTER TWO

THE CHURCH ESTABLISHED

THE martyrdom of Stephen was the occasion of a fierce outbreak of persecution against the church. Luke tells us, "And
there arose on that day a great persecution against the church
which was in Jerusalem" (Acts 8 : 1). One of the main protagonists of this policy of oppression was Saul of Tarsus, and his
zeal to exterminate the followers of Christ, whom he considered
a threat to the existence of the Jewish order, led him to embark
upon a journey to Damascus, armed with a letter of authority
from the High Priest, to arrest the 'heretics' and bring them
before the court of the Sanhedrin in Jerusalem (Acts 9 : 1-2).
It was as he was approaching Damascus that he himself was
arrested by the One he was persecuting and became one of His
most ardent disciples (Acts 9 : 3-9).

The persecution following Stephen's death was the means of
scattering abroad many of the saints in Jerusalem. Some travelled as far as Pheonicia, Cyprus and Antioch, preaching the
Gospel, and in the latter city a few of the believers, 'men of
Cyprus and Cyrene,' were led of the Spirit into a ministry
which found a particular response in the hearts of the Greeks
(Acts 11 : 19-21). The strength of the newly formed assembly
at Antioch is indicated by the repetition of the phrase 'the
Lord' in Acts 11 : 21-24. Christ as Lord was the centre of their
gathering. We must remember that this phrase meant much
more in the early church than often appears in the glib repeti-
tions of the present day. 'Kurios', the Greek word rendered in
the English New Testament as 'Lord' was also the word used
in the Septuagint for 'Jehovah', the most authoritative and
often used of the names of the God of Israel in the Old Testament. The significance of the acceptance of this title as applying to Christ, therefore, can hardly be overestimated. It at once
placed Christ in a position of complete supremacy in the
assembly, a position which could not be usurped by any man.
And His right to this title is attested by Scripture itself. Paul,
for example, in writing to the Philippians, quotes the prophet
Isaiah, applying Isaiah's use of the title 'Lord' directly to Christ

10

(cf. Phil. 2 : 2 and Isa. 45 : 22-23). Bowing to the Lordship of Christ is the essence of salvation, and this attitude of submission is foundational to the whole life of the church. Wherever it exists the Lord has ground on which to work, even although understanding of His ways be rudimentary; where it is absent there can be no real church. *auth.*✱

News of the remarkable move at Antioch was not long in reaching the church at Jerusalem, and Barnabas was at once sent forth to explore the situation. A man of spiritual stature and insight, he was not slow to discern the work to be of the Holy Spirit, and set his mind to building up and strengthening the believers in the things of the Lord (Acts 11 : 22-24).

It is in Antioch that Paul once again comes into view. After his conversion, he boldly preached Christ in Damascus the place to which he had gone with the express purpose of persecuting the Christians, but had to flee the city when it was known that the Jews were bent on taking his life. Returning to Jerusalem, and seeking the fellowship of the church, he was received, not altogether unnaturally, with considerable fear and distrust, but Barnabas, who was in Damascus during Paul's stay, introduced him to the apostles as a brother in Christ and testified to what God had been doing through him. Once again, however, Paul's preaching stirred up angry feeling, and further attempts were planned against his life, this time by the Grecian Jews. In the midst of all this the Jerusalem brethren accompanied him down to Caesarea and hustled him off home to Tarsus, no doubt with a sigh of relief that this troublesome character was at last off their hands (Acts 9 : 22-30).

Subsequent to Paul's departure from the country, the churches continued to grow both in strength and in number (Acts 9 : 31). God had His purpose in removing Paul from the public limelight for a time. It was to be fourteen years before he was to visit Jerusalem again (Gal. 2 : 1), and as far as we know, all of that period was spent in Tarsus up to the time when Barnabas sought him out and they returned as co-workers to the ministry in Antioch. There is reason to believe that Paul had been particularly active in preaching Christ to the Gentiles in the area of his native city, but possibly his twelve years of comparatively hidden ministry were years when, most of all, God ministered unto him, preparing him for the great task which lay ahead. On the other hand, it appears that the Jerusalem saints were much less concerned for Paul than they ought to have been. In fact they seem to have been almost completely

11

out of touch with him, otherwise Barnabas would not have had to seek for him so assiduously, and would have known more than the bare fact that he was still somewhere in or around Tarsus (Acts 11 : 25).

Under the ministry of Barnabas and Paul the church at Antioch continued to grow. A significant indication of its growth was the concern of the believers for God's people in other places, and this was given practical expression in the help that was sent to the saints in Judaea who were, at that time, suffering from the effects of a famine which was ravishing the land. This is all the more significant when it is remembered that the believers in Antioch were predominantly Gentile in background, while those in Judaea were Jewish. God had freed those in the Antioch church from considerations of class and race. They were unshackled by any loyalty to formal observances of the ceremonial law and saw, much more clearly than their Jerusalem brethren did, that fellowship in the church is on the ground of relationship with Christ alone. Those in the church at Jerusalem found it much more difficult to disassociate themselves entirely from the traditions of Jewish ritualism, and this obsession with outward form, as we shall see later, was both the beginning of the rot which was ultimately to corrupt the life of the church itself, and also helped to make the association between the early believers and the synagogues increasingly untenable, since it was clear to those who wanted to follow Christ wholly that any compromise with the religion of the past was a denial of the cross and the difference that it makes in the lives of those who believe.

The church at Antioch, therefore, was nurtured on separate ground from that of the synagogue, and from the very beginning there seems to have been a clear conception of the distinctive role the assembly has to play as a spiritual company in the basic unity of which natural and earthly considerations have no part. The names of some of the responsible brethren alone, as recorded by Luke in Acts 13 : 1 indicates the great divergence of background from which they came. God had fused them together into one 'New Man'.

The focus of the Spirit's working was unquestionably shifting from Jerusalem to Antioch, and it was from there that Paul and Barnabas, separated unto the ministry according to the Spirit's revelation in the church, went forth backed by the prayer and devotion of the saints. No such mark of fellowship had attended Paul's departure from Jerusalem, a symptom, no doubt, of the basic lack which was the reason for God's choosing Antioch as the launching ground for some of the greatest of apostolic missionary endeavours.

It may be conceded that the Jerusalem assembly had been wise, all these years previously, in peremptorily setting Paul on a ship bound for Tarsus, but it might have been expected that, if they had in any measure discerned that this remarkable man was one whom God could use, they would have given some indication of their concern for him, and certainly have upheld him in prayer. But as we have already seen, Paul was away from Jerusalem for fourteen years during most of which period the Jerusalem assembly did not even seem to be sure of his whereabouts, so it is unlikely that they spent very much time praying for him. On the other hand, it is only fair to remember that, when Paul and Barnabas visited Jerusalem with the help that had been so generously given by the saints at Antioch, they were given the 'right hand of fellowship' by the elders as they embarked upon their proposed ministry to the Gentiles. Yet in Paul's account of the meeting which he wrote to the Galatians (Gal. 2 : 1-10) there is more than a slight suggestion that the attitude of the Jerusalem elders was one more of tolerance than of the whole-hearted support one would like to have seen. Was there, perhaps, a little jealousy in Jerusalem, or pride of race which could have been embarrassed by the much needed help they received, and could not very well refuse, from Gentile Antioch?

Acts 13-14 tells how churches were established in the cities of Antioch of Pisidia, Iconium, Lystra and Derbe. These places were in the Roman Province of Galatia, and the assemblies established there through the ministry of Paul and Barnabas were the object of Paul's Galatian letter. It may be noted in passing how, in their preaching of the Word, the apostles concentrated on the large and influential centres which were situated along the great highways of the Roman Empire. There was no haphazard 'campaigning', for the apostles believed that from strategically situated groups of faithful witnesses the truth would speedily spread throughout the surrounding areas. That this was, in fact, the Spirit's guidance, is attested by the rapid extension of the churches.

The logical place in which to set about the task of announcing the good news in Pisidian Antioch was, of course, the synagogue. The congregation consisted both of Jews and 'God-fearers' (Acts 13 : 16), the section of the population which had

13

a particular interest in divine things, and many from both these communities accepted the message which (vs. 43), from the customary liberty of ministry in the synagogue, Paul had full freedom to proclaim. The most full-hearted response, however, came from the Gentile 'God-fearers', and there remained within the synagogue a hard core of truculent, Jewish opposition. The opposition came to a head the following sabbath when the Jews found themselves vastly outnumbered by the huge Gentile crowd which gathered to hear Paul and Barnabas, and Scripture records as the reason for the Jewish rejection of the message, not any honest inability to accept what Paul had said, but simply jealousy (vs. 45). Pride of race and the traditions of the past had been too deeply entrenched in the synagogue at Pisidian Antioch to give way to the undisputed sway of Christ as Messiah. A separate community, therefore, came into being, and the Jews, further incensed by this impudent piece of sheep-stealing, which was no more popular then than it is today, stirred up some of the sincere but gullible élite who should have known better, and hounded Paul and Barnabas out of the area.

Practically the same course of events followed their arrival in Iconium. Opposition came from both Jews and Gentiles, but the source of the trouble was 'the Jews that were disobedient' (Acts 14: 2), and the synagogue as a source of spiritual advancement was closed to those who believed. Separation was inevitable. From Iconium, Paul and Barnabas went on to Lystra and Derbe, and in these places also churches were established. Scripture does not speak of any contact with organized Judaism in these places, but there is little likelihood that such contact would have resulted in anything different than in Pisidian Antioch and Iconium, for the apostles found that some of their opponents from the latter two places were hot on their heels at Lystra bent on fomenting trouble. The inflexible defenders of Jewish orthodoxy were not such as to allow the faith of their more open hearted and spiritually discerning brethren to influence the well established order of the synagogue, and they were ready to sustain their position by a recourse to means which were beyond the scope of those who were disciples of the One full of grace and truth.

From Derbe, Paul and Barnabas retraced their steps through Lystra, Iconium and Pisidian Antioch, encouraging the churches which had been established, and setting apart elders in each place. The system of eldership was the same as had assured

14

the stability of the synagogues throughout the preceding centuries, so it was no arbitrary imposition on the assemblies by
the apostles; it was a pattern well tried which had stood the
test of time and, above all, had the seal of divine approval.

We must now leave Paul and Barnabas and turn our attention for a little to the church at Rome. Scripture leaves us
with no explicit account of the commencement of the Roman
church, but there is sufficient miscellaneous information from
which we can have a fair indication of its origin. It would have
been surprising had the momentous events of the cross and the
resurrection not had their effect in Rome at a very early stage,
for all roads led to Rome, and little of moment could happen
in the outside world without at least a tremor of its impact
being felt at the centre of the Empire. In all probability the
Gospel was first carried to Rome by those who were among the
crowd of visitors in Jerusalem on the day of Pentecost. The
' sojourners from Rome, both Jews and proselytes' whom Luke
mentions in his history (Acts 2 : 10) were, in fact, the only
visitors from west of the Bosphorous. Luke does not detail the
nationalities of the three thousand who believed and were
baptized, but no doubt there was a percentage of Romans
among them, and these may well have formed the nucleus of
the church in the great metropolis. Paul, writing his epistle
to the Romans in the year 57 from Corinth, addresses them as
a company which was already well established and thanks God
' because your faith is proclaimed throughout the whole world'
(Rom. 1 : 8).

Two people who were associated with the early days of the
church in Rome, and of whom the Scriptures give considerable
information, were Aquila and Priscilla. They were first mentioned as appearing in Corinth following the expulsion of the
Jews from Rome by the Emperor Claudius in the year A.D. 49.
Aquila was a Jew, ' a man of Pontus by race ' (Acts 18 : 2), but
it seems that he and his wife were followers of Christ before
they reached Corinth, for at once, on meeting the apostle Paul,
they find in him a kindred spirit, which had a much deeper
significance than the fact that Aquila was a leather worker, of
the same trade which Paul, as a Jewish teacher, had also practised on occasion. Aquila and Priscilla had, in fact, more than
a rudimentary grounding in the faith, for it was they whom
God used to lead Apollos, the eloquent and learned Alexandrian
Jew, into an understanding of the Gospel as it was revealed in
Christ (Acts 18 : 24-26).

15

It is likely that, at the beginning of the church's life in Rome, as in other places, it was associated with the Jewish synagogue. Aquila and Priscilla readily associated themselves with Paul's ministry in the synagogue at Corinth which is probably indicative of the practice they had followed in Rome. Rome, of course, had a sizeable and influential Jewish community which was in existence in the city in the second century B.C. and there were a number of synagogues. The Romans forbade the practice of any religion except it were specifically recognised by law, but Judaism was a recognised religion, and Christianity, legally, was but a Jewish sect. Its continuing association with the synagogues, however precarious, served to accord it a share in the standing of a 'religio licita' in Roman eyes.

Many centuries previously, Pharaoh, king of Egypt, had felt it necessary to adopt measures to control the rapidly expanding and influential Hebrew community within his borders, and the same problem was a recurring difficulty to the Roman authorities. Periodically they engaged in a tidying up operation which expelled the Jews from the city. There had, of course, to be a sufficient excuse, and in A.D. 49 the handy circumstance of continual, internal rioting among the Jews threatened to disturb the serenity of the Roman scene and compelled the Emperor Claudius to take stern action. The edict which was promulgated probably forbade the Jews to gather for the public synagogue worship, and that, of course, was tantamount to banishment.

But what was the cause of these internal disturbances? A later writer tells us that they were fomented by a certain 'Chrestus'. Here we are left to conjecture, but it is more than vaguely probable that 'Chrestus' signified the teaching of Christ, and that the hard core of orthodox, Jewish militants in Rome were indulging in the same riotous measures against the proclamation of the Gospel as are described for us in the Acts as having taken place in various other cities in the experience of the apostles. The pattern of separation which we have already noted was established in Rome also. When Aquila and Priscilla returned to Rome after the tumult had died down the centre of their fellowship was apparently the church that was in their own house.

The situation at Philippi forms about the nearest approach we can find to a synagogue's acceptance *in toto* of the Christian message, albeit to draw such a parallel here requires some little stretch of the imagination. A great Roman highway spanned

16

the Balkan peninsula from the Aegean Sea to the Adriatic coast. On this highway Philippi was situated, by the river Gangites in the north-eastern corner of Macedonia. It was the principal city of the area and had become a colony about forty years B.C. Actually, Philippi did not boast a synagogue as the Jewish community was apparently not of sufficient strength, and Jewish practice stipulated that the constitution of a proper synagogue required a minimum of ten men. There was, however, a recognised meeting place which was used for worship and prayer and was frequented mostly by faithful women, both Jews and 'God-fearers' (Acts 16 : 12-14). Most prominent among this little group was a Gentile lady, 'one that worshipped God' (vs. 14). Her name was Lydia, and she was a seller of the purple dye for which her native Thyatira was famous. Both she and her household accepted the message brought by Paul, were baptized, and the 'synagogue' prayer meeting became the nucleus of a church to which the Lord continued to add such as should be saved.

From Philippi Paul, Silas and Timothy moved on to Thessalonica, a city with a synagogue, and, as was Paul's custom, they identified themselves with the Jewish community. For three weeks Paul reasoned with them from the Scriptures (Acts 17 : 1-2). The Christian revelation was accepted by a number of the Jews as well as a very large number of the devout Gentiles, whereupon, the unbelieving Jews, for no higher reason than a bitter jealousy at the apparent success of the apostles' preaching, incited the city rabble, always ready for a fight for any or no reason, to help them, and caused a public uproar. These stalwarts of Jewish orthodoxy suddenly became gravely concerned for the welfare of the Roman Empire, and charged Paul and his companions with treason. They were, it was said, inciting the people to proclaim Jesus a rival Emperor. The rioters had wanted to bring the disciples before the rulers of the city, and with that purpose in view had besieged the house of Jason their host, but Paul and company were nowhere to be found, so they had to be content with dragging Jason and some other believers before the city fathers to bear the brunt of the charge. Poor Jason offered himself as security against the good behaviour of his guests and had them quickly despatched to Beroea.

In the synagogue at Beroea the disciples were courteously received. Their message led the Jews to a diligent examination of the Scriptures and many, including both Jews and Greeks,

17

believed. The peace, however, was soon shattered by the arrival of the Thessalonian Jews who, on hearing of Paul's reception at Beroea, hastened thither to assure that as few people as possible should be contaminated by this Christian heresy. Neither was Beroea lacking in a few hot-heads to rally round the unruly defenders of the faith. The believers escorted Paul as far as Athens (Acts 17 : 10-15).

The visit to Thessalonica had been quite a stormy event, but the believers who were left behind made remarkable and rapid progress. It is hardly to be supposed that they found much sympathy or fellowship in the synagogue which had been the seat of the bitter opposition against Paul and his companions. On the contrary, they suffered no little persecution as is clearly mentioned in the first letter which Paul wrote to them (1 Thess. 1 : 14; 2 : 4, etc.). Yet they at once began earnestly to propagate their new found faith, and Paul, writing from Athens but a matter of weeks later could say, " Ye became an ensample to all that believe in Macedonia and in Achaia. For from you hath sounded forth the word of the Lord, not only in Macedonia and Achaia, but in every place your faith to God-ward is gone forth (1 Thess. 1 : 7-8).

We have already noted the edict passed by the Emperor Claudius in the year 49 which led to the expulsion of the Jews from Rome. The effect of this edict was of limited duration, but Roman Jews had, nevertheless, to find a temporary home elsewhere, and some of them found their way to Corinth. Among these were Aquila and Priscilla. In Corinth, Aquila practised his trade as a leather worker and soon made the acquaintance of Paul who, on his arrival in the city, began to support himself from this same trade in accordance with Rabbinical custom. Together they attended the synagogue, and Paul, a distinguished scholar in his own right and known to have sat under the teaching of Gamaliel, one of the most noted and respected Rabbis of his day, was soon invited to expound the Scriptures. This he did week after week with considerable freedom, to the spiritual enlightenment of some and to the increasing annoyance of others. At last the opposition became so determined that Paul felt no useful purpose would be served by his continuing association with the synagogue. He did not have to look far for an alternative meeting place. Next door to the synagogue lived a Gentile God-fearer named Titus Justus who had been greatly influenced by the message Paul proclaimed. In his house the new community of Christians gathered and continued to grow.

When ' Crispus, the ruler of the synagogue, believed in the Lord with all his house ' (Acts 18 : 8), the opposition on the part of the Jews mounted, and they appealed to Gallio pro-consul of Achaia, preferring a charge against Paul of preaching a religion which was not authorised by law. This was a serious charge, and could it have been maintained, would have resulted in direct action by the Roman authorities against the Christians, for by law, no religion could be practised which was not licensed. Gallio ruled, however, that the dispute was purely an internal matter affecting the Jews alone, and drove those who brought the charge from the judgement seat (Acts 18 : 12-17).

This incident throws an important light on Paul's attitude to the revelation of the Gospel he had been divinely commissioned to preach, and on the relation of this message to the established Jewish community. From a natural point of view, the recognition of the Roman government for the infant Christian community was something to be prized, for had not Rome seen fit to accord the church its protection, it could at one sweep have outlawed the faith and scattered the believers at a time when, humanly speaking, it would hardly have seemed strong enough to survive such official disfavour. That this would actually happen was, of course, the hope of the Corinthian Jews in lodging their complaint. Rome, however, continued to look upon Christianity as but a sect of Judaism and to accord it Jewish privilege, so the church seemed safe as long as it would remain within the shelter of the synagogue. Yet Paul made no particular attempt to conciliate the synagogue authorities and to secure the church their patronage. His message was uncompromising, and he seemed little concerned that, in synagogue after synagogue, he was being branded as a heretic. Nor did he plead or have recourse to diplomatic subterfuges that he and his followers might be allowed to remain within the fold. On the contrary, he even took the initiative in leaving before the Jews had time to throw him out. Far from being conciliatory towards the tradition of which the synagogue was a stronghold, Paul's actions and attitude invited antagonism. His refusal to admit the ritual observances of the law, and his open defiance of the deep-rooted distinction between Jew and Gentile helped to widen the already expanding gulf between synagogue and church.

Paul was a far-sighted man, and could not have failed to see

19

that the policy he was deliberately pursuing was designed ultimately not only to make final the break between Judaism and
the church, but also to bring about the withdrawal of the recognition of the Roman government which the Christians had
been enjoying, for the moment this final cleavage between the
church and the synagogue became public, Christianity would
cease to be a religio licita, and Christians would have to re-
nounce their faith or become fugitives of the law. This is the
path along which Paul was deliberately leading the church, for
he saw that there could be no other which would leave un-
compromised the revelation which had been committed to him.

From Corinth, Paul, along with Aquila and Priscilla, set sail
for Syria. At Ephesus he entered the synagogue and reasoned
with the Jews, but, in spite of their pleading, did not consent
to prolong his visit, promising, however, to return at a later date.
Meanwhile, Aquila and Priscilla remained in the city and,
shortly afterwards, met the eloquent and learned Alexandrian
Jew, Apollos. Apollos 'had been instructed in the way of the
Lord' (Acts 18 : 25) but knew only the baptism of John. He
readily received the further revelation which God granted him
through Aquila and Priscilla, and he was subsequently much
used both in strengthening the saints and convincing the Jews
of the truth of the Messianic claim.

On Paul's return to Ephesus some months later he found
some disciples, numbering about twelve in all, who had received
a limited measure of the Gospel truth. It is possible that these
people were the fruit of Apollos' earlier ministry, for the limits
of their understanding seemed to coincide largely with what
Apollos himself knew before he was fully instructed (cf. Acts
18 : 24-25; 19 : 1-6). Be that as it may, they had open ears and
hearts to what Paul had to say, and were baptized in the name
of the Lord Jesus. These few formed the nucleus of the church
in Ephesus. As was his custom, Paul returned to the synagogue
and ministered freely for the space of three months. By the
end of that time, however, the now expected murmuring and
opposition was beginning to show itself, and it was soon evident
that there would be no further ready acceptance in the synagogue of what the apostle had to say. Paul did not try to resist
the inevitable. The church had to have free ground on which
to develop unobstructed by traditions which had outlived their
usefulness. The Lord provided an alternative place where the
disciples and others interested could meet, the school-room of
a sympathetic, local teacher, Tyrannus by name (or nick-name).

20

There the Word of the Lord was proclaimed with freedom, and from that small beginning the church at Ephesus grew.

In this chapter we have been concerned with an examination of the foundation of some of the larger churches established during the early years of the apostolic ministry, mainly those to which letters were later addressed by Paul, letters which have been preserved for us in the pages of the sacred canon. In this enquiry we have obtained a clear picture of the development of the relationship of those churches with the Jewish synagogue. Paul consistently began his ministry in the synagogue wherever one existed, but in every instance the association had to be discontinued and the church had to start afresh on clear ground. As has been sufficiently pointed out, there is no theoretic reason why this should inevitably have been so; in fact the synagogue seemed to inculcate a divinely designed mode of transition from the sacrificial symbolism of orthodox Judaism to the acceptance of the Christ as the one in whom all that symbolism was fulfilled. But somewhere along the line God's progressive revelation in the synagogue had been brought to a halt. Light which God had given had become crystallized in an unalterable tradition. The flow of life was stopped, and the only alternative to the church's bursting the bonds which held it and seeking a fresh channel in which to flow, was stagnation. At the beginning of the church's history we see a principle at work which is to be repeated continually through the succeeding centuries.

C

CHAPTER THREE

CHURCH ORDER

WHAT was the pattern of government adopted by the early churches? Does Scripture give any clear indication in this regard? The New Testament lays down basic principles for the ordering of the life of local congregations which were in common force in the days of the apostles. The basic order has a similarity to, and was, no doubt, in some respects, derived from the order which was followed in the Jewish synagogues, as we have already noted. Chief among the officers of the synagogue and of the churches were the elders. Strict standards governing the conduct of those eligible for such a position are clearly set down, but beyond this there is detailed instruction neither as to how these elders should be chosen, nor as to the limits of their authority and duty within the assembly. There is divine wisdom in this absence of any rigid code of procedure. The church was not organized into being; it was born through the working of the Spirit of God. It is not a mechanical contrivance but a living organism, and its life is dependent upon that element of spontaneity which a rigid and predetermined order denies.

The two Greek words translated in the New Testament as 'bishop' or 'overseer' (episkopos) and 'elder' (presbuteros) indicate the same office and are used interchangeably. At Miletus, for example, Paul called the ELDERS of the Ephesian church and exhorted them as those whom the Holy Spirit had made OVERSEERS of the flock (Acts 20 : 17, 28). In writing to Titus, he asks him to appoint ELDERS in every city in Crete, explaining the qualities which should characterise those who are fit to occupy this position of an OVERSEER (Titus 1 : 5-7).

Both in his letter to Timothy and in that to Titus Paul outlines these qualifications. An elder should be the 'husband of one wife'; a man concerned for the welfare of others, not simply for personal position or gain; a person of stable and unblemished character; one whose Christian standards were exemplified in a well-ordered, disciplined and God-fearing household; a brother of mature, spiritual experience who had both a

22

concern for the edification of the Lord's people and the ability to instruct them (1 Tim. 3 : 1-7; Titus 1 : 6-9).

The reference to an elder as the 'husband of one wife' has sometimes been taken to indicate that there were those in the early church who had more than one wife but who, as a consequence, were forbidden to hold any position of authority. It is unlikely, however, that this was what Paul was referring to. In the same letter he uses an identical form of words in laying down the conditions upon which widows could be accepted into a 'widows' order' which apparently existed in some of the churches at that time. A widow should, he states, have been 'the wife of one man', but it is not seriously contended that there were sisters in the early church who practised polyandry. Polygamy, although there were doubtless instances of it in the variegated society with which Paul came in contact, was not a common practice in the Graeco-Roman world. A believer who in his unregenerate days had married two wives and did not set the matter right on coming to Christ would, of course, be barred from eldership in the assembly, but what Paul wrote probably had a much wider application in that it was primarily meant to debar from church responsibility any who had been divorced and had married again although a previous wife was still alive. Moral laxity was rife in the Gentile world of Paul's day, and the contract of marriage carried with it little sense of lasting obligation.

Another important condition of eldership was that the brother concerned should have a well ordered household, and be able to rule well his own family. Paul makes a very valid and today oft neglected point when he writes, " But if a man knoweth not how to rule his own house, how shall he take care of the church of God ? " (1 Tim. 3 : 5). A man's home was the first place in which the life of Christ should be expected to have a practical effect, and if he did not recognise the essential responsibility of ordering his family according to God's standard, it could hardly be maintained that he was more than a novice in spiritual matters, which of itself would disqualify him from the position of eldership.

The New Testament cites no instances of the setting apart of elders which could justifiably form a precedent for all time. The idea that appointment to the office of eldership was an apostolic prerogative finds no support in Scripture. There is but one specific reference to elders being set apart by the apostles, that is in the cities of Lystra, Iconium and Pisidian

Antioch by Paul and Barnabas on their return journey from Derbe. Paul and Barnabas were here acting in their capacity as evangelists (Acts 4 : 20-23). In writing many years later to Titus, Paul charges him to 'appoint elders in every city' in Crete (Titus 1 : 5). Whether Paul was right, however, in making this charge, is open to serious question, and we have no indication that Titus was able to carry it out. We know practically nothing of the churches in Crete, if in fact there really existed churches at all, but the work never seems to have prospered. No hint is given as to how the elders at Jerusalem, Ephesus and Philippi came to occupy their position, while it appears in other places, Corinth and Thessalonica for example, that they were recognised without any formal appointment (1 Cor. 16 : 15-16; 1 Thess. 5 : 12-14).

The emphasis of the Scripture is that elders are the appointment of the Spirit (Acts 20 : 17, 28). They were marked out as the divine choice by their life and conduct, a choice which was accepted by all who were spiritual in the assembly. Thus relegating the choice directly to the Spirit according to the standard laid down in the Word on the one hand effectively debars the self-assertive from assuming a position of authority and, on the other, protects the work of God from the fallibility of human judgement.

In writing to the Philippians, Paul addresses his letter to 'all the saints in Christ Jesus which are at Philippi, with the overseers and deacons' (Phil. 1 : 1). This verse, along with the passage in Acts 6 which speaks of the setting apart of deacons in the church at Jerusalem, are the two portions in Scripture which specifically state the existence of deacons in two of the early assemblies. The purpose of the deacon's office may be gauged from the task to which they were appointed in Jerusalem, the carrying into effect of practical, 'business' details of the church's daily life, in this case the distribution of charity to certain of the saints who were in need.

Whether there were deacons in all the churches we do not know, but they obviously did not have the same place in the permanent order of the church as elders. There is no mention of Paul and Barnabas having set apart deacons in Lystra, Iconium and Pisidian Antioch when elders were set apart in these places. Nor does Paul mention the matter of deacons to Titus in his advice regarding the establishing of a church order in Crete. Deacons took their place in the Jerusalem church on account of a specific need, and it would seem that they held their position only so long as that particular need lasted. Certainly the indication of Scripture is that the office catered for exigencies in the life of the church which were not necessarily of permanent duration, so the deacons would function in their capacity for shorter or longer periods as the need required, but they were not an inevitably fixed part of the church's order. Nor is it to be assumed that the same people would be set apart for each separate need, but the gifts which particular people possessed qualifying them to act in particular situations would be taken into consideration. The need which arose early in the history of the Jerusalem church affected mainly the Grecian Jews, and the names of all those who were set apart as deacons to cater for the need shows that they too were from the Grecian section of the community. Obviously they were the most suited to meet the existing requirement, and were chosen on that basis. It is hardly to be supposed that in the whole of the Jerusalem assembly they alone would have been adequate to fill a permanent deacon's office. If, in fact, the deacons were being set apart as a recognised, permanent part of the church order, surely some of their number would have been Hebrews. It is highly improbable that the Hebrew section of the community contained so little gift as to exclude them completely from representation among the deacons, especially when it is considered that the Hebrews in the assembly were both numerically and otherwise more powerful than their Grecian brethren (cf. Acts 6 : 3-6).

It is well to notice the exacting qualifications demanded of deacons. They may not have been required to have the same ' aptness ' to teach as was expected of elders, but their personal lives and devotion to the things of God were governed by no less rigid a standard. In no sense were they of some lower spiritual strata, entrusted with more mundane tasks because of their inability to cope with anything higher. They were all men ' full of the Spirit and of wisdom ' (Acts 6 : 3), and at least two of them, Stephen and Philip, were teachers of outstanding ability. In the early church, every service to God required men who were wholly yielded to Him.

In the church of the New Testament, the public identification of believers with the Christian community was indicated by baptism. Luke tells us, " They then that received his word were baptized; and there were added unto them in that day about three thousand souls " (Acts 2 : 41). The practice seems to have been that each believer made a simple confession of the Lordship of Christ in public before baptism. Before Philip baptized the Ethopian Eunuch, the Eunuch affirmed, " I believe that Jesus Christ is the Son of God " (Acts 8 : 37 A.V.). True, this verse is but a later amplification of Luke's original narrative, and it is omitted entirely in the Revised Version, but it may, none the less, be a faithful portrayal of what actually happened. Similarly, Ananias exhorted Paul to be baptized, ' calling on His name ' (Acts 22 : 16).

The prime importance of this affirmation, of course, lies not in the form of words which was used, but in the reality of the experience that lay behind it. That it was no glib, ritualistic repetition we have already seen, for the acknowledgement of Christ as Lord had a tremendous, practical significance to the Jew and to others whose contact with Judaism had moulded their beliefs about God on the basis of the Old Testament revelation (see p. 10). This confession amounted to a clear proof of a life that had been made new in Christ. The proof of a consistent, spiritual life was just as indispensable a condition for baptism as it ought to be today. No doubt the apostles made mistakes. The incident of Simon recorded in Acts 8 is a case in point where Philip was obviously deceived, but the exception only goes to prove the rule. [Was Philip's sudden call to the desert (Acts 8 : 26) partly a discipline for his not too bright conduct of affairs during the latter part of his ministry in Samaria? Was God saying, " You had better come away for a while, Philip, and I will use you somewhere else "?]

The great commission given by our Lord to His disciples is much more explicit in its instructions concerning those who would follow Him. " Go ye therefore and make disciples of all the nations, baptising them into the name of the Father and of the Son and of the Holy Spirit " (Matt. 28 : 19). The purpose of this commission was not, of course, simply to state a baptismal formula, although the latter portion of the verse has been and is used as such. Our Lord's words extended not only to Jews and Gentile God-fearers, but to ' all the nations ', out into the pagan world where there was not even a rudimentary understanding of divine revelation, and they are a necessary amplification to the world at large of what was adequately summed up for the Jews and Gentile God-fearers as the Lordship of Christ. A person who had experienced that inner change wrought by divine grace would know God the Father as the Creator and Ruler of the world, the One whose condescending love had manifested itself in the incarnation. Christ had taught them so. They would know the Son as the One through whom the Father was fully revealed, and through whose eternal work they had been reconciled unto God by faith. They would know the Holy Spirit as the One through whom the standard of God was applied to their daily lives, granting them the grace and power to live lives as befitted children of God, and as the One through whom God's will was revealed and His presence manifested in their midst.

The mode of baptism does not here primarily concern us, but an interesting light is thrown on the emphasis of the early church in the Didache, a document of the beginning of the second century which deals with the teaching of our Lord to the twelve apostles. On the subject of baptism it says, " Baptize them in running water ' into the name of the Father and of the Son and of the Holy Spirit '. If you have no running water, then baptize them in other water : if you cannot do it in cold water, then do it in warm water. But if you cannot do it in either, then pour water three times on the head ' into the name of the Father and of the Son and of the Holy Spirit '." Obviously the importance of the meaning of the testimony outweighed considerations of form.

It is here important to recognise that Scripture is fundamentally a guide to principle, and in that sense is also an infallible guide to practice; but it is not a list of precedents which are to be mechanically and slavishly followed. We can only fully understand the application and implications of any Scriptural incident when we view it in the context of the circumstances in which it occurred. Otherwise we are prone to error. It is true that, in the Acts, baptism followed immediately or soon after believing, but to baptize today people who have made a mechanical repentance and profession of faith, and who can answer correctly a few questions on the nature of the new birth without showing any indication of a change which has affected their daily living, has no justification in Scripture, and is in no sense a parallel to the Scriptural practice.

Who were the first Christians, those whose baptism is recorded in the book of Acts? We have already seen that they were either Jews by birth or Gentiles whose spiritual hunger had led them into association with the synagogue where they had assimilated much of the Jewish outlook and the Jewish, Messianic hope. They were a people remarkably prepared for the revelation of the Gospel, and in accepting Christ as Messiah and Lord they were but entering into the fulfilment of that for

27

which they had longed and lived, and to which their God-fearing walk had been a constant testimony. To parallel the experience of these early Jews and God-fearers with the conversion experience of people today is to leave oneself open to misunderstanding the whole significance of baptism. Actually Philip made just that mistake when he baptized Simon the sorcerer. The early Jews and God-fearers, as that remnant in which the Spirit of God was active, may have been just as much the people of God before their actual acceptance of Christ as after it. Their entry was not so much into a new life as into a new revelation. The conversion experience of today, where people pass from a denial to an acceptance of the work of Christ, is first and foremost an entry into a new life of which the revelation is but a part. The proof of the reality of the experience is a consistent walk, and it is only in the light of a life which is obviously ordered by devotion to Christ that the testimony of baptism has any meaning.

The life of the church was also characterised by a second ceremony, the 'breaking of bread'. Instituted by our Lord Himself (Luke 22 : 19-22), this simple partaking together of bread and wine was a symbol to the disciples of the new covenant into which they had entered through faith in Christ. The relationship with Him which had brought an infusion of divine life had not only united them to God, but had welded them together in a common bond in the church, as partakers of a life which was from heaven, victorious over the sin which had divided asunder man from God and man from man. As the disciples took part in this simple ceremony, they testified to their present 'feasting' upon the Lord and to their common fellowship as having all alike been born into the divine family through a miracle of grace (John 6 : 48-51; 1 Cor. 10 : 16-17).

Baptism in the name of the Lord and the breaking of bread were the two outward ceremonies which characterised the groups of believers. Although in the early days succeeding the outpouring at Pentecost the followers of Christ were regarded, and regarded themselves, as but a party within the Jewish fold, they gathered separately in one another's houses to break bread (Acts 2 : 46), and it is probable that the disciples remembered the Lord in this way on the first day of each week. Of Paul's visit to Troas, Luke tells us, "And upon the first day of the week, when we were gathered together to break bread, Paul discoursed with them, intending to depart on the morrow, and prolonged his speech until midnight" (Acts 20 : 7). Although it is not explicitly stated, the implication of the verse is that it was the custom for the brethren to meet in this manner each Lord's day.

It is significant that the meaning of baptism and the Lord's table should have been the focal point of so much controversy in the years to come. The attitude of succeeding generations of professing Christians to these two symbolic acts has been a remarkably accurate gauge of the spiritual quality of their inner lives, whether faith has amounted to little more than a superstitous formalism, a belief in the efficacy of ritual observances, or has been of that enduring, eternal quality which sees Him who is invisible.

What did the early churches possess in the way of sacred Scripture, and to what did they look as their final authority in matters requiring guidance? They did, of course, possess the Scriptures of the Old Testament, and quoted from them unfailingly in maintaining the claim that Jesus was the Messiah. This acceptance of the Old Testament writings was based on no lesser authority than that of Christ Himself who, in all matters, upheld them as the highest court of appeal, and claimed to be the One in whom Scripture was finally fulfilled. The early churches, therefore, with every justification, confidently believed that they were the true heirs of the Old Testament, and continued to accept it as the unqualified Word of God.

Along with the Scriptures of the Old Testament, the first followers of Christ accepted the words of the Lord as binding upon them. Christ, after all, had come not merely as a spokesman of God, a prophet, but as the Messiah Himself, the incarnation of the divine Word. Then there was the word of the apostles. The Lord had seen fit to delegate His authority to certain of His disciples who, in exercise of that authority, were deputed to speak and to act in His name. The words of the apostles were likewise accepted by the early church as the direction of God, not always without challenge (Paul had to defend his apostleship on more than one occasion), but the general recognition of apostolic authority is clear enough. This type of inspired utterance was headed up in the gifts of apostleship and prophecy. In the church at Antioch, guidance in the setting apart of Barnabas and Saul came partly through the ministry of prophets, and in the same church some time earlier, through a prophet called Agabus, Barnabas and Saul had been guided to go up to Judaea with relief for the brethren who were suffering from the prevailing, severe famine (Acts 11 : 27-30). Later on

29

we again meet Brother Agabus as he prophesies concerning the sufferings to be inflicted upon Paul at Jerusalem (Acts 21 : 10-12).

The apostles also found occasion to convey their message through letters to various groups of believers or individuals as the need arose. Some of these we have preserved for us in the thirteen epistles of Paul, the anonymous epistle to the Hebrews, and the general epistles of Peter, James, John and Jude. As eye-witnesses of the life, death and resurrection of our Lord began to die out, it inevitably became desirable that there should be a permanent record of these events. Ultimately the four Gospels as we have them today began to circulate among the churches and were accorded general recognition. Luke also extended his narrative into the history which we call the Acts of the Apostles. Finally, there was the Apocalypse of John. Practically all of these writings had their spurious counterparts, but, in the course of time, under the guidance of the Holy Spirit, the divine character and inspiration of the twenty-seven books of our present New Testament became unalterably established among companies of Christians. It is evident, therefore, that the fixing of the canon of Scripture was not the result of an arbitrary decision made by some ecclesiastical Council. Long before any 'official' pronouncement was made the sixty-six books of the Bible had gained complete acceptance among the churches. When, finally, the Council of Carthage in the year 397 presumed to make a ruling on the matter, it but confirmed what was by that time an established fact.

The church and the Scriptures developed together, and the church ultimately recognised in the truth of the written revelation her complete foundation. The Bible is the expression of the divine Word, at one time spoken directly from the lips of Christ, and then through the apostles. The New Testament embodies the continuance of the apostolic ministry, the revelation of Christ which was completed with the commital to Paul of the mystery of the church (Col. 1 : 24-25). From this it follows that the ministry of apostleship and prophecy as embodied in particular people was but a temporary expedient. It was vitally necessary during the transition period when the written Word was being formulated and was gaining acceptance among believers, but the written Word completed, the particular ministry of the apostle and the prophet became redundant, just as the observation of the Old Testament sacrifices had to give way to their fulfilment in Christ. The principle came into operation, " But when that which is perfect is come, that which is

30

in part shall be done away " (1 Cor. 13 : 10). The functions of the apostle and the prophet still exist, but embodied in the written Word, not in any man. NOT !

The Gospel of Christ as revealed in the Scriptures means much more than the wiping out of a person's past sins; it means the possession of a divine life through the power of the Holy Spirit, a life whose ethical requirements are in all respects superior to the standards of others. This standard was earnestly inculcated in the early church, and that it was rigorously maintained is demonstrated in Paul's letter to the Corinthians where a serious lapse from the norm of Christian behaviour is dealt with. Such a departure from this high code of conduct was a denial of the Gospel, and meant the discipline of separation from the community. Fellowship could only be restored through repentance which was demonstrated by a decisive change of character. ~Right.

It is significant that the standard of conduct among Christians made an impression even among pagans who were not misled by the gossip of common scandalmongers. Even in the later persecutions which were perpetrated by the Roman authorities, officials were sometimes at a loss how to carry out the orders of the state, since the charges brought against Christians were so often unsupported by evidence. Theoretically, Rome's case against the Christians was that they were engaged in criminal activities, their refusal to accord reverence to the Emperor and to take part in state religious ceremonies being construed as treason. The mob, of course, who hated Christians just because they were different, had other complaints, and spread against them charges of incest and ritual cannibalism. The dilemma of officials was that, while crimes against the state were held to be essentially associated with a Christian profession, yet there does not seem to have been any law which specifically branded Christianity as a crime. Should then every Christian be considered guilty until he had demonstrated his loyalty to the powers that be by taking part in some prescribed ceremony, and in so doing given proof that he had denied his faith? But to demand this was wellnigh impossible, to such an extent had Christianity spread. The condemnation of Christians on the one hand, and the lack of any substantial proof of unlawful practices on the other, was a set of circumstances bound to perplex the mind of any official who was sincerely concerned with the administration of justice.

This perplexity, and the high ethical standard prevailing

31

among Christians, are well illustrated in correspondence in the year A.D. 112 between the Roman Emperor, Trajan, and Pliny, governor of the province of Bithynia. Pliny had sought the Emperor's counsel on the matter of dealing with the Christians and asks, "Whether the very profession of the name is to be punished, or only the criminal practices which go along with the name." He then goes on to tell of an anonymous letter he had received containing a long list of names. On interrogating these people, he found that many of them had renounced Christianity years before. What is most interesting, however, is the account they gave of their abandoned faith. " But they maintained that their fault or error amounted to nothing more than this : they were in the habit of meeting on a certain fixed day before sunrise and reciting an antiphonal hymn to Christ as God, and binding themselves with an oath—not to commit any crime, but to abstain from all acts of theft, robbery and adultery, from breaches of faith, from denying a trust when called upon to honour it. After this, they went on, it was their custom to separate, and then meet again to partake of food, but food of an ordinary and innocent kind." In his reply to Pliny, Trajan says, " . . . Indeed, no general decision can be made by which a set form of dealing with them could be established. They must not be ferreted out. . . . Anonymous documents which are laid before you should receive no attention in any case : they are a very bad precedent and quite unworthy of the age in which we live." Plainly, the confusion caused by the Christians was not because of their criminal activities, but because of their good character. revolution of Righteousness

The churches in early days were not linked by any type of federal organization, although they were closely united by the bonds of Christian fellowship. No one church had precedence over another, yet those assemblies which had been longer and more solidly grounded in the faith were naturally respected as sources of advice and spiritual counsel in time of need. In the pattern of evangelism which is outlined in the Acts, the Gospel was first preached in the strategic centres, and from there it penetrated into the surrounding areas. The church which had been used to initiate the spread of the truth in a particular district would naturally have a parental concern for the infant churches it had brought into being, and would in turn receive due spiritual recognition from the weaker groups, but that did not in any sense presume overlordship of one church upon another : it was simply an expression of the concern of fellow-

32

ship through which all developed together in the things of the Spirit.

The earliest quest for advice of which we read is when a delegation was sent from Antioch to consult with the apostles and elders at Jerusalem over the matter of the circumcision of Gentile converts, certain Judaistic teachers having insisted that this was necessary for salvation (Acts 15 : 1-35). It is obvious from the account given by Luke that the brethren at Antioch were simply desirous of some mature counsel on a question that was causing considerable perplexity. They also wished to prove the *bona fides* of the visiting teachers who apparently claimed the authority of the apostles at Jerusalem for what they said (Acts 15 : 1, 24). There is no indication that they were looking for some *ex cathedra* pronouncement from Jerusalem which should arbitrarily be accepted as divine law. Had the church in Jerusalem felt it was their place to dictate on matters of doctrine, they would almost certainly have attempted earlier to formulate some opinion on such an important question as circumcision, for they could hardly have been unaware that circumcision was not practised among the believers at Antioch, while those in the church at Jerusalem had conformed to this Jewish rite. Yet when the matter is raised before the Jerusalem elders, the ensuing discussion makes it perfectly clear that little if any previous attempt had been made to find the mind of the Spirit. The need for a thorough examination of the question had not hitherto arisen since it had caused no problem in their own midst. There had been no previous consideration of examining the question in order to legislate for others.

In the resultant letter sent from Jerusalem, however, there is an unmistakable air of authority. This would have been perfectly in order as an apostolic pronouncement, the position of the apostles being what it was at that particular period, but the church at Antioch had the word of the apostle Paul who had been with them when the question of circumcision was so acutely raised, and Paul was in no doubt as to the mind of the Spirit on the matter. The letter from Jerusalem, of course, was not an apostolic pronouncement; it was a letter from the church (Acts 15 : 23) addressed and circulated to the brethren in Antioch, Syria and Cilicia, with ' advice ' which was expected to be obeyed. And the ' advice ' was obeyed for, after all, it was good advice. The whole background of the incident shows that the church at Jerusalem did not think it their position to act as an ecclesiastical authority for churches in other places, but when their counsel was sought it was given with the air that it ought to be accepted without question. And 'advice' which is always and inevitably obeyed is, of course, a command. But more of this in the following chapter.

Even at a later period in the history of the church when a monarchical bishopric had been established, the independence of individual congregations was maintained. Churches may have consulted freely with one another on numerous matters, but once the consultations were over, there was no accepted rule that the pronouncement of one body should dominate over the rest. There were not infrequent instances of individuals trying to make their own judgment in some matter binding upon all, but that this attempt should be made at all proves that the churches did not recognise any human pontiff or any 'mother church' as the mouthpiece of God. To quote but one example from the post-apostolic era : in the year 231 Origen, one of the most gifted and spiritually-minded teachers of any age, was excommunicated by the jealous Demetrius, Bishop of Alexandria. Demetrius sought recognition for his action from the whole Christian world in an attempt effectively to curtail Origen's influence, but the support he desired was generally denied, and Origen continued to earn the respect of those he taught till he died in the year 254.

There were many opportunities in the early years of the church's history for the believers to minister to one another in practical matters. Right from the beginning a sense of mutual responsibility was developed. In the church at Jerusalem there was a voluntary pooling of resources from which the requirements of those in need could be met (Acts 2 : 44-45), and some of the first believers to be set apart for particular service were deacons whose job was to oversee the distribution of charity.

This common sense of obligation soon manifested itself outside the local church, in the desire of one church to minister to the needs of others. The churches in Jerusalem and Judaea seemed to be inflicted with a chronic poverty which made them the object of much assistance from others. Barnabas and Saul were deputed by the believers in Antioch to deliver a gift to Jerusalem to relieve the church during a time of severe famine (Acts 11 : 29-30). Later, Paul organized a collection over a wide area for the Jerusalem saints, believers in many places contributing generously in their concern (Rom. 15 : 25-26; 1 Cor. 16 : 1-4). It does not seem that one of Paul's main objects in organizing this collection was realised, namely, the forging of more intimate bonds between the predominantly Gentile churches and the peculiarly class-conscious Jews of the church at Jerusalem, but the gesture was, nevertheless, a mark of the sense of responsibility to one another which existed generally throughout the churches, and if the recipients were not blessed as much as they ought to have been, it was certainly a blessing and strength to those who gave.

As well as the settled administration of the local churches which was in the hands of elders there was, as we find from the New Testament, a ministry exercised by gifted brethren who moved widely among the various assemblies. Paul and some of the apostles, among others, were engaged in this type of ministry. The book of the Acts gives a clear idea of the function it served. In his epistle to the Ephesians Paul enumerates the gifts which are used for the establishment and building up of the church. They are apostles and prophets, whose ministry is now embodied in the completed canon of Scripture (see page 30), and evangelists, pastors and teachers, whose ministries in all ages are exercised according to the enabling given by God to His servants (Eph. 4 : 11). These gifts had a local expression in the elders of each assembly, and an extra-local expression in the itinerant ministries of Paul and others who formed a spiritual link of great value between the people of God in the various churches. They were not officials of any ecclesiastical organization, but ministers of Christ who were accepted, and whose authority was recognised because the mark of the Spirit was upon them. The effectiveness of their ministry was dependent solely upon their spiritual worth. They occupied no legal position which could have afforded them a guarantee of continued status should their devotion to God and their spiritual vitality wane.

Finally, a word on what the early believers were called. The church in apostolic times maintained a plea for namelessness which has been continued right up to the present day and which, in itself, would form a most interesting, historical study. Their desire has again and again been denied them, but there has never lacked someone to espouse the cause that the Lord's name is sufficient to denote the Lord's family. It has always seemed to be a losing battle, yet the battle still continues.

The believers in the early churches used various names to describe themselves, but the most commonly used in the epistles are 'saints' and 'brethren', terms which denoted simply that they were people in whose hearts a divine work had been

35

wrought, and that they were bound together in the family of God. A name that was foisted upon them in Hebrew society was 'Nazarenes', no doubt from the fact that they were followers of Jesus of Nazareth. Luke, however, in the Acts, speaks of the 'disciples' and in Antioch they were first given the name 'Christians' (Acts 11 : 26). They spoke much of Jesus as the 'Christ', a term full of meaning to the Jews but strange-sounding and of little significance to the Gentiles. The Gentiles, therefore, called them 'Christianoi', Christ's people. The name was peculiarly apt. What more would Christ's people want to be called than simply that, Christians?

CHAPTER FOUR

SIGNS OF DECLENSION

HUMAN nature being what it is, and this world being what it is, it cannot be expected that the work of God will remain uncontested. The child of God and the church are born into a life of continuous, spiritual battle, and whatever God establishes man ultimately wants to prune and shape to his own liking. The New Testament adequately reveals the constant drag of the world upon the church to pull down what is of heaven to the level of the earth, and the strength and insistence of its efforts.

Long before the apostles had completed their ministry there were destructive forces assiduously working upon the church from within. The faithful record of Scripture has left for our profit a warning, applicable to every age, of the subtleties which would sap the spiritual energies of the church till it is reduced from the divine to something that is purely human. The problems encountered in the churches of the apostolic era are set down for our examination in the epistles. They are typical of the heedlessness to divine principle which, down through history, has been at the root of the ultimate decay and declension of practically every movement of the Spirit of God. It is, unfortunately, almost impossible to trace the exact course of the life of the churches in the years immediately following New Testament times. From the point to which Luke conducts us in his history of the Acts till the latter part of the second century there is a conspicuous lack of historical information on the development of the assemblies. When we emerge from this period of uncertainty, we find a church in many respects quite different from the churches of the New Testament. Wide and far-reaching changes have taken place, and there is an unmistakable move in the direction of the institutionalism of later years. This crystallization of Christianity is, in turn, the prime reason for the emergence of fresh expressions of the life of the Gospel. Where the vitality of spiritual life could not be contained within the increasingly restricted limits of a humanly imposed organization and rule, it burst the bounds and found

37

D

its fuller expression in an atmosphere of direct and free communion with God.

One of the most instructive accounts recorded for us in Scripture is that of the development of the church at Jerusalem, its relative place in the early Christian picture, and its relationship to the other churches which were the eventual result of the spread of the Gospel. The Jerusalem assembly as the 'mother' church occupied a unique position. It had the privilege of being most intimately in touch with those who had personally known the Lord, and naturally contained a greater wealth of mature, spiritual experience than existed in many of the newer congregations. The advice of the Jerusalem brethren on difficult questions was valued by others as we have seen. Yet gradually, but unmistakably, we find the focus of God's work moving from Jerusalem to Antioch, an assembly with a predominantly Gentile background. Antioch, above all others, was the assembly that gave impetus to the great missionary endeavours in which Paul was a prominent figure, and Antioch stood firmly behind the work of the Lord in prayer and fellowship. More and more the church at Jerusalem occupies the position of a spectator of the great advances of the Gospel, a very interested spectator no doubt, and one who feels a particular right to have a hand in what is taking place, but there is little active spiritual involvement in the spread of the truth outside Jerusalem or Judaea.

If any church should have been actively concerned in the great missionary journeys of Paul which were so signally fulfilling the Lord's command to preach the Gospel to every creature, surely the church at Jerusalem should have been so concerned. But there are other concerns which seem to have taken first place. Why is it that, with the Jerusalem church's unique privileges and potential, her basic significance to the expanding work of the Gospel should be so evidently on the decline? It hardly seems satisfactory to put this down simply to an arbitrary choice on the part of God. There are other and much more probable explanations.

Christ was the fulfilment of all God's dealings with Israel, and it was to Israel, through the institution of the synagogue, as we have already seen, that the Gospel was first presented. Many of the early believers did not recognise, as did Stephen and Paul, the radical cleavage that was inevitable between the church and the synagogue. They considered the church to be little more than a new party within the Jewish community, and as long as they maintained their allegiance to the ceremonial law they were accepted by the Jews, with whatever reservations. We have noted how Paul's insight into the nature and implications of the Gospel and the church led him to pursue a policy which resulted in a clear and final break with Judaism. In Jerusalem we find the opposite tendency, a continual working for conciliation. This gave rise to the peculiar contradiction which existed in the life of the Jerusalem assembly. On the one hand, they could not deny the working of the Spirit of God among the Gentiles, in fact it had been foretold in the Scriptures, but on the other, they could not rid themselves of a sense that it was obligatory upon Jewish believers to observe circumcision and other parts of the ceremonial law, although they admitted that these things were not necessary for salvation.

There are a number of indications that the Jerusalem church's anxiety to hold intact a tolerant relationship with the Jewish community was carried to such an extent that it blunted the edge of its witness and its lasting spiritual effectiveness. When Paul first visited Jerusalem after his conversion, we have seen how the believers summarily shipped him off home to Tarsus when his presence began to cause embarrassment. Then what of the Judaizing teachers from Judaea who caused so much perplexity in Antioch and among the churches of Galatia? (Acts 15 : 1; Gal. 2 : 12). Some of these men had apparently brought a message from James, the most prominent among the Jerusalem brethren, leaving the impression wherever they went that what they preached had the backing of the Jerusalem elders. In the letter that is subsequently circularised from Jerusalem this is, of course, categorically denied (Acts 15 : 24), but are we to believe that these preachers, trusted as they were to be the bearers of some tidings from James, were perpetrating a deliberate falsehood, or did they sincerely feel that they had substantial support in Jerusalem for their emphasis on circumcision as necessary for salvation? There seems no reason to doubt their sincerity, and every reason to believe that they were by no means unjustified in drawing the conclusions they did on the Jerusalem church's agreement with them.

In the Jerusalem church there was a small but vociferous group of 'Pharisees who believed' (Acts 15 : 5). As with most strong minded groups of people, they could make a noise and an impression out of all proportion to their size (which, of course, is good when they happen to be right, bad when they happen to be wrong). They clung tenaciously to the requirements of

39

the ceremonial law, and had a very substantial following (Acts 21 : 20). When the deputation from Antioch arrived at Jerusalem to discuss the matter of circumcision with the elders of the church, some of this group of 'Pharisees who believed' apparently having learned somehow of the reason for the deputation's visit, made a plea for the enforcement of the rite of circumcision and the ceremonial law. This petition seems to have been completely unsolicited, and was made before the apostles and elders gathered together to consider the matter, so it is obvious that these zealots for the law represented a strong section of opinion within the assembly (Acts 15 : 5-6). They were used to making their voice heard, and they were used to being listened to.

But what was the attitude of James to this state of affairs, James who, as we have seen, had come to occupy the leading position in the Jerusalem assembly? In the recent persecution which had been instigated by Herod against 'certain of the church' (Acts 12 : 1), James was left unmolested. Yet Herod executed James, the brother of Peter, and Peter himself was imprisoned, and that too to the pleasure of the Jews (Acts 12 : 2). Clearly, James and his followers occupied a position of respect among the general populace which had been forfeited by Peter and others. The reason for this is that Peter, in obedience to the vision that God had given him, was consorting with the Gentiles, grievously offending Jewish susceptibilities in the process, while James had maintained an attitude of strict compliance with the law. While James full well accepted the basis of the Gospel as faith in Christ, and was under no illusions as to the observance of the ceremonial law being necessary for salvation, yet his attitude was conciliatory to those who took an extreme line. If, in his own heart, he did not agree with them, yet he did not oppose them, so it is not difficult to understand how the teachers who appeared in Antioch and Galatia could believe that what they taught had the general backing of the Jerusalem assembly and of James himself.

James, of course, was no bigot. He was a man renowned for his sacrificial life, of grace and gentleness of character. 'James the just' he was afterwards called. His dealing in the circumcision dispute certainly shows him to be a man who did not lack in down to earth common sense. But just this very combination of admirable qualities had its drawbacks. He was an excellent keeper of the peace, for he always saw both sides of the picture, and respected the other side with a graciousness and conviction that was wellnigh irresistible. Of course he knew that circumcision and observance of the ceremonial law were not necessary to salvation, but, on the other hand, that did not mean that those who kept these observances were unsaved. They too belonged to Christ if they had faith in Him, so why be the means of antagonizing them? James' weakness was probably that his desire to keep the peace predominated over his responsibility to continue proclaiming the positive truths of the Gospel. And it is the truth alone that brings real and lasting freedom.

We must not underestimate the strength of this conciliatory influence of which Jerusalem was the centre, nor what a grievous weakness it was. Its real root lay in a limited understanding of the purpose of Christ. However obvious it was from the Spirit's working that the Gentiles were equal sharers in God's plan, however much the Jerusalem believers assented to this in theory, at heart they could never rid themselves of the idea that Christ was specially for the Jews, and if Gentiles were to have a part in His saving work they should enter into that privilege as Jewish proselytes. The same type of attitude has, of course, been common in every age. Traditional belief or superstition, however unreasonable it may be, dies hard. In some parts of the world there are numerous superstitions regarding certain wholesome foods, that if eaten at a particular season, or in combination with other things, they will lead to illness. Attempting to dislodge these unfounded beliefs is an interesting exercise. The person concerned may be highly intelligent, the arguments advanced may be quite conclusive, but after he has assented to everything he will go away as convinced as ever that his traditional belief is right. The inability on the part of the Jerusalem church to appreciate the scope of the work of Christ explains the contradiction in the standard they accepted as of God for the assemblies in the Gentile world, while yet holding on to a different standard for themselves. What would have happened, one wonders, had God not moved the focus of His working from Jerusalem to Antioch. The situation in Jerusalem really amounted to a traditionalist party led by James which would have confined the church to a mere Jewish sect. It was through the vision and ministry of Stephen, Barnabas and Paul that the influence of traditionalism and the attempted centralization in Jerusalem of the church's life were overcome, leaving the church free, and the Spirit free to work within it.

The experiences of Peter and Paul also provide us with illuminating examples both of the strength of influence of the

Jerusalem church's stand, and of its unfortunate potentialities. It was to Peter that God had, in a very startling manner, revealed that the Gentiles as well as the Jews were heirs of the Gospel. At first Peter, as an orthodox, law-abiding Jew, withstood the implication of the vision he had received, but then accepted it as the Word of God. When he related his experience to the brethren in Jerusalem, they too were left with no alternative but to accept what God had spoken, and they 'glorified God' (Acts 11 : 1-18). Yet later, in Antioch, we find the stalwart Peter abandoning his stand because of the pressure of the Judaizing teachers who had come down from Judaea. Before their arrival he had freely mixed and eaten with the Gentile believers, but afterwards he separated from them and would eat only with the Jews. In fact a little Jewish clique began to gather round him. Even Barnabas was led astray. It is surprising how easily Peter was diverted from the way God had explicitly shown him through a visit of people who certainly did not have his apostolic standing, and most probably did not have anything like his spiritual maturity. But they came from James, and that fact overshadowed everything else. The church at Jerusalem still had a particular aura of superiority and authority in the eyes of Peter.

Paul rebukes Peter in no uncertain terms. His relationship with the church at Jerusalem was one of close fellowship, but not such that he was overawed by the sense of a superior authority. By no standard could Peter's action be justified, and it was, in reality, a denial of the Gospel (Gal. 2 : 11-17). Peter seems to have taken the admonition in good part, and we hear no more of such untimely appeasement.

However, Paul himself is also put to the test. It was his last visit to Jerusalem, and he had gone there with brethren appointed from other churches to deliver what had been received from the collection he had organized for the relief of the poor in the Jerusalem assembly. Actually, Paul had been advised to stay clear of Jerusalem as his ministry and fellowship among the Gentiles had engendered much feeling in the city against him.

Paul and the party were graciously received. The day following their arrival they had a session with the elders, and Paul, thrilled by what he had seen of the working of the Spirit, related to them all that God had done through his ministry to the Gentiles. "Wonderful! Wonderful!" they said, "Praise the Lord! Now, look here, brother. Do you see the thousands of believing Jews we have here in Jerusalem who are zealots for the law?"

42

And they went on to tell him how much offence had been caused through the stories circulated about him. "Why can't you show them that you are as good a Jew as anyone?" It so happened that there was an excellent opportunity of doing so. Four of the Jerusalem brethren had taken a temporary Nazarite vow and were about to discharge that vow in the Temple. Paul could go along with them, take part in the ritual cleansing, and thereby demonstrate both to the traditionally minded church and to the Hebrew populace that he had not abandoned his old loyalties. Such was the plan, and Paul agreed. Should he have done so? If he were right in doing so, one may well ask why God did not honour the step he took, for it signally failed to accomplish the purpose for which it was intended. Instead of allaying the suspicions of the people, it caused a public furore (Acts 21 : 17-32), hardly calculated to increase his popularity with the section of the church he had particularly set out to win.

Unlike most human biographers who almost inevitably tend to stress one aspect of character at the expense of another, the Bible is completely honest, and portrays men as they really are. The apostles' failings are faithfully portrayed along with their strengths. His visit to Jerusalem was one occasion when Paul made a mistake. It is, of course, easy to be wise after the event, but Paul's mistake can teach us some salutary lessons. We may well sympathise with his dilemma. He was the guest of the Jerusalem believers who were being stigmatized by his action, and here was an opportunity to remove some of the odium from them. He himself was a Jew who loved his people after the flesh. Might he not identify himself with them to some extent and win a good word not only for himself, but also for his Lord? Then, what the elders said was so reasonable, their concern was so great, their attitude so gracious. And who could resist James? He could melt a heart of stone, and Paul's heart was no stone. Paul was graciously badgered into a compromise.

Two things are further emphasized through the experiences of Paul and Peter just related. First is the occupation of the Jerusalem church with the desire to conciliate the Jews, to the extent that the vision of the church as a divine company called out of every race was obscured. It is true that the provisions arrived at as an outcome of the discussion on circumcision had been eminently reasonable (Acts 15 : 23-29; 21 : 25). They recognised no obligation upon Gentile believers to observe the Jewish ceremonial law, yet in the midst of this clear declaration on the complete efficacy of faith in Christ there existed, as we have already noticed, this obvious contradiction in the daily life of the Jerusalem assembly. In fact if not in theory, they did not accept the regenerated life of the Spirit as the one thing that united all those who were in Christ, irrespective of whether they were Jews or Gentiles. Could we say that the Jerusalem church was the first Christian denomination? To the relationship of spiritual life it added the necessity of conformity to a prescribed ritual.

Secondly, Peter's experience in particular demonstrates the almost unconscious tendency to look to Jerusalem as the centre, not simply in a healthy spirit of fellowship, but in a spirit of subservience. So far, in fact, did Peter regard Jerusalem opinion, that he did violence to his own conscience and disobeyed the explicit command of God given to him in one of the most graphic, spiritual experiences he had known. This was certainly not the type of relationship that the Spirit was fostering between the churches, yet if Peter with his experience and maturity found himself bereft of spiritual judgement through a temptation to a misplaced, earthly loyalty, what could be expected from the community of ordinary believers who would shortly be overawed by the same authority that had overawed Peter? The standard set by the Lord was of an entirely different order. The community of believers, however small, and wherever they met, was His dwelling place through the Spirit. As they remained subservient to Him they could always know His mind, " For where two or three are gathered together in my name, there am I in the midst of them " (Matt. 18 : 20). We find this worked out, for example, in Antioch, where the will of the Lord was clearly revealed as the brethren ' ministered unto the Lord ' (Acts 13 : 2).

Looking at the situation from the other point of view, that of the Jerusalem church, there is little question that they felt they occupied a special position of authority in relation to the other assemblies. When Peter and Paul were given the right hand of fellowship in their ministries to the Jews and to the Gentiles, the brethren at Jerusalem had made one request, that they should remember the poor, the poor, of course, being themselves, for as already mentioned, the Jerusalem assembly seems to have suffered from a chronic poverty (Gal. 2 : 7-10). Paul says that this same burden was much upon his own heart, and in this connection he discharged his obligation faithfully, as we know. Yet it is doubtful whether Paul and the Jerusalem brethren understood the same thing by ' remembering the poor '. While

44

to Paul it was a spiritual obligation which should mark the love, fellowship and concern which exists among all true believers, to the mind of those in Jerusalem it was almost certainly more in the nature of a tribute which they felt was owed to them because of their special position, just as the Temple at Jerusalem received tribute from Jews scattered throughout the world.

We may also question the attitude of the Judaizing teachers who caused such a stir in Antioch and throughout Galatia. Did they feel that their message carried special weight because they came from Jerusalem? We know that they over-stepped the terms of their commission, whatever that was, for it is specifically stated in the letter from Jerusalem on the matter of circumcision, but that alone does not explain the perplexity their teaching caused. It also has to be remembered that, although the Jerusalem elders clearly censured the doctrine which these men preached, yet they did not disassociate themselves from them, for they had been sent out at least on the authority of James (Acts 15 : 24; Gal. 2 : 12). The only explanation that fully satisfies the conditions is that these teachers from Jerusalem did, in fact, carry with them an air of authority and superiority which was not simply spiritual, but legal, all of which points to a very early tendency towards centralization, with Jerusalem at the head. That this tendency did not, at this stage, gain further ground, was due to the strength of the assembly at Antioch and to the fact that God had moved the focus of His working there from Jerusalem.

It may be idle to speculate on what would have happened had the authority of Jerusalem at that time succeeded in dominating the development and life of the other churches, but it is not difficult to realise what serious difficulties could have arisen from the strong sympathies in Jerusalem to the ritual observances of the law, and the lack of a real, heart acceptance of the Gentiles. However admirable and reassuring the letter sent from James and the elders to Antioch and other assemblies, it would have required to be backed by a more practical compliance with its standard on the part of the Jerusalem church itself if it were to have had a permanent effect among communities which looked to Jerusalem for a lead. Otherwise, the contrary conduct of the Jerusalem assembly would almost inevitably have been the means of perpetuating the difference throughout the Christian community, and the cause, ultimately, of widespread division.

In summing up our examination into the reasons why God

saw fit to replace Jerusalem by Antioch as the spring-board for the great missionary endeavour of apostolic times, there are three things which have been emphasized as a grave danger to the life of the church and a curb on the working of the Spirit.

1. The practical refusal to recognise that life in the Spirit is the only and indispensable ground of fellowship. Spiritual life, of course, is not simply an acknowledgement of the claims of Christ. It is an acknowledgement which produces a divine change. A holy life is inseparable from the possession of spiritual life, and where a practical walk which honours Christ is combined with an open acknowledgement of Him and submission to Him, there remains nothing else which should be demanded as a condition of fellowship.

2. The tendency common to all human nature to be man centred instead of God centred. It would be difficult to over-emphasize the importance of fellowship in the life of the church. Regeneration is essentially an entrance into a life of fellowship. It is through the mutual dependence of fellowship in the church that God has ordained to make His mind known, but the purpose of fellowship is to enable us to see the hand of God and make us more dependent upon Him. When the church becomes dependent upon the means of God's grace instead of upon God Himself, fellowship degenerates into dependence upon man, or hero worship, and becomes a snare.

3. The move towards centralization of control and ecclesiastical authoritarianism. This ultimately leads to a dispute with the Lordship of Christ, for He is the Head of the church and is actively present by His Spirit in the midst of His people. Christ alone stands as the Mediator between God and men. The church is vested with the authority to represent God to the world, but no human being or group of persons has the authority to represent God to the church, for Christ dwells there in person. Since ecclesiastical authoritarianism detracts from the incentive to direct dependence upon God, it is not conducive to the healthy development of spiritual life, for it encourages a mechanical attitude to spiritual truth which ultimately reduces faith to a dead formalism.

As we pursue the course of the church down through the centuries, we will see these three tendencies again and again assert themselves, and the Spirit of God, hindered in His work-

46

ing by humanly imposed limitations, move afresh to reveal the fuller purpose of Christ on freer ground.

A brief review of some of the difficulties encountered in two other churches of New Testament times will suffice to illustrate the subtle means by which Satan seeks to devitalize the witness of the assembly. Jerusalem apart, Scripture leaves us a fuller account of the establishing of the assemblies at Corinth and Ephesus than of any others, and we have, furthermore, the three letters written to them by the apostle Paul, as well as the message of the Spirit of God to the church at Ephesus recorded for us in Revelation 2.

The Corinthian assembly had been invaded by the evils of *Corinth* immorality and dissention which were a well-known feature of the life of the city itself. The Corinthians' brains were mostly employed on a business level (when they were not empty-mindedly indulging in gratifying the flesh), but the city was a keen rival of nearby, intellectual Athens, so many of the citizens were preudo-philosophers. This, no doubt, was the source of much of the hair-splitting wrangling that took place in the church. But these things were really no more than symptoms *don't indulge* of a much more basic evil. The Corinthians' playing at being *in fleshly* philosophers had so increased their self-importance that they *philosophy.* had, in practice, denied the Lordship of Christ. That is why Paul commences his first letter to them, not by slating them for their follies, but by exalting Christ in an attempt to shame them into a recognition of their own pettiness and stupidity by lifting their eyes from the mire to the glory of God. In the first ten verses of his letter alone Paul refers to Christ as Lord no less than six times. Paul's salutary epistle was the means, in God's hand, of restoring the Corinthians' perspective, and their first love to the Lord was recovered. Their experience shows us that anything that would detract from the Lordship of Christ in the assembly, even an occupation with truth itself, is a potential destroyer of God's purpose in His people.

The lesson of the Ephesian church is essentially the same. Paul addresses his letter ' to the faithful in Christ Jesus ' showing in this simple phrase that the very nature and purpose of the church is dependent upon their being a people who are subservient to the Lord. The Ephesian assembly was outstanding for its spiritual progress and maturity. In the book of Revelation it is commended for persistent zeal, patience and spiritual discernment, but in spite of all these things there could be a lack of heart devotion to Christ which would make the assembly

47

useless to God. The very truth which they knew so well could be held in pride and self-sufficiency, and the very energy with which they propagated it could be the energy of the flesh which, denying the Lordship of the One, true Head, effectively staunched the flow of the Spirit's life, and left the church itself a castaway.

Pride or self-sufficiency is the basic evil which denies God His rightful place. It may take many forms, all of them outwardly plausible; the expedient of human organization to facilitate the functioning of the assembly and protect it from error; dependence upon a man or a human hierarchy, guised as humility and fellowship; a zeal for a particular aspect of truth which will deny the right of fellowship unless that 'truth' be imposed upon everybody. All of these deny the Lordship of Christ, and to dethrone Him from His rightful place in the midst of His people has been the cause of the great, spiritual warfare of the ages. How often the arch-enemy has seemed to succeed, but when man has apparently prevailed, and the corn of wheat of the Lordship of Christ has been cast to the ground as dead, it has but sprung up again to yield forth a more abundant harvest.

CHAPTER FIVE

CHANGE

IN the previous chapter we have been concerned mainly with the attitude of conceit which, finding place in certain sections of the church in early years, opened the way for debilitating changes which were gradually to establish themselves in the churches' order. We will now see what these changes actually were.

Although there is very little historical information on the growth and development of the church from the end of the apostolic period till late in the second century, the extent of the spread of the Gospel was, without doubt, phenomenal. In a letter written by Pliny, Governor of Bithynia to the Roman Emperor, Trajan, about the year A.D. 112 he deals specifically with the problem the spread of Christianity was posing in his administration of the province. He says, "For many of every age, every class, and both sexes are being accused (i.e. of being Christians) and will continue to be accused. Nor has this contagious superstition spread through the cities only, but also through the villages and the countryside." Pliny then goes on to say how temples were practically deserted, and there had been a slump in the trade of fodder for the sacrificial animals, since the offering of heathen sacrifices had lost its vogue. True, many 'Christians' were 'reclaimed' because of the persecutions of the period, indicating that all who took the name of Christ and had, for a season, abandoned their pagan practices, had not experienced a true regeneration, but the extent of the influence of the Gospel up to the end of the second century is, none the less, evident. If such was the case in the province of Bithynia, the position was almost certainly similar elsewhere in Asia Minor and farther afield. What Paul wrote to the Thessalonians may well be indicative of the general zeal and diligence with which the early church set forth to propagate the faith. "For from you hath sounded forth the word of the Lord, not only in Macedonia and Achaia, but in every place your faith to Godward is gone forth" (1 Thess. 1 : 8).

The communities of believers, large and small, continued their work and witness in the same, simple dependence upon the

49

ever present Lord, in fellowship with one another, and guided
by elders obviously sealed by the setting apart of the Spirit, as
they had seen in the first churches established through the
ministry of the apostles. It was not long, however, before the
wind of change began to blow. There were always those who
remained faithful to the Scriptural ground of meeting, but as
the Christian community increased in size, so the face of the
church in general began to alter. The transformation, of course,
took place gradually, and in some places there was a continuance
of the apostolic pattern, or some aspects of it, into the second
century.

We have seen the basic attitude behind the changes, but what
was the outward reason for them? The outward reason for the
majority of ecclesiastical changes was simply expediency. When
the Lordship of Christ ceases to be the sole impetus of the
church, and self-sufficient man takes over, there are bound to
be changes in the spiritual pattern which suggest themselves
in the name of efficiency, for the spiritual pattern just does not
work when man, and not God, is in control. Human expediency, however, has never proved a good hand-maid to spiritual
progress.

The tendency towards the heading up of the government of
a church in one man is seen first in Jerusalem. The assembly
was, no doubt, ruled in theory at least, by a plurality of elders,
but in the references we have to these men in the Acts of the
Apostles we find that increasing pre-eminence is given to one
man, namely James. In the earlier mention of the church at
Jerusalem reference is made to the apostles (Acts 9 : 27) or to
'the apostles and the brethren' (Acts 11 : 1). Later, however,
James comes in for special mention along with the others who
had the oversight of the community. "Tell these things unto
James, and to the brethren," says Peter, announcing his deliverance from gaol (Acts 12 : 17). Likewise, on Paul's final visit to
Jerusalem we read, "Paul went in with us unto James; and all
the elders were present" (Acts 21 : 18). James also appears as
the main spokesman or chairman in the discussion on circumcision (Acts 15 : 13). It is, of course, necessary that, when the
need arises, one of a company of elders should act as spokesman
for the group (it is hardly practical that all should speak in
unison), but James ultimately occupied a position which was
much more than this. He became more even than first among
equals; he became first pure and simple, and emerged distinctly
as leader of the group.

Transition from eldership to authoritarian leadership is not difficult to understand, and from a human point of view, such change is almost inescapable. The Scriptural principle is demonstrably unworkable apart from the Spirit. Whenever humble dependence upon the Lord slackens, the eldership degenerates into no more than a human committee. Committees have all sorts of interesting possibilities. If all the members are weak, no one will decide anything; if all the members are strong, no one will allow anyone else to decide anything; if there are but a few strong personalities, the committee is likely to disintegrate in an explosion of invective; if there is but one strong personality, all the rest become 'yes-men' and the committee, to all practical purposes, gives up in favour of one man rule. Committee rule is notoriously weak unless there is one strong mind which can take the lead, and when his position is recognised and perpetuated, the committee naturally melts unassumingly away and leaves him to it.

It is interesting to find, however, that James' benevolent rule in Jerusalem did not permanently establish the idea of leaving control in the hands of one man. The church, of course, was scattered by the terrible war and destruction of the city in the year A.D. 70 but the war over, some of the Christians returned, and the church of Jerusalem was reconstituted. A brother called Simeon for many years seems to have occupied a similar place of authority in the assembly to James, but from the time of his death in 107 to 135 it appears that the church was, once again, ruled by a plurality of elders, an indication that the Scriptural principle which had early been in force had not been forgotten. The fourth century historian, Eusebius, quotes a list, compiled some hundred years before his time, of thirteen men who were leaders of the Jerusalem church during these twenty-eight years. He assumes that they were Bishops in the monarchical sense which predominated in his own day, but a little mental arithmetic will show both how highly improbable it is that thirteen people should rule consecutively in one church with an average term of office of little more than two years, and also how strong a fixture the idea of monarchical Bishops had become by the time of Eusebius. It is much more probable that the thirteen names are simply a list of the elders of the Jerusalem church over the twenty-eight-year period.

Another danger in the early church, and one which is no less common today, was the danger of self-appointed leadership. There must be few assemblies where there is not some self-assertive, and maybe eminently capable brother, who is certain he can manage affairs much better than those who are doing so, or than anyone else. If the eldership is weak, he will soon dominate the scene, and if there are no elders, he will do the work of half a dozen elders rolled into one with a will and a gusto that drives everything before it, and ultimately drives everyone away. John writes of such a person in his third epistle, Diotrephes.

Brother Diotrephes was quite a character, and John sighs in sorrow at the chaos he is causing. Diotrephes loved pre-eminence (such people never seem to think much on the difference between true pre-eminence and notoriety), and, of course, he knew much more and much better than any of the apostles. When John wrote to the church, Diotrephes took charge of the letter and said they were not going to waste their time having anything to do with him. Had they not heard the stories that had been going round about John? They are not going to receive John, nor any of his followers either for that matter, and if there are any in the church who want to receive them, they can go and join them—outside (3 John 9-10). Diotrephes ruled with an iron hand.

The picture is only too familiar. But what is the answer to this type of situation? Why, the answer is to elect, or set apart, or for God to choose (different people prefer different terminology) someone whom everybody likes, everyone, that is, apart from Diotrephes, to take charge of the assembly. This seems to have been the solution that was adopted at a relatively early stage in the church's history, for there can be little doubt that the establishment of monarchical Bishops was, among other things, designed to combat the very real evil of the self-appointment in church matters of able, spiritual despots. Whether a despot who is chosen is any better than a despot who is not chosen is, of course, a debatable point.

The tragedy of this course was that it was a purely human expedient, the easy way out, for the natural way is always easier to the flesh than the way of the Spirit. The only way in which the Scriptural order can be made to work is through constant subjection to the will of the Lord, but that is the only way in which the church can be expected to grow and develop healthily. If certain evils have been more easily counteracted within the church through recourse to human expedients, the church itself has, in the long run, suffered much more through spiritual dearth in other directions.

The writings of Ignatius contain the first clear mention of the monarchical Bishop, and in this sense Ignatius himself was Bishop of Antioch. In the year 115 on his way to execution in Rome, he wrote to various places letters stressing the great importance of the Bishop's office. To him, a single Bishop in the church was indispensable, and his authority was absolute. He alone could administer baptism and officiate at the Lord's table. Even a love feast required his presence. The uncompromising vehemence with which Ignatius defended the position is clear proof that the position must have been very strongly assailed. He may not have been, by any means, a lone voice in championing the Bishop's cause, but the idea had obviously not taken such firm root that it could be allowed to develop quietly without protection. By the middle of the second century, however, the view of Ignatius commanded wide acceptance.

At least until the year of Ignatius' martyrdom the church at Rome was ruled by elders, and shortly after that time Polycarp, writing to the assembly at Philippi addresses, not a single Bishop, but the elders. Yet Polycarp, as Bishop of Smyrna, held a position parallel to that of Ignatius in Antioch, and both of these men had known some of the apostles. Polycarp had been taught by John. It is in some ways strange that men of such ability and devotion who had contact with the very sources of divine Scripture should hold so strongly to a position, in Ignatius' case at least, which had so little Scriptural justification, but it shows again how even a person's zeal for the propagation and defence of the truth may drive him to devices of human expediency to the neglect of divine order. Polycarp, an old and venerated servant of the Lord, was put to death for his faith in Smyrna in the year 156.

The early monarchical Bishop was, of course, different to the Bishop of modern days with his oversight of a large diocese. The fitting modern parallel would be that of a parish minister or parish priest. Otherwise it would obviously have been impossible for the Bishop to officiate at every celebration of the Lord's Table as Ignatius lays down to be a necessary part of his duties. Neither was there any thought in those early days of an episcopal succession. Even when this latter idea first came into prominence, it was a conception completely different from the present idea of apostolic succession. Irenaeus, writing on this subject towards the end of the second century, was concerned simply with the historical continuance of a line of Bishops in any particular place. The view widely held today in episcopal com-

E

munions of an actual ordination perpetuated through the consecratory act of a Bishop which can be traced right back to the time of the apostles, and which has vested all those thus consecrated with apostolic authority is the product of someone's imagination at a still later stage in the history of the Church.

The establishment of the monarchical Bishop soon gave rise to the recognition of two classes within the church, and also opened the way for other evils. These two classes have been perpetuated down through the centuries in the distinction between clergy and laity. It is interesting how singularly inept the word 'clergy' is in this connection. It is derived from the Greek word 'kleiron', a word used by Peter in his first epistle and rendered in the English A.V. by the word 'heritage'. The revisers have translated the verse, " Neither as lording it over the charge allotted to you " (1 Peter 5 : 3). This is part of Peter's exhortation to elders (vs. 1) and nothing could be more clear than that the charge allotted to them, or God's heritage, is the believers in the assembly as a whole, yet through some strange etymological perversion, from a word which indicated the great unity and privilege of the church as a whole, there has been derived a word which means practically the opposite, and is used to denote a class of people with special privilege within the Church itself.

There can be no doubt that in Ignatius' desire to see a clerical system firmly established his motive was pure. He was concerned, above all, to protect the church from the prevalent heresies of the day. But however worthy his aim, the method he employed to assure its success was mistaken, and played right into the hands of the forces he was seeking to counteract.

The labyrinthal speculations of Greek philosophy produced much heart discontent, and there were many who sought peace of heart and mind in other directions. This, as we have already seen, was one of the main reasons for the influx into the Jewish synagogues of the Gentile God-fearers, many of whom were among the first to accept the Gospel. There were, however, other and less desirable effects of Greek thought. It gave rise to numerous cults or 'mystery religions'. Something of a similar nature has occurred in Japan since the end of the last world war. The disillusionment which spread with the collapse of State Shinto has given rise to a phenomenal growth of 'new religions', small sects of a wide variety and mixture of beliefs, all offering some measure of spiritual comfort and peace. The Greek cults had a wide influence and a popular appeal, and the blessings which they offered were entered into through the undergoing of various initiatory rites performed by a priestly class set apart for such ministrations.

Christianity has always been open to heathen influences to the extent that it has departed from the divine pattern, and the departure which Ignatius so zealously encouraged fitted in admirably with the aura of mystery which surrounded the fashionable cults of the day. It is easy to understand how, to pagans who assumed the Christian faith, a regime of clerics could take on a much different significance from what was ever intended by Ignatius and others of his persuasion. From being a special class of people it was a short step to their being considered a class with special powers, and the ceremonies at which they officiated, baptism and the Lord's table, naturally came to be associated directly with the powers they were supposed to employ. The power of the Spirit having gone, these rites took its place; baptism came to be understood as a means whereby regeneration was miraculously conferred, and the Lord's table, with the bread and wine miraculously transformed into the actual flesh and blood of Christ through the power of the Bishop, became a further means of the magical impartation of divine grace. All this was a direct inheritance from heathenism, for nowhere in the New Testament is there any hint that the administration of baptism or the Lord's table should be restricted to any special class of people, neither are the supposedly miraculous associations of these ordinances at all in accordance with Scriptural teaching.

Thus the rot set in. Baptismal regeneration was being taught early in the second century, and a variation of possibly slightly later origin was the baptism of infants, another practice for which there is no authority in the New Testament. Tertullian, writing in the year 197, condemns the practice along with the practice of baptizing the dead, yet another innovation.

But the cause of Christ was not lost. The leaven had been introduced into the fellowship of the church, and was doing its insidious work, a process that was to continue till the 'whole was leavened'. This corrupt church, however, was only what appeared outwardly to the world as the result of the Gospel. In the midst of an increasing denial of the life that is in Christ, God had His people who were not carried away by the assimilation of heathen ways, and these, down through the centuries, were to bear the torch of testimony. As we follow the course of this witness through the years, it will become increasingly

55

evident that it diverges very far at times from the organized institution of Christianity. The history of the working of the Spirit of God is not the history of any organization, and what usually goes by the name 'Church History' is only too often a sorry tale of bigoted quarrels and selfish intrigue. Yet the history of the two, the spiritual movement, and the earthly institution, are sometimes so closely intermingled that it is impossible to give an account of one without referring to the other.

While there was a constant activity of devitalizing forces within the church, there was one thing which slowed down their progress for the first three centuries. That was the onslaught of persecution to which the believers were constantly subjected. The first violent outbreak of persecution against the Christians perpetrated by the Imperial power took place in the year A.D. 64 during the reign of Nero. Persecution extended throughout the Empire, and was often systematically pursued. There were periods when the violence abated to some extent, and other times when the storm died down altogether, depending largely on the successive Emperors who occupied the seat of power, but till early in the fourth century in the reign of Constantine, the church, outlawed by law, lived under the constant threat of the severest and most cruel penalties. Christians were tortured and put to death; all their property was confiscated, and every attempt was also made to destroy the Scriptures.

There is no need to digress at this point to go into details of the unmentionable sufferings inflicted upon the believers. The opportunity for Nero's cruel oppression in 64 came with the great fire of Rome. Rumour spread that the Emperor himself was guilty of incendiarism, so Nero used the Christians as a scape-goat and accused them of setting the city on fire. Whether the Emperor was guilty of the crime as rumour suggested we do not know for certain, but a man who so openly went to the utter limits of bestiality could have been guilty of any outrage, and he was, at the same time, clever enough to have used the very incredibility of the charge laid against him as a means of covering up his own guilt, for he had known more than his worthy share of popularity. There was, however, a sufficient strength of popular opinion against the Christians for Nero to carry the people with him in the terrible slaughter that he instigated. Christians were unpopular. The whole of Roman life was bound up with heathen practices in which they resolutely refused to take part, so social ostracism was the

56

result. Their separate life cloaked them with an aura of mystery to the ordinary Roman citizen, and malicious rumour, cloathed with the fearful refinements of the inevitable gossip, served to complete the picture of a people who were the enemies of mankind and not fit to live. The exemplary life of the Christians gradually broke down this popular hatred, but these were early days in the history of the church, and distrust was at its height. Even so, the orgy of cruelty let loose by Nero awoke a feeling of pity within the hearts of the general populace. They had had their fill of gore and the revolting reek of roasting, human flesh. There was left a feeling of disgust that all this carnage was but to satiate the savagery of a human beast. It was during this outbreak of persecution that the apostles Peter and Paul were martyred in Rome. Nero finally committed suicide in the year 68 to escape the death to which the Senate had sentenced him.

One of the most dreadful aspects of Nero's cruelty was that it served as a terrible precedent for later Roman rulers who wanted to pursue a policy of repression against the Christians, and there were not a few who bent all their efforts to exterminate the faith.

As in Japan up to recent years, so also in the Roman Empire the Emperor was regarded as divine, and it is round this fact that many stories of martyrdom are centred. To call upon the Emperor as ' Lord ' was something that no Christian could do, nor could he offer the few ritual grains of incense in his honour. These, therefore, were the tests that were often applied, and compliance or refusal meant life or death.

From the great army of martyrs of these early days one of the best known is Polycarp. Taught by the apostle John, he was later Bishop of Smyrna where he was put to death in the year 156. His great confession of faith has challenged many down through the centuries. As he was led to the scene of execution he was besought to recant and save his life. The pro-consul of Asia in person pled with the venerable old servant of God but to acknowledge the Emperor, deny Christ and be set free. Then Polycarp uttered these memorable words, " Eighty-six years have I served Him, and He has done me no wrong; how then can I blaspheme my Saviour and King? " He was led away to the stake. Polycarp's death signalled the end of persecution in Asia for a time. It seems that the sight of so saintly a man being led off to execution for his faithfulness, produced a public conscience against the organised slaughter of Christians, and

57

the churches entered upon a period of respite from fear and destruction.

The tide of persecution ebbed and flowed with the passing years, but it was becoming increasingly clear that it would be the Roman Empire, not the church, that would have to give way. Whatever the official attitude, to many ordinary men and women the Christian way had a distinct appeal. The Christians were not allowed to give public expression to their faith, but their consistent way of life was breaking down the old prejudices with which they were assailed, and gave the lie to the slanders that had been spread against them. The years of peace were years when many were added to the church, and Christians penetrated practically every level of society. When persecutions did break out again they increasingly lacked the support of the common people, and ultimately of the officials also whose job it was to carry them out. It is true that Christians in every part of the Empire did not enjoy this increasing freedom. In Palestine and Egypt the fiercest of all persecutions was in the early years of the fourth century, but viewing the situation in the Empire as a whole, repressions against the believers were declining in severity.

A fresh wave of persecution broke out in the year 202 during the reign of Septimius Severus following his issue of an edict which forbade conversion either to Judaism or to Christianity. This is interesting as the first appearance of legislation which specifically outlawed the holding of the Christian faith. Christianity had for a long time been separated from Judaism in the official mind and was, therefore, an 'unlicensed religion'. Christians had been condemned, officially according to Roman law, on a point of law and order, but the edict of 202 made Christianity itself a crime.

After almost half a century of rest, the onslaught against the church was again renewed during the short reign of Decius. The Roman Empire was beset by enemies on two fronts, the Goths on the north, and the Sassanids on the east. Decius decided to rally people to the call of the Empire by demanding that they demonstrate their loyalty to the State religion. Christianity must be crushed, and all must sacrifice to the State gods. In this test some Christians recanted, others stood firm, but for the first time participation of the mob in acts of persecution was lacking. Some pagans even sought to help their Christian neighbours escape the scrutiny of the officials. The old suspicion and bitterness of years was giving way at last. The meek were inheriting the earth.

The last violent attempt to destroy Christianity commenced in 303 during the reign of Diocletian. So numerous had the Christians become, that it was obvious something had to be done at once, or not at all. In a now-or-never attempt to deal with the situation, edicts were promulgated first for the destruction of all Christian places of worship and of the Scriptures, then for the arrest of the clergy, and finally for all Christians to sacrifice to the State gods on penalty of execution. The strictness with which these measures were enforced varied from place to place, but the Christians began to command the sympathy not only of the ordinary pagans, but of the officials themselves. Eventually the Emperor Galerius rescinded the anti-Christian edicts in 311. With this the Imperial persecution came to an end. Rome had been defeated.

How did the standard of the church as a whole fare during these centuries of trial? There were bound to be many who were attracted by the Christian ethic who yet never reached the stage of faith where they experienced true regeneration. Such people easily lapsed into their old position when the day of testing came. Others recanted only under the severest provocation. Yet, on the whole, the Christian testimony remained unshaken, and the fortitude of many of God's people in suffering broke down popular opposition.

About the middle of the second century an anonymous writer wrote to an enquirer called Diognetius, giving a description of the life of the Christian community. His words aptly sum up the judgement which the whole Roman world ultimately had to accept. "Christians," he said, "display to us their wonderful and confessedly striking method of life. They live in their own countries, but simply as sojourners, yet endure all hardships as foreigners. Every foreign land is to them as home, yet their every home land is foreign. They pass their days on earth, but they are citizens of heaven. They obey the laws of the land, and at the same time surpass the law by their lives. They love all and are reviled by all." The blood of the martyrs had watered the seed of the Gospel, and the fruit of the Spirit was the testimony of the church.

59

CHAPTER SIX

HERESIES

As early as New Testament times the life of the churches was disturbed by various forms of erroneous teaching. The Graeco-Roman world of apostolic days was full of philosophic speculations, and many of the intellectual *élite* indulged their minds in 'superior' forms of learning which theorized on the nature and problems of life. The common 'cultural' spirit of the day is nicely captured by Luke when he writes of Athens, " Now all the Athenians and the strangers sojourning there had leisure for nothing else, but either to tell or to hear some new thing" (Acts 17 : 21 marg.). These religious speculators borrowed from a great variety of sources in an attempt to devise some theory of God which satisfied the human mind, and were not hesitant to draw also from Christianity. Greek thought in this way made an effort to penetrate into the church, and the ultimate attempt to interpret Christianity in terms of 'modern, enlightened thought' gave rise to various heresies which for many years stood in opposition to the 'faith once delivered to the saints' Paul's epistle to the Colossians, and John's first and second epistles, for example, give warnings against these prevalent forms of error which were the source, consciously or otherwise, of a number of difficulties with which the churches of the New Testament were beleaguered.

To understand the future course of the church, it is necessary that we should know a little about some of these heresies, not because they themselves were successful in modifying the character of the church, but because of the means adopted by the church to counter their influence. These counter measures, much more than the heresies themselves, were responsible for the changes which were eventually to lead the assemblies so far away from the simplicity of church life as it was in New Testament times.

Gnosticism

Underlying much of the heathen philosophy which pertained in the Graeco-Roman world of apostolic days was the idea that

[handwritten annotations:] fear of error ruins a person and the church.

[handwritten annotations at bottom:] Page 64 shows how han to protect against heresies— have strong spiritual life to Christ Jesus - the Truth.

concern to not err and prayerful...ness about the things that sound... error is good and necessary but not fear the material world was intrinsically evil or worthless, and the body, therefore, being material, was morally neutral. This idea, of course, had a still earlier origin, and is a familiar facet in some schemes of Oriental thought. Around this basic, fallacious premise, were developed numerous interpretations (or misinterpretations to be more precise) of the Christian message. These intepretations became known as Gnosticism.

'Gnosis' is the Greek word for 'knowledge', and had to do specifically with a nonsensical cosmology (as we would consider it today) which embodied the 'scientific outlook' of the age. This theory of the universe held that each planet was a spirit ruler exercising each an influence over a particular sphere, and separating the earth from the ultimate reality. The idea even then, of course, not a new one, forms the basis of that pernicious superstition, astrology. It is very easy to see how all this fitted into the idea of a separate, spiritual reality and an indifferent, material order. Far outside the realm of the planets lived God, high and above the contamination of this material world which was the creation not of the supreme God, who could not deign to be interested in such things, but of some inferior, demi-god. Christianized 'gnosis', or gnosticism as it came to be called, looked upon the body as the prison of the soul, and Jesus as the representative of the divine who condescended to enter this lower realm of the earth in order to release the captive soul and reunite it once again to the eternal spirit.

In its practical application to daily living there were two possible ways of interpreting gnosticism. First, it could be interpreted to mean that, since the body was amoral, the extent to which it was indulged was of no consequence, or secondly, that since the body was of no real value, its demands should be denied or subdued as far as possible. Gnostics generally followed the latter interpretation. They were known, therefore, for their stringent discipline and asceticism. It is to this that Paul refers in writing to the Colossian assembly where there was an attempted infiltration of gnostic ideas, when he speaks of the danger of being brought into bondage to ordinances by those who were urging them " Handle not, nor taste, nor touch " (Col. 2 : 21).

Another erroneous teaching which the churches of early years had to combat was called Docetism. Docetism shared the basic presuppositions of Gnosticism, and its characteristic view was that the incarnation was but an appearance (in the sense of unreality) of God. Christ, it said, did not actually come in the

61

flesh. This was the doctrine that John so strongly condemned in his first epistle.

It may be mentioned in passing how a remnant of Gnostic thought has been carried over into Christianity right up to the present day. It is often most evident where there is a greater depth of spiritual teaching and where people have sought to be true to the Word of God. We must always be careful against an assumed spirituality which exalts that which is ' spiritual ' and denigrates everything of the material and earthly order into something completely worthless. The material part of our being, the body, is much more necessary to spiritual wholeness than many suppose. Scripture never discounts the material order while exalting a spiritual order alone as being the only and absolute, ultimate reality. The present world order is fallen and, in consequence is, we know, one day going to pass away (1 Peter 1 : 24-25), but its place is going to be taken, not by a spiritual nothingness, but by a new creation, and that new creation will be enjoyed by a new, resurrection body (1 Cor. 15 : 42-44).

The failure to appreciate this wholeness of spiritual life which should envelop, renew and sanctify the earthly aspect of our being as well, led to the extreme asceticism which at times has occupied a prominent place in the history of the church. It is also the source of the tendency of believers in some parts of the world in particular to sweep aside everything of beauty and order as being ' worldly '. The Christian life, above all others, should be a life of true beauty and order.

Marcionism

During the second century a teacher called Marcion wielded a great influence in the Christian world, drawing after him many followers whom he formed into rival churches. Marcionism was an influence which had to be reckoned with for many generations.

Marcion himself was a native of Asia Minor, born about the year 85. He was brought up among the churches of his own province, and in his concern over the great problems of sin and evil gradually developed a teaching that was peculiarly his own. These ideas he brought to Rome about the year 140, but they were totally unacceptable to the believers so, severing his relationship with the churches, he began to gather people together in separate congregations.

Marcion had been deeply influenced by gnostic thought, and based his teaching on the hypothesis of the material order being essentially evil. This, he said, was created not by the God whom Jesus proclaimed, but by an inferior god who was none other than the Jehovah of the Old Testament. He is the first person we know to have claimed that the God of the Old Testament and the God of the New Testament were different Beings. The *wrong!* Old Testament God was to Marcion a cold, stern God of judgement, ever seeking to bring people into bondage, while the New Testament God was a God of love and forgiveness who desired the liberty of mankind. Inevitably, Marcion's belief led him to abandon entirely the Old Testament Scriptures which he thought were essentially pernicious. Jesus, he said, had come to liberate man from the bondage which had been brought by the God of the Jews and by Judaism. Jesus, incidentally, was the Jesus of docetic theology who was but an appearance of God and had not actually come in the flesh.

The one thing, above all others, which gave Marcion's teaching a distinctive character, was the esteem in which he held the apostle Paul. As we have seen, he rejected the Old Testament in its entirety, and most of the New Testament suffered the same fate. The disciples, he held, were deceived into thinking that Jesus was the Jewish Messiah and the fulfilment of Old Testament prophecy. What practically all the New Testament writers wrote was designed simply to perpetrate the old, Jewish deception and had, therefore, to be scrapped along with the Jewish Scriptures. Only Paul really understood the Gospel which had been a special revelation to him, and only one man *a common* really understood Paul. That man, of course, was Marcion. *thing w/*

All this meant that what Scripture Marcion did accept had to *cults-one* be subjected to the most drastic treatment. He formulated a *guy gods* canon of his own which was composed of two parts, the first part *the special* consisting of Luke's Gospel, and the second part of the first ten *revelation and* of Paul's letters. All of these had to be suitably expurgated in *only he has it* order to rid them of anything that might be taken as a complimentary reference to Jehovah, or of anything that would lend authority to the Old Testament, so even what should be accepted as divine revelation had been corrupted by Judaizers who wanted to make Scripture serve their own ends. It all required the discerning eye of Marcion and the judicious application of his red pencil. To this canon he added a work of his own called the 'Antitheses' in which he enlarged on his system of belief based on the contrast between the God of the Old Testament and the God of the New.

Why did Marcion command so great a following, and why did his influence last so long? Some of his popularity, no doubt, was due to a remarkable personality. When we consider that he was almost sixty years of age before he began to gather his followers together into distinctive groups, it is evident that he must have been a man of considerable enthusiasm and energy to wield such a lasting influence. On the other hand, a foundation had almost certainly been laid in earlier years through his influence within the churches during the period in which he was developing his teaching.

There was, however, another factor that contributed much to his success, and that was the growing influence of clericalism and worldliness in the churches. Churches where spiritual life is at a low ebb are good ground for the seeds of wrong teaching and especially if, as is nearly always the case, the wrong teaching has a little mixture of the truth and is accompanied by practices which commend themselves to those who are seeking after spiritual satisfaction. Marcion, following the general trend among gnostics, advocated strict asceticism, and enjoined celibacy upon his followers. Baptism and the Lord's table were observed, and his groups returned once again to a greater simplicity of worship reminiscent of earlier days. Since Marcionism forbade marriage, it could not be perpetuated through the ordinary course of family life, and had to depend, therefore, on the diligent propagation of its teachings for its continued existence, which is but another indication of the popularity and vitality it enjoyed.

Manichaeism

Late in the first half of the third century, a new religion called Manichaeism made its appearance. Mani was born in 216 in Babylonia and exercised an influence which extended from Spain in the west to China in the east. Strongly influenced by gnosticism, he held to the gnostics' general concept of dualism. He considered himself to be in the line of the great sages who had lived down through the ages bringing to the world an increasing understanding of the continuously developing revelation of God to mankind. He also identified himself with the Holy Spirit whom the Lord promised His disciples to send after He was taken from them.

64

Mani drew his ideas from different sources, not only from Christianity, but also from Zoroastrianism and Buddhism. In fact, his vision was to establish a universal religion which included the 'truth' culled from all these different faiths. His followers were violently persecuted both in the east and in the west, but the religion spread rapidly nevertheless. Mani exercised a considerable influence in Persia but was at last put to death there by crucifixion in the year 276.

Manichaeism had an undoubted attraction for the philosophically minded seeker after truth. Augustine, later to exert such a powerful influence on Christian history, was a Manichaean before he was converted to Christ, and Priscillian, the great Spanish reformer, also showed some interest in the teaching of Mani before he became a Christian. As the Church gradually took the shape of an ecumenical movement with its centre in Rome, organizational unity and human authoritarianism taking the place of spiritual power, 'Manichaeist' became a very convenient epithet with which to brand all who refused to identify themselves with the Roman community but who, instead, insisted on maintaining the simple order and spiritual standard of the Scriptures. Many of the groups of believers whom we shall have cause to mention later on were stigmatized as Manichaeist, among them the followers of Priscillian mentioned above, although the accusation was completely baseless. Manichaeism gradually declined in influence, although there was a revival of the teaching in the middle ages and some of its tenets, of course, are still held today in theosophy and some forms of universalism.

Arianism

Arius was a presbyter in the church of Alexandria early in the fourth century, and the controversy which surrounded his name and teaching was destined to shake the whole of Christendom. Gnosticism, Marcionism and Manichaeism which we have considered so far, were such mixtures of Christian and heathen ideas that they were soon not to be recognised as basically Christian in character at all. With Arianism, however, we come to an essentially different type of heresy, for the dispute had to do, not with the nature of the Christian revelation, but with the interpretation of an accepted fact of the Christian revelation, namely the trinity.

The fact of the trinity, the Father, Son and Holy Spirit in the one Godhead was readily recognised in Scripture, but the

> we need to fall radically in love with Jesus so we can fear Him and go get souls!

question then arose as to the nature of the relationship between these three Persons. Christians were being accused of worshipping not one God, but three Gods, and this charge had to be refuted. The resultant enquiry produced the struggle which still goes on to find words sufficient to do justice to the divine revelation. Inevitably man is limited whenever he makes an attempt to explain eternal truth. Our words must fall far short even of our understanding, and our understanding must fall equally short of the reality. It is hardly surprising that, in the effort to put into human words what God had shown, there should arise different schools of interpretation, and that some of these should go to unwarranted extremes by emphasizing the oneness of the Godhead while giving insufficient place to the Son and the Holy Spirit.

During the period we are considering, there existed two famous theological schools at Antioch and Alexandria. Arius had been trained under the noted scholar Lucian at Antioch, a school which laid great emphasis on the truth of the humanity of Christ. This emphasis was particularly necessary to combat the influence of gnosticism and suchlike erroneous views which denied that Christ had come in the flesh. There was, however, a considerable divergence of emphasis between Alexandria and Antioch, so when Arius came to Alexandria he ultimately, in the year 318, came into conflict with the theological views of the Bishop Alexander whom he accused of heresy. The particular brand of heresy with which Alexander was charged was Sabellianism which, in turn, belongs to the Monarchian school of thought. Monarchianism taught that the Son and the Holy Spirit were but emanations from God the Father, or different means whereby the Father had periodically decided to reveal Himself, and Sabellianism said that Father, Son and Holy Spirit were merely three characters in which the One God manifested Himself, as three parts in a drama might be played by one person.

In his reaction to this one extreme, Arius went equally far in the other direction, but basically his scheme of teaching seems to have been influenced by Greek thought. Arius' concept of God was more gnostic than Christian. God, to him, was too far removed from men to have any direct relation with them. The Son, he said, was a created being, the first and highest of all created beings, neither God nor man, but the mediator between the two. The error of Arianism is, of course, that in denying Christ's divinity, it denies His saving power. Arius was deposed

66

from his position as presbyter in Alexandria in the year 321. He did, however, have a considerable following, and we will have occasion to remark later on on the way Arianism rocked the early Christian world.

Yet these abstruse, theological controversies, important as they were, were not the immediate concern of ordinary believers, and many who were Arians in name were devoted to the Lord, zealous in witness, and carried out a remarkable missionary work in the northern kingdoms of Europe. Arianism was a deadly menace to true faith nevertheless, and once its implications penetrated the day-to-day life of the church, could leave no room for the life of the Spirit. An interesting sidelight is the way Arius sought to popularise his views. Instead of leaving them to the mature and prayerful consideration of spiritual minds, he couched them in not too poetic verses which were sung to popular tunes by the Alexandrian Christians.

Pelagianism excuse - BM

Pelagius, a native of the British Isles, was born in the latter part of the fourth century. A man of sterling character and integrity he was shocked on visiting Rome, revered as a great centre of the Christian religion, to see the standard of morality that prevailed in the city. In Rome, in the early fifth century, he developed his teaching. Pelagius' views were a reaction to the encouragement to careless living which he felt was given by the orthodox doctrine of man and sin. If, he argued, sin was the result of a fallen nature inherited from Adam for which man, therefore, could not be held responsible, then there was every excuse to be content with a low standard of morality, and little incentive to overcome evil. The sinful nature, he said, was not inherited. All were innocent by birth, and only became implicated in Adam's sin in that, by a conscious act of their own volition, they followed his bad example. Salvation, therefore, was dependent simply upon man's will to choose the right.

The greatest of Pelagius' antagonists was Augustine, who, incidentally, readily admitted Pelagius' sterling character. It was in his refutation of Pelagius' views that Augustine developed the doctrine of divine grace. The dispute between these two great men was the root of the great controversy which exists right up to the present day in various guises, the controversy between the sovereignty of God and the free will of man. Augustine, as did the apostle Paul, had a most startling conver-

67

sion, and his own experience was a proof of the matchless grace of God and the inability of man to do anything for his own salvation apart from the exercise of the divine initiative in irresistible love. Pelagius, on the other hand, probably had no such radical, spiritual experience, and he so emphasized the freedom and responsibility of man to choose that, in his scheme of teaching, the grace of God became completely unnecessary.

While there was much that was true in what Pelagius taught, his basic premises were contrary to Scripture, beclouded man's understanding of himself, gave a boost to his pride by making him believe he was able to save himself, and detracted from his sense of dependence upon God. Actually, Pelagianism is very common in the world of today, the idea that man can be saved by ' doing the best he can '.

Sacerdotalism

Augustine has been hailed as the greatest Christian teacher since New Testament times. Of his spiritual stature and intellectual ability there can be no doubt, and the contribution which he has made to Christian thinking is certainly immense, yet the very greatness of his name has been the means of perpetuating the grossest error which he himself propagated. More than anyone else, Augustine has encouraged the pernicious doctrine of salvation through the sacraments of an organized, earthly Church, which brought with it priestcraft with all the evil and miseries that has entailed down through the centuries. We will, however, have cause to return to Augustine later, and sacerdotalism did not originate with him, but was a development which went back to earlier years and found encouragement in the utterances of earlier teachers.

We have seen in the last chapter how clericalism began to take shape in the early churches, and how the special position accorded to a Christian *élite* within the local congregation tended to establish the belief that they were endowed with special powers. Ignatius, although he had known some of the apostles personally, was strong in his insistence upon the dominance of a Bishop in the local church, and held that baptism and the Lord's table were only validly administered when he was in attendance. This paved the way admirably for the exaggerated importance given to priests and priestly administered sacraments.

Between the end of the early history recounted by Luke in

the Acts of the apostles and the end of the second century lies a period of which no consecutive account of the development of the church is available. At the end of that time, however, when we once again see the situation clearly, it is a situation very different to what existed in apostolic days. Different factors have worked together to bring about a crystallization of much of the Christian testimony. What we find is not only a number of independent, Christian congregations linked together in the bonds of fellowship and spiritual life, but also an ecumenical body, the Catholic Church, possessing a clearly recognised canon of Scripture, and an increasingly well-defined statement of doctrinal belief. Apart from these there were, of course, also the definitely heretical groups, more heathen than Christian. Of the believers who remained symbolizing the reaction of spiritual life to the increasing formality and lifelessness of the Catholic institution, we shall see more later, but a hundred years before the time of Constantine there existed the concept of an organized, Catholic Church which excluded from it all who would not conform to its practices. religeous spirits

One of the sternest and most unbending protagonists of this early Catholicism was Cyprian. Born about the year A.D. 200 Cyprian was brought up in a pagan environment, but a few years after his conversion to Christianity was consecrated Bishop of Carthage. In this we find a flagrant departure from the clear principle of Scripture, even laying aside the fact that Cyprian's Bishopric was something much different from that envisaged in the New Testament and putting it simply on the plane of an elder's position of responsibility. One of the conditions laid down for eldership in the Scriptures is that the elder should not be a 'novice' (1 Tim. 3 : 6), and it may well have been the clinging influence of certain ideas from paganism, so recently abandoned, that helped Cyprian to adopt his rigid views on the authority of the Bishop, the supreme place of the Catholic Church, and the efficacy of the sacraments that were such a distinct advance along the road to papal supremacy.

Cyprian held that the authority of the Bishops was exactly the same as the authority of the apostles. He accorded a special dignity to the Bishop of the Roman Church as the successor of Peter, but did not allow that the Bishop of Rome or any one Bishop could exercise authority over another Bishop. To him the Church was the rule of the established succession of Bishops in toto in their various seats of authority, and anything outside the authority of that established succession, or any schism from

F

religeous
spirits.
"Oh! you leave
the organized
religeon and
you go to hell.
That is evil.

it, cut off those who left the fold from the possibility of salvation. This Church alone had valid sacraments, and since salvation was conferred through the sacraments, there could be no salvation outside the Church. This Cyprian held to be true whatever the life or doctrine of those who seceded. In belief and practice they could be identical with the Catholic communion, they might be of exemplary Christian character, but the very fact of their having separated from the sphere of apostolic authority separated them also from the grace of God. This sphere was the Church of Christ and, as Cyprian said, " He who is not in the Church of Christ is not a Christian."

A century and a half later, Augustine, in his polemic against Pelagianism, was to quote Cyprian in support of his own erroneous views. Sacerdotalism has been perpetuated down through the centuries, and has probably been the greatest menace of all to the growth of spiritual life.

CHAPTER SEVEN

REACTION

THE impact of these various forms of teaching on the life of the church was the cause of a complexity of reactions which we must now consider. In all, two questions dominated the church's deliberations. First, what is the truth? Secondly, how can the truth be best defended and preserved? The effect of this enquiry, which was to extend over many years, was partly good and partly bad.

One of the good effects of Gnosticism was that it stimulated Christian leaders into a greater effort to understand their faith, and to set down in writing reasoned accounts of what they believed. This fresh, intellectual activity, however, was not without its dangers, for it gradually began to take the place of devotion to Christ, and Christianity more and more came to be a matter of understanding, of assent to certain truths, rather than of dedication and love to the Lord.

[margin note: mental assent w/o an encounter of the heart does nothing]

Although this untoward intellectualisation of faith was, in the first instance, produced by the need to combat gnosticism, almost inevitably it would have occurred in any case, if not at that precise period in history, certainly later. It is, in fact, one of the most subtle dangers which continues to afflict the church, and its insidious encroachment can be seen whenever, in any company of believers, the spontaneous devotion to the Lord which accompanies the inflow of the Spirit's life, begins to ebb away. In a preoccupation with resisting error it is only too easy to forget that correct belief does not insure spiritual life.

Recent years have seen a great resurgence of evangelical truth in many parts of the world. This is much to be welcomed, but alongside this return to Biblical doctrine there is unmistakably developing an evangelical orthodoxy which is spiritually dead. People may have all the language of new birth and regeneration without having experienced anything of the work of the Spirit through which alone they are made partakers of the divine nature. Assent to the most accurate statement of Scriptural truth, or the mechanical profession of an experience of God's working, is no substitute for the life of Christ.

71

The church's reaction to Marcionism pre-eminently centred round Marcion's Scripture canon. We have already seen how Marcion rejected the whole of the Old Testament and a large part of the New, suitably edited what was left to fit into his own ideas, and acclaimed this, with some additions of his own, as holy writ. Now, if Marcion's claim was untrue, if the writings for which he claimed direct inspiration were not, in fact, inspired, then it was up to the church to indicate the writings for which divine inspiration could be legitimately claimed. This was done, and various lists of canonical books have come down to us compiled by various church leaders in the early centuries before the Council of Carthage in 397 made a final listing of the twenty-seven New Testament books as we have them today.

It should be remembered that the New Testament writings were not vested with any extra authority by their being officially recognised by the Church. The opposite is the case. The recognition of the canonical books was simply the acceptance of a well attested fact. The authority of Scripture had already been established through its application by the Holy Spirit to the experience of the believers. By accepting the writings of Scripture as canonical, the church recognised their authority as paramount in all matters relating to faith and conduct. They formed the norm by which every doctrinal claim could be tested and every dispute decided.

While the increased understanding of the faith and the specific recognition accorded to Scripture were both important steps forward, the way in which early, ecumenical Christianity emerged as the self-appointed guardian of the faith and the Word is less to be commended. We have seen how, at a very early stage in the church's history, the primitive, Scriptural pattern was assailed and gave increasing place to the domination of a clerical order. Once this departure from the divine plan had been established, the new, spiritual hierarchy became the obvious protectors of the faith and custodians of the Word. So what had been gained in the church's defence of its spiritual life against falsehood was now to be constricted within an exclusive, ecumenical circle which, on the one hand, gained in authority and prestige by being the supposed guardian of the faith and the Word and, on the other, began to arrogate to itself the exclusive right to define the faith and interpret the Word, excommunicating from its fellowship all who did not own unquestioning loyalty to its findings. It is a fact to be pondered

72

that even after nearly twenty centuries of Christianity we have not yet fully learned that the only adequate defence of the truth is the practice of the truth. Wherever there are those who live lives of subservience to Christ, the Spirit can be trusted to protect the faith and the Word without the need of any human organization. Man's well intentioned desire to protect the truth by making it captive to his own limited understanding of it within some human organization is doomed to failure. Truth cannot live in captivity.

As the ecumenical concept of Christianity increased in strength, those who remained outside this organized development were viewed with increasing distrust as heretics, however loyal they might be to the faith, and however exemplary their lives. It was not unusual to accuse such people of Manichaeism. The greater awareness of the nature of the truth and of the authority of the Word also brought a greater awareness of heresy and, unfortunately, lent encouragement to the practice of witch-hunting. Heresy hunting is an extremely dangerous pursuit, not simply for the heretics, but particularly for those who engage in it. It proved a very potent, destructive force in the life of the early church, for the dominating factor quickly became the passion to root out the evil instead of to build up the good. A Christianity which becomes engrossed in the negative is destructive to its own nature. Our Lord's parable of the darnel has a very pertinent application to His people in all ages (Matt. 13 : 24-30). We need not think that tares are good, but uprooting them is not the main concern of the church. Darnel will exist within Christendom till the end of the age, but it will have less room to develop where the wheat is growing strong and hardy. The prosperity of false cults is very often a symptom of the decadence of the church, and the answer is not in trying to uproot them in the energy of the flesh, but in a fresh inflow of spiritual life. Had the church of the early centuries expended in positive, spiritual growth the energy which was used in trying to uproot all that its hyper-sensitive age branded as heresy, it may have been more fit to combat the subtler evils it was later to encounter.

It must be conceded that, in the first battles against false systems of teaching, the churches were largely united. To a certain extent, the church in which the Spirit was moving in life and power still corresponded to the outward organization, in spite of the early signs of departure from apostolic pattern. Gnosticism, Marcionism and the rest were such confused mixtures of truth and error that there could be no question of their relationship to those who were one in the life of the Spirit. They were definitely outside the pall. It was when controversy arose over the theological questions to which these erroneous views gave rise, that the field of battle changed and the church became the scene of civil strife. The tendency to over-intellectualization of the faith and the heat engendered through the resultant controversy led to an inflexibility which cut at the very root of fellowship. Mind was triumphing over spirit. It did not seem to be sufficiently appreciated that finite man has a limited capacity to contain infinite truth, and that in all theological speculation, important and edifying as it may be, grace plays an absolutely essential part. Grace is the only basis on which fellowship in the Spirit can be maintained. When this necessary element of grace was absent, it became inevitable that controversial issues, which were magnified and became more extreme through a hard, unflinching attitude, should be submitted to human arbitration. The machinery for this arbitration was all ready to be assembled with the departure from Scriptural principle that had already taken place, and the emergence of an ecclesiastical hierarchy which could be gathered together in one place as representative of the church ecumenical. The theological controversies of the early centuries, therefore, culminated in the great Church Councils which are such a well known part of Church history.

The reason behind the gathering of many of the Church Councils was the demand for a precise statement of certain facets of Christian truth which would exclude the prevailing heresies of the day. On that level they performed an important and vitally necessary service. They also symbolized, however, the human authoritarianism of the ecumenical Church, and it is with this that we are here primarily concerned.

There is no need at the present juncture to detail the various questions which occupied the deliberations of these Councils over the centuries, but a brief review of the first of them, the Council of Nicaea in 325, will serve to reveal the rule of human law over the things of the Spirit which the perpetuation of these gatherings of ecclesiastical dignitaries represented.

In the previous chapter we have dealt with Arius and the doctrine which he developed. Arius had been deposed from his position as a presbyter in the church at Alexandria in 321, but continued to command widespread respect in the eastern part of the Roman Empire where many of the Christian leaders

74

shared with him a common loyalty to the theological school of Antioch. So powerful, in fact, did Arius become, that the eastern Church was threatened with schism, a prospect which greatly concerned Constantine who by that time exercised un-disputed rule over the entire Empire. Constantine, with a maximum of good will and a minimum of theological under-standing, sought to avert the threatened division by attempting to bring Arius and Alexander, Bishop of Alexandria together. He met with complete failure. It was then that he called together to consider the question the representatives from churches throughout the known world who met in Nicaea in Asia Minor. Somewhere in the region of three hundred Bishops were in attendance, representing both sides. Arius personally led his own deputation, and the Council was presided over by the as yet unbaptized Roman Emperor, Constantine himself.

The result of the Council was the formulation of a statement of doctrine which explicitly rejected the Arian view and con-cluded with the anathemas of 'the holy Catholic and apostolic Church' upon those who assented to it. Arius and the only two Bishops who refused to sign were excommunicated, but Arius succeeded in gaining the Emperor Constantine's patronage, and the controversy was continued. Nevertheless, Nicaea was a culmination of the inevitable movement towards centralization in the ecumenical Church's authority. At last one body of men had succeeded in speaking as the voice of the world Church. Their pronouncements may not have been universally obeyed, as the continuance of the Arian controversy shows, but the voice was unmistakably a voice of authority, and when the second Council, held at Constantinople in 381, received Imperial back-ing for its declaration that the statement of Nicaea was the one, lawful religion, centralization of the control of the Church was further strengthened.

Various factors had also been working to ensure that the control would be centred in Rome. The Roman church alone among the churches of the west was able to claim that it had been founded by the apostles, and it doubtless deserved the respect that it earned from its consistency of teaching and the practical nature of the Christianity that was exhibited by the Roman Christians in the early days. For the younger, develop-ing churches of the west, the church in Rome was the natural place to go when they needed advice, since Rome was the capital of the civilized world. It also seemed natural on that score to accord the church there a special measure of prestige. Add to this the patronisation of the Emperor when Constantine began to favour Christianity, and the enhanced dignity which the Roman church took over from the Imperial court when Constantine moved his capital in 334 to the newly constructed Constantinople, named after him. Then the Council of Nicaea had taken up other questions apart from the Arian heresy. Of these, some had to do with Church government and the precedence of its Bishops. The sees of Rome, Antioch and Alexandria were acknowledged as occupying a leading position. Finally, in the closing years of the fourth century, as the political power of Rome declined, the ecclesiastical power of Rome increased to wield undisputed authority throughout organized Christendom. The ecumenical process was complete. What had been attempted in the church's infancy, imposition of central control from Jerusalem, but had been graciously forestalled by God's working, now became a reality.

Already in this chapter we have ranged over a considerable period of history, but only in so doing has it been possible to. see clearly the eventual outcome of the apparently small departures from Scriptural principle of the church's earliest years. The expediency of human organization was the beginning. Then came the excessive intellectualization of the faith in the attempt to counteract the effect of Gnosticism and other heresies. The steadily expanding organization of the church with its centralizing influence was invoked to lend authority to the doctrinal formulae which were produced. One reacted upon the other. The organized Church served to emphasize the importance of correct belief which in itself amounted to no more than cold orthodoxy, and the formulation of ever more precise definitions of divine truth depended on an increasingly powerful Church organization to enforce them. Rome was the inevitable result. Thus surely, yet almost imperceptibly, spiritual life as the basis of the church gave place to mental assent to a creed, and this was enforced by the ecumenical Church as law.

The great fallacy of a Church whose final appeal is to its organization for the maintenance of its life is that it is completely out of consonance with the very basis of life in the Spirit. Human organization can deal only on the basis of law, and has jurisdiction only over the outward acts of a man, not over his inner thoughts and motives. There is certainly a place for law in the church, but it is always subservient to the life of the Spirit. The church is the sphere of the rule of Christ who dwells in the midst of His people. Where subservience and devotion to Him

76

Holiness

remain the basic factors and rule of the church's life, His rule reaches down into the spirit and soul of a man which are the source of all his actions. Where this rule of the Spirit is denied, corruption is the inescapable result. How prone is man to deny this law of spiritual life and try to manage the work of God in his fleshly, efficient way, is one of the great lessons of Church History. Pelagianism, which we have noticed in the last chapter, was a human reaction to the failure of this human denial of Christ's lordship in the church. Sacerdotalism was the logical machinery required in a vain, make-believe attempt to confer the blessings and vitality which were denied to the working of the Holy Spirit.

We must now retrace our thoughts, and against the background of the picture just portrayed, the picture of an increasingly complex and decreasingly spiritual, ecumenical Christianity, see the ways in which a witness to the life of dependence upon Christ was maintained. To whatever extent truth tended to become submerged in ritual and organization, or practical Christian living tended to become enveloped in a cloud of theological speculation, the witness of an individual or corporate testimony was never extinguished. Sometimes it may appear that the line adopted by these men and movements was unduly severe, or lacking in a liberality which would have allowed the outward appearance of a united fellowship to continue, but their true significance can only be guaged when they are viewed against the much wider background of Church history, not simply against the background of immediately contemporary events. When this is done, it will be seen that the true, spiritual history of the church often takes its course through the generations of those who were despised by organized Christendom, and not through the edifice of traditional Christianity.

In spite of the early departures from the simple, Scriptural order, an understanding of the true basis of the church was not altogether lost. Ignatius' sentence, "Where Jesus Christ is, there is the Catholic church," is one indication that, in his thinking, he had not departed from spiritual life as the sole foundation of the assembly, although in matters of church order he had departed considerably from New Testament practice. Ignatius, as we have already seen, entertained an exalted idea of the place of the Bishop in the life of the church. It is well to note here that the deviation from a Biblical pattern did not mean the quenching of the life of the Spirit. Pattern is always second in importance to life, and that is the reason why, down

77

through history, there has not infrequently been a flow of spiritual vitality in a religious system which has little in common with anything that the apostles envisaged. On the other hand, we must not conclude that pattern is unimportant. The revelation of the life of the Spirit will be unavoidably restricted if it does not have an adequate 'body' through which it can be expressed, and where that is so, the ultimate effect must be the weakening of life till it dies out, or its bursting forth from the hampering limitations to find fuller expression elsewhere. The first departures of the early church from the divine order did not put an end to spiritual life, but they opened the way for the debilitating ills which were to sap the church's energy at a later stage in its development.

Origen

Certainly the greatest Christian scholar of the early centuries was Origen of Alexandria who was born in A.D. 185, the son of godly parents through whose faithful upbringing he came to an early experience of the Gospel. Leonidas, his father, who first taught him in the Scriptures, was martyred for his faith when Origen was less than twenty years old. In later years Origen became, for a time, head of Alexandria's great theological school, and applied his agile mind, trained both in the Scriptures and in Greek philosophy, to the searching questions of the faith. From his pen we have the first attempt at the construction of a systematic theology. A presbyter of the church of Alexandria and a layman, he was a man of extraordinary devotion whose learning commanded the respect of men of position in the Church. But his great ability did not lead to a harmonious relationship with ecclesiastical dignitaries who presumed that the right to teach was their sole prerogative, or who saw in the esteem given to Origen a usurpation of the respect they felt should have been accorded to them. Origen succeeded in rousing the jealousy of Alexandria's Bishop Demetrius who deposed him from the office of presbyter in the year 321. He spent the last twenty-three years of his life continuing to exercise his greatly valued ministry in exile in Palestinian Caesarea. There he died in the year 254 from the result of tortures inflicted upon him during the persecution instigated by the Roman Emperor, Decius, in A.D. 250.

Origen had a particularly clear idea of the nature of the church. The church, he held, was spiritually based, and all

78

those who were recipients of divine life belonged to it. It was not to be blandly equated with a human organization. A teacher of Origen's stature and acknowledged respect and saintliness was bound to have had a wide influence wherever he went and taught among those who had a genuine desire to maintain an active testimony to a resurrection life.

It should not worry us that some of Origen's views were later stigmatised as heresy. There must be very few men particularly used of God who have not, at some time in their career, been called heretics, often by those who have an equally sincere desire for the truth. The practice is even yet not dead, but it will be a great day when some of the well-intentioned defenders of the faith find that some of their much maligned heretics have been allotted even ever so small a corner of the heavenly home.

Novatians

In A.D. 250 the Emperor Decius, in an attempt to insure the security of the State by demanding a demonstration of universal loyalty to the State religion, promulgated an edict which instituted a severe persecution of Christians throughout the Empire. Under the strain of this official harassment many Christians denied the faith by offering the prescribed sacrifice to the State gods. For some whose Christianity was little more than a thin veneer covering a heathen heart, and who had come to swell the Church's ranks in the preceding years of peace, the open acknowledgment of heathenism was a matter of course, and stirred within them no qualms of conscience. Others, however, succumbed only under severe threats of violence and torture. When the period of persecution was over, the question naturally arose of the re-admission into the communion of the church of those who had denied the faith under duress. The weaker brethren, whose courage had been unequal to the stress of the times and who had saved their bodies at the price of a suffering conscience, returned with genuine repentance, desiring a re-establishment of the fellowship they once knew. No doubt other, one-time Christians of the purely nominal variety also wished to be re-installed, for less worthy motives.

Should those who had once lapsed be received? The question was the subject of grave discussion within the churches, and of strong divergence of opinion. On the one hand were the rigorists who said that no person who had denied Christ should be re-admitted to communion. They found an able leader in

79

the Roman presbyter, Novatian. A more lenient policy, however, was adopted by a majority of responsible, Church leaders and won the day. Novatian and those with him who stood for a pure church fellowship found themselves ostracised from the Church Catholic and formed communities which extended from Asia Minor to Spain. These groups of that particular age, and indeed for about two and a half centuries later have come down to us in history known as Novatians, but it is certain that they represented a movement much wider than the influence of one man, although Novatian was a recognised leader in their midst and was the one around whom, in his own lifetime, controversy centred.

Another name given to them was Cathars, or Puritans, although it is doubtful whether the congregations themselves were much more ready to adopt that tab than they were ready to accept the name 'Novatians'. Cathars, however, is a name which we find recurring down through history, and was often given by the Roman Church to the heretical sects (to their way of thinking) which seemed to persist through the ages, who lived lives which even their enemies had to admit were beyond reproach, and who claimed that the spiritual origin of their communities went right back to the days of the apostles themselves. We shall meet the Cathars again in a later chapter. The Novatians of the middle of the third century should not be viewed as an entirely new protest against the increasing laxity of the Church. Rather did they reinforce a protest that was there already in existence of groups of Christians who had never abandoned the simple faith and practice of apostolic times.

It is easy to simplify the incident of the Novatian secession into accepting that Novatian was unduly harsh, while the general run of the rulers of the Church reflected the true spirit of Christ. This, in general, may be true, but it is equally true that much deeper issues were at stake. There can be no doubt that the rigorist party was willing to show less grace to those who had fallen than was the Lord Himself. After all, Peter denied the Lord under much less provocation than those who suffered under the persecution of Decius, yet repentance brought restoration and a subsequent life of distinctive usefulness. Man rarely approaches God's readiness to show mercy and forgiveness.

On the other hand, we must take into account all that was implied in the more lenient view adopted by the majority of Bishops when seen in the light of the standard of Christian life held widely in the Church. They ruled that those who had fallen be subject to a period of probation, and then fully restored to fellowship. This was eminently reasonable, provided the probation was the means of establishing, through the discernment of the Spirit, the existence of a consistent devotion and loyalty to the Lord. But was this the case? We do not in the least need to doubt that many who were restored to full communion were genuinely devout believers, and that their restoration was right and proper, but it seems more than a little probable that a person could be restored simply by an outward conformity to certain stipulated forms which may or may not have been an indication of true spiritual life. This may not have been the case always, but the lenient attitude adopted by the majority of the Bishops, although in itself perfectly right and justified, seems, unfortunately, not altogether disassociated from the growing idea that spiritual life was conferred through the rites of the church, and that it was the observance of these rites that was of paramount importance.

The importance attached to baptism as a grace conferring ritual is aptly illustrated in the great controversy on the subject between Stephen, Bishop of Rome, and Cyprian, Bishop of Carthage. Cyprian held that the one, Catholic Church possessed valid sacraments, that there was no salvation outside it, and that, therefore, under no circumstances could baptism conferred by those who had separated from the mother Church, or had been pronounced heretics by the Church, be recognised as valid. Stephen held to the contrary view. Both views, however, presuppose the rite as a direct means of the impartation of divine grace, Cyprian's view because of his concept of the nature of the Church, and Stephen's view because of his insistence that it was the rite itself that was important, not the circumstances in which it was administered. The dispute came to an end with Stephen's death in 257 and Cyprian's martyrdom the year following. Stephen's views have ever since been accepted in the Roman communion.

Following on Cyprian's concept of the Church was his attitude to Novatian. Novatian had never been looked upon as a heretic. In fact he was strictly orthodox in outlook, and was one of the great minds who applied himself to stating the relationship between the three Persons of the Trinity. His orthodoxy, however, made little impression on Cyprian who insisted that orthodoxy, character, everything, was spiritually meaningless since he was out of fellowship with the one, Catholic Church. To Novatian, the basis of the church was consistency of spiritual life, to Cyprian the basis of the Church was in her grace-conferring rituals, and Cyprian's view was symptomatic of the belief that was to establish itself so firmly as the accepted doctrine.

Granted that the Novatian reaction to receiving those who had lapsed in time of persecution was unduly severe, yet viewing the issue in its wider perspective, we can see in the Novatian division a stand for the principle of spiritual life as the sole basis of church fellowship which was vitally necessary if all Christianity was not to degenerate into a ritual of sophisticated heathenism. If we condemn Novatian unreservedly, we likewise condemn every subsequent effort to reclaim a testimony of holiness from a church which was to become the depository of every imaginable corruption. On one memorable occasion during the infancy of the church, God saw fit to act in judgement in a way which today would be considered unduly severe, in order to save the church from a premature corruption (Acts 5 : 1-11). It may well be that the severity of the Novatian reaction was just as necessary at its particular time in history to protect the integrity of a witness to Christ when it was being assailed in many and subtle ways.

Montanism

Montanism, a movement which arose within the Catholic Church about the middle of the second century had this in common with the Novatians, that it expected a high standard of Christian living from those within its fellowship. This again was a reaction against the growing laxity which was evident within the organized Church. As organization increased, and more and more authority was exercised by the Bishops, there was a consequent emphasis upon a spiritual efficacy of rituals performed by the Bishops, particularly the rituals of baptism and the eucharist. This tended towards an inclusiveness of Church fellowship which the Montanists rightly recognised as a danger posing a threat to the church's whole spiritual life. The Spirit's working, they felt, was being replaced by dependence upon organization and ritual.

The people called 'Montanists' were given their name from Montanus who began to teach in the mountains of Phrygia in the year 156. Considering the condition of the Church, as Montanus saw it, it was not unnatural that he should lay great emphasis on the place of the Holy Spirit among the people of

God. Nor are we to think that this emphasis was unhealthy. On the contrary, it was much needed in view of the inordinate occupation with form, and dependence upon learning which was slowly paralysing the church's life. Montanus did, however, in some respects, carry his emphasis to an unwarranted extreme. According to him, the age was the dispensation of the Spirit who continued to work miraculously no less than in the days of the apostles, and who spoke through prophets of whom, of course, Montanus was one. The second coming of the Lord was near at hand, and He was going to set up the New Jerusalem here on earth.

The one thing which, more than any other, disturbed the staid and stolid Church, was the activity of Montanist prophets, or even more particularly, the activity of Montanist prophetesses. In this, of course, we see clearly the peak of Montanist reaction to increasing ecclesiasticism. The Bishop was the epitomy of formalism; the prophet was the epitomy of the Spirit's working. Prophecy occupied a recognised place in the life of the church of apostolic times. We have in the New Testament, for example, a figure such as Agabus (Acts 11 : 27-28; 21 : 10). Nor must we relegate all prophecy to the past. Rightly understood as a gift of the church (Eph. 4 : 11) in conjunction with the Scriptures, prophecy is still active where the clear exposition of the Word is marked by the unction of the Spirit which relegates the Scriptures from the realm of the dead letter to something which is intensely practical and vital. That this element of prophecy has so largely departed from the preaching of the present day is nothing of which to be proud. It is, in fact, but a symptom of the spiritual lethargy which is so often accepted as a norm of church life. No doubt, of course, the Montanists majored in the more ecstatic and unpredictable variety of prophecy, of which Agabus' pronouncements can be taken as a fair example.

What we must remember, however, is that, with the exaltation of the Bishop's power, less room was being left in the church for either type of prophetic ministry. Ignatius, himself not altogether lacking the marks of an enthusiast, so emphasized the supremacy of the Bishop that if spiritual gift were not to be channelled through this Church dignitary it is difficult to see how it could gain expression in the church at all. In this way, the opposition between the orthodox Church and the Montanist movement tended to head itself up in the struggle of Bishop *versus* prophet, or ecclesiastical rigidity *versus* the spontaneity of spiritual life.

Montanists, again like the Novatians, were not classed as heretics. They were orthodox in regard to basic truth, and had not departed from the foundation of the apostles. But if Ignatius or some of his fellow Bishops were alive today, they would probably have called them one of the 'fringe sects'. The fires of persecution did not have the same effect on Montanism as on the rest of the Church. They were never troubled by the perplexing question of large numbers of their followers denying the Lord in time of trial, and seeking re-acceptance into the fellowship when the threat of persecution had subsided. Montanists, on the contrary, tended to seek martyrdom, and to look down upon such actions as were adopted, during the Decian persecution, by some Church leaders who, not unreasonably, decided it was better to lie low for a while that they might be of service to the church again when the wave of persecution had died down.

It is not altogether difficult to enter into something of the spirit of the Montanist groups, their passion for morality, their contagious enthusiasm, their warmth of fellowship, their zeal for the Lord. They had their roots in a part of the world that was noted for its ebullient spirits, and they lived well up to its reputation. The manifestations of Montanism have been repeated at other times down through history, and can be recognised in the Pentecostal movements of the present day. There we often find the same excesses and the same warmth of spirit. However much Montanism was deplored by formal Christianity, there was yet something in its life which bore unmistakable witness to the power of God. It is noteworthy that voices were raised within the organized, Catholic Church against taking too severe a line with the Montanists, lest the Church be in danger of quenching the Spirit. No doubt this measure of sympathy enabled the Montanist groups to continue for a longer period as a spiritual movement within organized Christianity. Ultimately, however, it became plain that the new wine of the life of the Spirit could not indefinitely be contained in the old wineskins of formal religion. The Montanists, who began as groups within the Church where those devoted to the Lord could find true spiritual fellowship while maintaining their allegiance to organized religion, became distinctly separate congregations. This separation took place first in the east, probably because there the greater exuberance of Montanist groups forced the issue more quickly. In the west the Catholic connection continued for a longer period, but there too the final break was inevitable.

Montanism commanded a widespread following and survived, at least in Phrygia, the country of its origin, into the sixth century when it was forcibly destroyed by the Emperor Justinian. By the end of the second century it had spread to the Roman province of Africa. It may well be that the Montanism of Africa was of a more mellow variety, not quite so marked by the turbulent enthusiasm of its Phrygian congregations. No doubt the passage of years, and experience, served to temper some of the excesses to which it was prone, particularly in its beginnings. It is certainly significant that, in Africa, at the commencement of the third century, Montanism won the fellowship of Tertullian, the great Carthaginian theologian. Tertullian severed his ties completely with the Catholic Church and found among the 'men of the Spirit' a fellowship from which he continued to carry on his work. It is hardly creditable that a man of Tertullian's calibre and experience would be deceived by the frothy superficiality which is sometimes pictured as Montanism. That he should have so completely thrown in his lot with the movement is indicative of a stability and robustness of Christian character in Montanism which made it the witness it was and its survival worthwhile. When finally the followers of Christ called Montanists had to lay down the torch of testimony, there were others ready to take it up.

Life and revival in the Holy SPIRIT w/ stability and character of Christ Holiness onto Him makes it last, longer than a quick fly by, turning quickly to something else when it was done.

G

CHAPTER EIGHT

THE CHURCH FLATTERED

THE early fourth century was to see the church enter upon one of its severest tests. It is a period which, at one and the same time, exhibits both triumph and defeat. The drama that was enacted found its focus in the Roman Emperor Constantine's espousal of the Christian cause. The church had undergone nearly three hundred years of tumultuous development. There were Christians who still retained the simplicity, devotion and loyalty to the Lord which had characterised the congregations of apostolic times. On the other hand, there is also evident the effect of the hand of man in the things of God. Spiritually, it was inevitable that such a test should come, for faith must be tried. If the foundation and fabric of the church as it stood in the year 313 had not been tested by the temper of the new era which was then ushered in, they were bound to have been tested in some other manner.

The patronage of the Roman power extended to the Christian Church may have resulted in much that can quite understandably be called tragic, but behind it all there was the hand of God. It was for the ultimate good of the cause of Christ that weaknesses which had developed over the previous three centuries should not continue unexposed. On the positive side, the accession of Constantine was the admission of the world that the life of Christ in His people is indestructible. The fires of persecution could not quench it, nor the floods of oppression overwhelm it. The enormous capacity of the spiritual life of the church to survive and to triumph over all the carnal means of the world hurled against it, stood as an unassailable fact. And the victory was won with spiritual weapons alone; truly it was the triumph of the cross, the weakness and foolishness of God overcoming the strength and wisdom of men. The church had won. The great Roman Empire had to bow its head in defeat.

The other side to the picture is seen in the profound changes which had taken place within the church, and the effects of these changes when the church entered a new sphere of popularity and worldly acclaim. The life of the Spirit is greater than any pattern, and the grace of God overrules many of man's follies, but we must not deduce from this that pattern is altogether un-important, and that the grace of God can be unconditionally counted upon, to whatever extent man goes in meddling with spiritual order. The steady departure from primitive pattern did not altogether put an end to the life of the Spirit within the church as the history of the first three centuries amply shows, but the early order was established in the wisdom of God parti-cularly to withstand stresses and strains with which the church would ultimately and inevitably have to deal. Where the simplicity of a spiritual community began to give way to the complexity of a human organization, the resistance of the church to certain ills was lowered to a point where eventual catastrophe was unavoidable. This we shall see as we pursue our subject. God organized the church for catastrophe; man organized the church into catastrophe.

The Roman Empire of the west was the scene of internal rivalry, and in the year 312, Constantine marched south against his opponent, Maxentius. Constantine was a worshipper of the sun god, his patron deity, and owned the title of High Priest of the Roman State religion, but before embarking upon his campaign against Maxentius he had a vision in which he said he saw the form of a cross in the sky. Then on the eve of the decisive battle of Milvian Bridge he was given, in a dream, a 'divine' command to mark the shields of his soldiers with a monogram consisting of the first two letters of the Greek name of Christ, an 'X' superimposed by a 'P'. Constantine went into battle with the belief that he was, in a special sense, under the protective care of the Christians' God. He was victorious, and the victory vindicated the belief which he was to hold throughout the remaining years of his life. This is the first time that we have God's sanction invoked upon warfare, and none too happy a precedent it proved to be. In the Roman Empire, many Christians refused to serve in the army, and since they were, in any case, often suspected of disloyalty because of their general refusal to take part in prescribed, religious cere-monies, the unfriendliness of the authorities did not extend to the Christians' being coerced into soldiering, a policy which the Romans might have been afraid was too apt to rebound upon themselves. Warfare is something which seems strangely in-consistent with the life and teaching of Christ. In these modern days, most Christian leaders manage to admit as much, at least in time of peace.

Constantine's victory at Milvian Bridge and his consequent mastery over the western part of the Roman Empire was immediately followed by an edict bringing all persecutions of Christians to an end. The next year, 313, he and his eastern counterpart, Licinius, met at Milan to promulgate a further edict allowing freedom of religion throughout the Empire, and requiring the restoration of Christians' property which had been confiscated in the previous persecutions. The Milan agreement, however, did not bring final peace. Conflict ensued between Constantine and Licinius, the latter finally embarking upon further persecutions of the Christians believing, not unnaturally, that they favoured the western Emperor who showed more toleration towards them. Constantine's power steadily increased, and in 324 he gained authority over the whole Roman Empire. His success was celebrated with a fresh pronouncement of religious toleration.

Constantine's espousal of the Christian cause did not mean that he himself publicly accepted Christianity. True, he was much more than a sympathiser; he believed that he owed a peculiar debt to the Christians' God, but at the same time he retained his High Priestly title of the pagan, State religion. It was not till the year before his death in 338 that he accepted baptism and thus openly declared himself as a Christian. The effects upon the Church of the new-found, Imperial favour were many and various, but two things in this connection particularly need to engage our attention.

First, Christianity became fashionable. Although Constantine himself was not a committed Christian, he encouraged others to accept the faith, and there were plenty of people ready to accept anything if, in doing so, they earned the commendation of the State. There was therefore, a great influx of pagans into the Christian Church, pagans who had been Christianized by learning the rudiments of the faith and being baptized, but who, nevertheless, were still pagans at heart. The way, of course, had been prepared for such an influx by the over-intellectualization of the faith and by the increasing tendency towards sacramentalism. We have already noticed the development of both these factors. The ingress of pagan ideas which accompanied this enlargement of the Christian sphere could hardly fail to affect the Church substantially. Something of its extent can be imagined when we take into account that, on

Constantine's accession, the masses in many of the great cities of the Empire became 'Christian' within a remarkably short period.

Secondly, the State was accorded a recognised say in Church matters. In their gratitude to Constantine for his patronage, the Church leaders allowed him a place of prominence in Church affairs which was in no way his due. Again, however, it must be remembered that the ground had already been well prepared. Had centralization in the organization of the Church not been fostered, it would have been impossible for Constantine to have been offered, or to have exercised the measure of control he did. The prominence given to Bishops, and the regard in which a few of these were held above others, giving them, in fact if not in theory, control over their more humble brethren, made for an easy means of communication between the State and the Church, and also an effective means of control by the State once its authority in the Church was fully recognised.

There was an interesting parallel to this in Japan during the last war. The organised groups of Christianity in the country were federated into one, large system, approved and controlled by the State. There were, however, a large number of Christian groups who stoutly maintained a claim to the independence of each local congregation. The truth of this claim was attested by the fact that the Japanese Government found it impossible to include them within their federation and had to deal with each local group separately. The leaders of some were imprisoned, and their literature confiscated, yet others continued to meet quietly in homes as was their custom. They still exist in Japan today, having survived the ordeal of war with a testimony unsullied, and a faith intact.

The development of a hierarchical form of government within the Church inevitably brought with it a sense of quasi-political rivalry and a lust for power, with all its corrupting tendencies. With the weight of emphasis now on the organizational aspect of the Church instead of on its spiritual nature, the way was further opened for the scheming type of aspirant to leadership, and he found, within the Church, full scope for his arts and crafts. It was but a small step from this religious manouvering into an alliance with the political world that had now taken on a Christian veneer. The degeneration of the Church had set the stage for the unholy alliance between Church and State. The Church had bartered its liberty for popularity and, as a consequence, was to come under a much worse and more insidious tyranny than it had even previously known, the tyranny of a worldly ecclesiasticism.

With the weight of the general populace in the great cities ' Christian ' and ready to be swayed by anyone who could command their fleeting loyalty for a brief moment, it is not long before we find Church leaders exploiting the vagaries of the mob in their own favour as it had been exploited in favour of the Imperial power.   In a previous chapter it has been noted how Arius, in the great theological controversy which his views engendered, flung the whole thing, as it were into the market place to be sung and shouted about by any seekers after petty excitement.   The majority probably knew little more of Arius than his name, and still less about the rights and wrongs of the theology they so loudly advertised.   But it was the spirit of the day.   Eternal truths became matters of street gossip, and elections to ecclesiastical office became matters of popular, brawling rivalry, as the election of Damasus to the Bishopric of Rome in 366.   Unfortunately, the spirit of the early fourth century was not a passing phase.   It had come to stay, and it is all dismally familiar down through the pages of Church history, nor is it yet an unfamiliar part of Christendom.   Intolerance within the Church began to grow at an alarming rate, and with it that unreasonable insistence upon non-essentials and upon uniformity which is ever the mark of a lifeless religion.   Conformity to the every whim of a central, religious authority became the mark of orthodoxy, and those who would not conform came increasingly to be regarded as rebels, either to be coerced into submission or to be exterminated.   The irony of the situation is tragic in its intensity.   The Church which had been so violently persecuted, and had won for itself such a well deserved freedom, was itself to adopt the role of persecutor and deny to others, even within its own ranks, the freedom it had so lately won.

It is difficult to point to one particular time as the date when papal supremacy was finally established.   The ultimate rule of Rome was the consummation of a process of development which had been going on over a considerable period.   Rome had, at first, been a quite legitimate source of advice for other churches in need of counsel and fellowship, but with the development of Roman prestige, the advice gradually took on a new authority.   It was venerated to the point where to dream of questioning it would have been thought presumptuous.   And advice which is automatically accepted is a command.

If, however, we are to look for a time when the papacy was finally established, there would be considerable grounds for putting it during the time of Leo the Great who was Bishop of Rome from 440 to 461. Roman supremacy was, no doubt, a practically established fact prior to this, but it was Leo who set the fact upon a theological foundation. It was he who found the authority for the Roman Church in his interpretation of our Lord's words to Peter in Matt. 16: 18-19, " Tho art Peter, and upon this rock I will build my church: and the gates of Hades shall not prevail against it. I will give unto thee the keys of the kingdom: and whatsoever thou shalt bind on earth shall be bound in heaven: and whatsoever thou shalt loose on earth shall be loosed in heaven." Peter was the founder of the church at Rome and the Roman Bishops inherited his authority, including that particular supremacy which was indicated in our Lords' giving him ' the keys of the kingdom of heaven '. Thus ran Leo's argument. It is almost certain that Peter visited Rome, most probably more than once. It is also very likely that he had a share in the founding of the Roman assembly. Unfortunately, these facts tend to be clouded in the minds of many Christians by prejudice. But they still do not make Leo's argument true, nor his interpretation of Scripture a justifiable one.

It may well be asked what all this has to do with spiritual Christianity. The answer, of course, is, " Very little." Yet it is just for this reason that it has been necessary to mention this grimmer side of fourth century Christianity, for it demonstrates how far organized Christianity had departed from a spiritual faith. From the fourth century on, the spiritual movement is much more distinctly defined from the organized religion. The picture prior to that time is, in a sense, much more confused. As church organization had developed, there were always those who remained unaffected by the process and maintained the original simplicity, free from entanglement with the emerging Church system. Yet it is obvious that, in the years of grim transition from a spiritual church to a worldly Church, the movement of the Spirit and the visible representation of the church as generally recognised, should not infrequently coincide. In spite of the weaknesses and troubles which beset Christianity in the first three centuries, the picture includes much that is of life and victory. We need not hang our heads in shame. How different it is in the centuries following. There were still great souls within the Roman communion to whom we, even today, under God, owe a tremendous debt, but their position was an anachronism. Some, out of a mistaken loyalty to 'Mother Church' suffered persecutions unto death within the fold; others such as Augustine, themselves helped to strengthen the Church in its error; yet others found solace from the whole, sordid round in the seclusion and service of monasticism. But the great spiritual movement, the expression of the church in the New Testament sense, is now generally to be found separate from organized Christianity as it recognised and centred in Rome.

After Pentecost, the preaching of the Gospel spread far beyond the bounds of the Roman Empire. In its great and powerful neighbour, the Persian Empire, congregations of Christians were established and continued throughout the first three tumultuous centuries cut off from much that had influenced the churches of the west. Various factors contributed to their isolation, among others the atmosphere of distrust which existed between the two Empires, and the difference in language. The result was that these eastern churches, for a much longer period, maintained the simple character of apostolic times. Even through the third century when the ecclesiastical system of the west was rapidly developing, the eastern congregations seem to have held on to their individual independence, and to have been active in propagating the truth farther afield.

A move to unite the churches in the Persian Empire under one head was initiated early in the fourth century, but it met with strenuous opposition, and although the proposal continued to be urged, other events served to delay its acceptance for a considerable period. When Christianity earned official sponsorship within the Roman Empire on the accession of Constantine, there was a violent reaction against Christians within the Empire of Persia. It is not difficult to understand how the Persian kings began to suspect Christians, who professed a belief alien to Persia's native Zoroastrianism, of sympathising with the rival, and greatly feared, Roman power. This distrust finally broke out into a terrible persecution which lasted for forty, dreadful years, during which about sixteen thousand Christians are supposed to have died because of their faith. Persecution came to an end in 399 with the accession to the Persian throne of Yezdegerd I. Yezdegerd never accepted allegiance to Christ as did Constantine, but his attachment to his old religion did not prevent what had already happened in the Roman world, an alliance between church and State, albeit an alliance of a looser and somewhat different nature.

In Yezdegerd's friendliness, the Roman Emperor saw an opportunity to ease the severely strained relations which existed between the two Empires because of the persecutions, and sent as an ambassador of peace a Bishop Maruta who proved himself a very skilled negotiator. Maruta, however, had more in mind than obtaining relief for the oppressed Christians of the east. He was also concerned that they should be brought within the fold of Rome-centred Christianity, and after more than a generation of the severest trial, the Persian churches were only too ready to welcome anything which seemed to be an expression of fellowship. Isaak, the Metropolitan of Seleucia-Ctesiphon, the capital of the Persian Empire, together with Maruta, approached Yezdegerd I and received permission to call together a synod in the year 410 for the purpose of reorganizing the Church. Yezdegerd recognised Isaak as head over the entire Christian community within his Empire, and the synod joined together in praising this heathen monarch for his munificence. In the new Church organization that was established, all deviation from the settled rule was forbidden under penalty of excommunication from the body of Christ and discipline at the hand of the Emperor. Yezdegerd was granted virtual control over the whole Church.

Maruta had brought with him a letter from the Bishops of the west setting forth principles of ecclesiastical practice and doctrinal requirements that would bring the eastern churches completely into line with western developments. All Christians were to be organized into one system from which there could be no dissension. Those who disagreed were condemned. Rules were laid down for the succession of Bishops who would have jurisdiction over prescribed areas. In each parish no more than one congregation would be allowed. The will of the Persian Emperor was acknowledged, and the religious supremacy of the western church centred in Rome. Thus were the Churches of both east and west drawn into one fold. Early in the church's history the tendency towards centralization was seen in Jerusalem. By the early fifth century the process had reached yet another significant stage in its development. Roman Christianity apparently dominated the Christian scene in both the Roman and Persian Empires.

Constantine's attitude to Christianity was predominantly determined by his political mind. The sincerity of his rudimentary allegiance to the Christian's God need not be questioned, but his interest was by no means purely spiritual. Christianity, as a religion, should be one of the unifying forces of the Empire. It was important, therefore, that the Church under Rome should be one. Constantine's concern for this is clearly seen in the part he played in the Donatist dispute.

The Donatists, as they came to be known after two leading men among them, both named Donatus, arose in North Africa after the severe persecution under Diocletian in the early years of the fourth century. They had been much influenced by the teaching of Novatian of some fifty years before and took a similar line with regard to those who had weakened in times of terror. Ultimately they separated from the Catholic communion, having objected to the appointment as Bishop of Carthage in 312 of Caecilian, against whom they preferred certain charges. Constantine had tried his best to mediate in the dispute, but when two commissions of Church dignitaries which he called to formulate a judgement made their pronouncement in favour of Caecilian, the Donatists, adamant in their position, proclaimed themselves the one, true Catholic Church 'excommunicating' practically the whole of Christendom in the process. In Carthage, Donatus was consecrated Bishop in opposition to Caecilian. The movement continued for many years. Imperial force was used against it in the early fifth century in an effort to coerce its adherents back into the Catholic fold, but not until the Muhammadan invasion in the seventh century did the Donatists finally disappear from North Africa.

Constantine must be held responsible in some degree for the dreadful intolerance which has disfigured the history of Christianity down through the centuries. His flattery of the now highly organized Church encouraged it to arrogate to itself over the souls of man an authority which belongs to God alone, and the political necessity that the unity of the Church should be first in importance to its spiritual character further fostered a spirit of intolerance with whatever could be labelled schismatic. Constantine set a precedent which was to be followed by succeeding Roman Emperors, all of whom, with one exception, outwardly acknowledged the Christian faith. His patronism of Christianity did not extend to those who would not fit into the religious system which could be used to further his own political ends.

Donatists, at the beginning of the movement, were characterised by a high standard of Christian conduct, but their insistence upon a pure communion within the Church was later coloured by factors which were much less desirable. They never rid themselves of the hierarchical organization which was to

94

such an extent both an outcome and a cause of the degeneracy within the Catholic party. They were subject to the baneful influence of party spirit which had become such a common feature of the organized religion. The Donatists made a loud profession of standing for spiritual liberty and had a slogan, " What has the Emperor to do with the Church," but this hardly seemed to measure up with the consistent appeals they had made to the Emperor in their dispute. It appeared to be little more than a sign of their frustration at the Emperor's having turned down their case. The Donatists formed a major part of the Christian community in North Africa, but continued in strife till Christianity in that part of the world was blotted out by the followers of the Prophet.

In holding that spiritual life and character, not sacraments, are the basis of the church, the Donatists were right, but their idea of separation did not extend to a repudiation of the desire to be recognised by the secular power as the true, Catholic Church. It may be idle to conjecture what would have happened had they received such recognition, but if the experience of others is a valid teacher, the Donatists too would have found that power corrupts. As it was, the desire for that power was a corrupting influence which left Donatism more of a negative than a positive force in Christian history. It is ever hard for Christians to believe that part of their life is to bear the reproach of Christ in a world that does not recognise Him, and the humility of the Lord displayed in the church is an essential requisite to a fully effective testimony. The life of Christ which is the basis of the assembly is not simply the absence of sin and compromise with evil, but the existence within regenerate men and women of the graces of Christ by which they live their daily lives.

CHAPTER NINE

RELIGION AND THE GOSPEL

WHILE the Catholic power was strengthening its hand, Christianity continued to expand.   On the one hand, there were eager ambassadors of the Gospel through whose ministry there was an undoubted diffusion of spiritual life; on the other, the various factors which had brought about a common departure from the simplicity of the Scriptures meant that, with the spread of the Gospel, elements of weakness were introduced into the very foundation of new churches with the inevitable, disastrous results.

Nestorius

One of the most remarkable missionary movements of all times had its origin in Nestorius of Antioch who was appointed Bishop of Constantinople in 428. A man of boundless energy and great eloquence, Nestorius gained wide popularity and respect, but also succeeded in rousing bitter opposition from those who were jealous of his increasing influence.   This was particularly true of Cyril, Bishop of Alexandria.   There was a traditional rivalry between the sees of Alexandria and Constantinople, and Cyril was ever on the watch for an opportunity to increase his own status and discredit Nestorius.

Nestorius belonged to the Antioch school of theology which, as we have already seen, laid particular emphasis on the humanity of Christ.   This was a necessary emphasis in order to counteract a common tendency of the day to make the manhood of Christ unreal, but Nestorius, in his stress on the two natures of Christ, was accused of teaching that Christ was two persons.   He was arraigned before the Council of Ephesus in 431 on a charge of heresy.

There was in the church of that time an increasing aptitude towards the worship of the Virgin Mary.   This was strenuously opposed by some, including Nestorius, and although Mariolatry had not been ' officially' condoned, yet its condemnation ran counter to popular sentiment.   It was a very cunning stratagem

96

on the part of Cyril of Alexandria, who dominated the Council of Ephesus, that Nestorius' orthodoxy should be judged by whether or not he was willing to allow Mary the title of 'Theotokos', or 'Mother of God' as it is loosely translated. Nestorius, of course, protested that Mary was the mother of the Man Christ Jesus, but not of His deity. He was condemned and banished, living the remainder of his life in impoverished circumstances in the Egyptian desert. During his exile he wrote an account of his beliefs entitled 'The Treatise of Heraclides of Damascus'. The proceedings of the Council of Ephesus were grossly unfair and only served to satisfy the selfish ambition and bitter rivalry of Cyril.

There were many Bishops, however, who refused to accept the judgement passed on Nestorius. These were likewise expelled, and found refuge among the Christians of Syria and Persia who, from then on, were stigmatised as Nestorian. The Persian rulers, recognising that this division in Christianity precluded the Persian churches from outside sympathies which might pose a threat to the security of the Empire, allowed the churches an added measure of freedom. This gave an impetus to the zeal for preaching the Gospel which was to carry the Nestorians to the far corners of the globe with the message of salvation. These indefatigable missionaries spread down through Arabia, across the plains of central Asia, south into the Indian peninsula and Ceylon, and on eastwards into China which they reached in the first half of the seventh century. Part of their labour was the translation of the Scriptures into several languages.

While the record of the Nestorian missionary ventures is a story to inspire us all in our witness for Christ, yet their work was hampered and ultimately failed because of their adherence to ecclesiastical tradition which had become such a major factor in the life of the Catholic Church. New churches were organized under one head, and Bishops appointed in accordance with the old, hierarchical order. The years saw a strengthening of misplaced faith in episcopal authority and in the efficacy of the sacraments to bring salvation. Whereas the separations of the Nestorians from the Catholic system had accorded an opportunity to return to the pattern of Scripture, coming under the authority of the Spirit through whom the Lord dwells in the midst of His people, they yet continued to maintain their link with the secular power and pursued the same downward course as the Church within the Roman Empire.

Records of Nestorian missionary enterprise tell of the missionaries bringing not only sacred books, but images as well. In this we can see something of the extent to which they had departed from the purity of the Gospel. The number of converts increased, but moral character declined. The churches founded by the Nestorians degenerated as a testimony to the life of Christ. ' Christian ' idolatry was little witness to heathen idolaters, and all paved the way for the great wave of Islam which was to sweep over vast territories, blotting out everything in its path. But maybe Islam was but the judgement of God upon a Church which had so degenerated and departed from the truth as it is in Christ Jesus as to have been better destroyed than remain as a reproach to the name of the One it professed to own as Lord.

Twenty years after the condemnation of Nestorius at Ephesus, one of his most virulent opponents, Eutyches, was himself charged with being a heretic and condemned at the Council of Calchedon for holding that Christ had but one nature. This doctrine, called Monophysitism, still finds expression in the Coptic churches of Egypt and Ethiopia. Although Christianity had spread down into Ethiopia in early days, it suffered a similar fate to that of the Nestorian churches, having become bogged down in an allegiance to ritual and tradition.

In the western and northern outposts of the Roman Empire, the message of Christ had spread at a comparatively early stage. Of how or by whom the Gospel was preached we know very little, for no great names have come down to us as associated with missionary labours of early days in these parts. We know, however, that the Gospel had penetrated into the regions beyond. In 314 at the Synod of Arles, three Bishops attended from Britain, indicating that there already existed an established Christian community in that country. The Goths who sacked Rome in 410 were a partially Christianized race, and it may be thanks to that fact that anything at all of the old, Roman civilization was allowed to remain. Certainly the Christianity of the Goths, and the coming to Arles of Bishops from Britain may, of themselves, indicate no more than the presence of a debased form of religion such as was now centred at Rome, but it does show that the message of Christ had spread, and, as we shall see, amidst the dross of superficial religion there was also that of much greater spiritual value.

Much too little importance is usually given to the part played by ordinary men and women in the advance of the Gospel.

So often the history of the church is portrayed as simply the organized advance of organized religion. The life of Christ, however, should pre-eminently find its expression in the day-to-day lives of those who have submitted to His Lordship, and this witness should be the most potent power for the extension of the Gospel. This has always been true, and still is where spiritual life has not degenerated to the realm of the purely formal. The fellowship thus established between men and God and between believers together is something much higher and greater than can be expressed in any humanly sustained, ecclesiastical system.

Travel throughout the Roman world was restricted only by the speed of horse or man. One could go from the borders of Scotland to Mesopotamia completely free from the hindrance of international barriers, and there was a constant flow of traffic in the interests of trade or the normal running of the Empire. It was most probably from Gaul, through traders plying in the ordinary course of their business, that the Gospel first reached the British Isles. Meanwhile, from south eastern Europe and Asia Minor the Gospel, in a similar manner, spread up through Bulgaria and into Russia.

Augustine

Having viewed generally the expansion of the Christian faith in different parts of the world, we must now return to look at the development of policy within the Roman Church, for it is here that we find the centre of opposition to the growth of a spiritual faith. In few places can we find the life of Catholic Christianity more aptly epitomised than in the life of Augustine. In Augustine we see the confusion of spiritual life and ideals with ecclesiastical barbarism. Probably no man has made such a great contribution to Christian thinking as Augustine, and probably no man has made such a great contribution to the establishment of the Roman Church and the perpetration of centuries of ruthlessness in the name of Christ. Augustine had an experience of Christ which granted him a deep insight into some of the most glorious truths of Scripture, yet he not only condoned but also perpetrated some of the gravest of errors.

Augustine was born in 354 in Numidia, north Africa, the son of a pagan father and a saintly, Christian mother, Monica, who hoped and prayed steadfastly for him as she saw him grow up into a life of spiritual emptiness and profligacy. In his frustra-

99

tion with life, Augustine was successively influenced by many of the different philosophies of his day, but found satisfaction in none. At the age of thirty he was appointed as a teacher of rhetoric at Milan where he came under the influence of the great Bishop Ambrose. Two years later, through reading the closing verses of Paul's Epistle to the Romans, chapter thirteen, he was soundly converted. Ambrose baptized him in 387. The following year he returned to his native Africa, and in 395 was made Bishop of Hippo where he lived for the remaining thirty-five years of his life.

Augustine developed, in particular, two lines of doctrine, the doctrine of grace, and the doctrine of the Church. His emphasis on the former has been the source of much spiritual enlightenment; his treatment of the latter has equally been the source of great spiritual darkness.

It is very understandable how Augustine's thinking should be dominated by the grace of God. His dramatic conversion, and the radical nature of the change that took place immediately in his life, served to emphazise the great gulf which had existed between him and God, and the terribleness of the sin which was its cause. Only the boundless grace of a loving God could have bridged such a gap. Augustine had no difficulty in understanding the teaching and experience of the apostle Paul, for Paul's experience had been his own. He knew that there was no good thing in him which could in the least have merited his salvation. His development of the doctrine of grace, however, was also the outcome of his reaction to Pelagius whose teaching we have already noted. Pelagius denied the fact of original sin and, consequently, saw no need of divine grace to free man from sin's bondage. Salvation, or following God, he said, lay completely within the power of man's own will. Augustine employed all his powers to withstand this unscriptural doctrine, and wrote a number of treatises on the subject.

Augustine gained impetus to develop his doctrine of the Church first from his concern over the Donatist movement which had broken away from the Catholic organization, and secondly from the disastrous fall of Rome in 410 which presaged the collapse of the western Empire. It was this that inspired him to write his great treatise *The City of God* in which his views on the nature of the Church are expanded.

In his answer to the Donatists' insistence upon a pure communion, Augustine upheld an inclusive theory of the Church through which alone the grace of God is mediated to men by means of the sacraments. Outside this Church, he asserted, there could be no salvation, whatever a person's righteousness, or however strong his faith. In his book *The City of God* he contrasted Rome, the greatest city on earth which was bound to pass away, with the Church. But the Church which he figured as *The City of God* was not the spiritual unity of believers, but the ecclesiastical organization of Catholicism. To bring men within the sphere of the Catholic system Augustine even sanctioned the use of force. It was preferable, he said, that people should be brought to acknowledge God's way through teaching, but if they did not respond to this then compulsion was allowable. To substantiate his point, he quoted the words of our Lord, " Compel them to come in " (Luke 14 : 23 A.V.). When it was proposed to use force against the Donatists he at first demurred, but afterwards consented. His view of the Church as an earthly organization and a purely visible unity led him to adopt earthly expedients to see it built up and its power sustained. The unspeakable suffering to which this error led, and the rampant evil which it condoned, were to darken the history of Christianity throughout succeeding centuries.

Augustine lent his authority to traditionalism and sacramentalism, fostered belief in purgatory, and encouraged the use of relics which, in the hands of unscrupulous priests, was to become such a disgraceful and lucrative trade, playing upon the incredulity of superstitious people to fill the coffers of Catholicism and the pockets of her prelates. Yet these things were so strangely inconsistent both with some aspects of Augustine's teaching and his own experience. On the one hand, he magnifies the grace of God who chooses and grants salvation to whom He will; on the other, he restricts salvation to an earthly, ecclesiastical organization which dispenses grace through its sacraments as the sole means of God's working. In his own conversion he had experienced the power of God bringing conviction through His Word, and through this grace alone he found peace and reconciliation. Yet later he is willing, indeed advocates, to replace the working of the Spirit by the fear of pain inflicted by man, and accepts an extorted confession as saving faith. Augustine's life is an example of the unwarranted extremes to which a man of strong devotions and passionate zeal can go when, be it with every good intention, he departs from the principles of Scripture.

The doctrine of the Church as expounded by Augustine found full expression in the Catholic system. Everybody who did not

101

own allegiance to the ' one and only Church ' was a heretic, and every group of Christians who maintained a Scriptural independence and bowed only to the Lord who dwelt in their midst was schismatic. By intrigue, persuasion, or by persecution, the Roman Church sought to bring all under its sway. But God was not without a witness. Even within Catholicism there arose men of great devotion to the Lord who spoke out against the flagrant evils that were commonly practised. They had a genuine burden to minister the Gospel, but very often, through a misplaced loyalty to the degenerate Church in which they had been born and nurtured, their testimony was compromised, their service frustrated, and their spiritual insight darkened by the shroud of an ecclesiastical traditionalism which they were unable to shake off. Beyond the pall of Rome, however, there were those who, in simple dependence upon the Lord through His Word, maintained the light, life and liberty of the early churches, and it is in those, who form the stream of the spiritual movement of the church down through the centuries, that our main interest lies.

Monasticism

The decline of spirituality and the increase of worldliness within the churches led to the separation of groups who sought to maintain their communion with God and with one another on simple, Scriptural lines. It led others to withdraw themselves entirely from the affairs of the world and to give themselves over to ascetic lives of study and solitary worship. This developed into monasticism, which found a lasting place within the organized, Christian communion. A proportion of these monastic orders laid emphasis on simplicity but not asceticism, and were given over to service rather than the sole development of their members' own spiritual lives. Some men of great saintliness who remained within the Roman fold found, in the monastic communities, a freer opportunity to serve God, and a haven from the sordid intrigue and corruption of the Church at large. These monastic orders, however, generally followed a common course. Beginning in a spirit of self-denial and service, they became rich, worldly and proud, and abused the authority they had won. In reaction, another order would be founded to return to the same principles, and the same cycle would be repeated.

Priscillian

About the time of the birth of Augustine in 354, a remarkable move to return to sole dependence upon the Word of God was taking place in Spain and was to spread into France and Portugal. An outstanding man associated with this move was a wealthy Spaniard of great learning and eloquence named Priscillian. Priscillian had abandoned the old, pagan beliefs, yet felt no attraction for Christianity, and sought spiritual rest and satisfaction in some of the other philosophies prevalent in his day. His search, however, brought him back to the Christ whom he had previously rejected, and he entered upon a new life of ardent devotion to the Lord. He became a great student and teacher of the Scriptures. Many people were attracted to his gatherings where the sincerity of his preaching and the practical nature of his expositions were used, in the hands of God, to make new life in Christ a reality to many.

Priscillian was a layman, but his ability was noted by the Church, and he was appointed Bishop of Avila. His saintliness of life, his teaching and his popularity, however, drew a strong reaction from the Spanish clergy, and in 380 an accusation of Manichaeism was brought against him. This, of course, was a favourite charge with which the Catholic Church condemned those who refused to acknowledge its absolute supremacy. The charge, however, was not found proven, but the attack was renewed in 384 at the Synod of Bordeaux when Priscillian's adversaries, joined by the evil Bishop Ithacus, accused him and his followers not only of heresy, but also of immorality and sorcery. Appeal was made to the Emperor Maximus, but he, being desirous for political ends of ingratiating himself with the Spanish clergy, ratified the sentence of execution. Priscillian and six other ' Priscillianists ', as they were called (although they themselves took only the name of ' Christians '), were beheaded, and Priscillian's voluminous writings were assiduously sought out and destroyed.

This outrage was not perpetrated without protest. Two of the most noted Churchmen of the day, Martin of Tours and the fearless Bishop Ambrose of Milan, strongly protested against such wickedness and refused to have fellowship with those Bishops who had been party to the persecution. Popular feeling among those who had known Priscillian was roused, and when the Emperor Maximus was overthrown, the Bishop Ithacus who had connived at Priscillian's execution was deposed. The

103

Roman Church, however, years later, gave official sanction to Priscillian's execution and handed down to posterity the patent falsehood that he and those who were his companions in faith had been punished for their heresy and wickedness. The real cause of the execution was simply the desire of the Catholic party to suppress all that diverged from the tradition of Rome.

The discovery in 1886 of some of the writings of Priscillian has thrown a great deal of light upon his character, his teaching, and those who were associated with him. It is unfortunate that much of the information we have concerning groups of Christians down through history who deviated from the institutional Church comes from their enemies and must, therefore, be suspected of bias. When Rome persecuted separate movements of Christian believers, she sought also to destroy any records which might make them appear in a favourable light to subsequent generations, so it is very probable that, in the centuries of Rome's religious dominance, there were many more gatherings of spiritual folk living out their lives of testimony in simple dependence upon Christ than those of which we have present knowledge. Some of the facets of Priscillian's teaching are most illuminating, and reveal a man of saintly character with a very clear insight into the meaning of Scripture, in a day when so much of spiritual truth was beclouded by tradition and human perversion.

Priscillian based what he taught squarely upon the Word of God which he accepted as the sole rule in matters of doctrine and of daily living. Christians are called to a holy life which is the outcome of communion with Christ. This communion is entered into, not through sacraments, but through living faith. Priscillian recognised no spiritual distinction between laity and clergy. All believers alike are partakers of the Spirit who instructs them through the Word, and the ministry of the Word is, therefore, open to all according to the Spirit's pleasure. It is not hard to see the divergence of these views from the accepted teaching of the Church, and to understand how the preaching of Priscillian and the holy lives of those who were associated with him cut at the very roots of clerical domination, the doctrine of apostolic succession, and sacramentalism. That the Catholic Church should deny them was inevitable, for Priscillian's Scripture-based concept of the church was diametrically opposed to that of Rome.

The death of Priscillian and his companions did not bring to an end the work which he had done, and the popular revulsion at the shameful massacre of godly people served for a time to temper the wave of persecution. Later it was renewed with increased ferocity, but the companies of believers known to themselves as 'Christians' and by others as 'Priscillianists' continued for some two centuries.

Christianity in Britain

Patrick and Columba

Earlier in this chapter we have noted how the Gospel spread to the British Isles. Christianity in England was at first comparatively free from Catholic influence, but much of it was destroyed in the Anglo-Saxon invasions from the middle of the fifth century. About the year 385 in a village called Bannavern, the exact location of which is unknown, was born Succat, or as he is more commonly known to us today, Patrick. Patrick's parents were simple, devout Christians, but their son, during his early years, took little interest in their spiritual instruction. When he was in his teens, he was carried off by a band of marauding Irishmen and sold as a slave into a pagan clan. It was there, separated from every outward Christian influence, that he recalled to mind the lessons of his boyhood and yielded himself to Christ. Patrick was twice a captive and twice rescued. Eventually, back among his own people, he heard the call of God to return to Ireland with the Gospel.

Patrick reached Ireland again in 432 and commenced his work of evangelization. He was not altogether free from the errors of his time, but there is no indication that he accepted the authority of Rome, and the churches which were established were certainly of a vastly different and purer order. The Gospel which Patrick proclaimed was not the Gospel of traditions or sacraments, but the message of the Word of God which was used to bring many to repentance and allegiance to Christ.

Over a hundred years later, in one of these Irish churches, there arose a man of great piety named Columba. With the urge to proclaim the Gospel burning within him, Columba and several other zealous Christians embarked from Ireland in 563, landing on Iona, an island off the west coast of Scotland. There they found already settled some Christian Culdees who had found refuge in Iona from the factions of the Picts and Scots on the mainland. The Culdees were Christians whose history went back to the earliest days of Christianity in Britain. They owned the Lordship of Christ alone, not that of any Church system, refused luxury and extravagant living, maintained themselves by honest toil, and were zealous in the ministry of God's

105

Iona

Word. In these circumstances there was established a community of Christians from which the light of the Gospel was to shine forth on to the mainland of Britain and over into the continent of Europe.

The Christian company of Iona is often pictured as a monastic community, but this is misleading, for it differed widely from the monasteries of Catholicism. There was no support in Iona for the sacerdotal system which had engulfed much of the Christian world. Columba was but a first among equals, and the community was governed by presbyters or elders. It was the Spirit of God, he held, not the ordination of man, who made servants of God. The importance of rituals was discounted, and the Scriptures were the rule of faith and daily living. From Iona, men were set apart as chosen of God to take the Gospel to other regions. No doubt there were features in their work which were foreign to the pattern of apostolic times, but they were free to follow the Lord, and with the Scriptures as their guide they proclaimed the news of the Gospel over into northern and central Europe.

England had been overrun by the pagan Anglo-Saxons and now lay between Rome and the independent churches of Britain. The energetic Pope Gregory I was determined to convert the English and, through them, bring the already existing communities of Christians in the north and west under the dominion of the Catholic Church. To this end, in the year 597, he despatched a mission led by Augustine, an accomplished and zealous man who was possessed of a mixture of piety and a consuming ambition for himself and for Rome. He was, at the same time, a skilled diplomat. Augustine seemed to feel that the advancement of the power of the Church should take precedence over matters of Christian character. The mission was, in some respects, a great success. In less than a year Ethelbert, king of Kent, and thousands of his subjects had been converted after the Romish fashion. There was, however, a fierce conflict between the old, British churches, and the system which Augustine introduced. He died having failed miserably to bring the Christians of Ireland and Scotland under the dominion of the Pope.

Efforts were continually renewed to subdue the free churches of Britain. As the years passed, their spiritual strength waned and their resistance weakened. Some held out longer than others, but by the beginning of the eighth century it could be said that the vast majority of Christians throughout the British Isles owned the sway of Rome.

The fire of the Spirit, however, was not quenched, nor can it ever be, and there remained those in the mountains of Caledonia and elsewhere, separated from what the world at large recognised as the Church, but maintaining their witness and refusing to accept the mediation of any human institution between themselves and God. These faithful people, and those who came after them, were to incorporate their faith in the spiritual movements of a later day. The torch of testimony continued to burn, and was to be taken up in succeeding centuries to burn with a much brighter light.

CHAPTER TEN

TORCH BEARERS

Islam

In Old Testament times God not infrequently used heathen nations to judge the degeneracy of His own people. In the second and third chapters of the Book of Revelation, the messages of the Spirit of God to the seven churches warns of God's judgement in removing the lampstands of witness if His people do not persevere in their devotion to Him. There are incidents in the history of the Church which well may be interpreted as a divine intervention to blot out that which had become a reproach to the name of Christ. By the seventh century, much of the Church was ripe for judgement.

Muhammad was born in Mecca in 571 of an *élite* family. In his youth he travelled with trading caravans along the main trade routes of the Arabian peninsula, and in Syria and Palestine had considerable contact with Jews and Christians. He was not impressed by his encounter with Christianity, mixed as it was with superstition and idolatry. A visionary, and one who was incensed by the degradations of the idolatrous polytheism of his own race, he embarked upon a life of reform. His efforts were spurred on by direct revelations which he claimed to receive from God and which were committed to writing to form the Qur'an.

Whatever may be said of Muhammad, and there can be no doubt as to the contradictions of his own character, he instigated, on a social level, a much needed reform among the Arabs of his day. God, he said, was One, and he was His prophet. His fierce denunciations of idolatry and other blatant evils so stirred up opposition in Mecca that, with a company of his followers, he fled in 622 to Medina. From that year the Muslim era is dated, and indeed his flight, or 'hijra' as it is called, proved to be the turning point of his career. By the time of his death in 632 practically the whole of Arabia lay at his feet.

Muhammad's successors as Kaliphs took up the cause, and Islam spread with bewildering rapidity. Damascus fell to the

108

Muslim forces in 635, and then the great bastions of Christianity, Jerusalem, Antioch and Alexandria. Thousands of church buildings were destroyed or turned into mosques. The tide swept across north Africa practically obliterating Christianity. Few communities survived. Those who refused to deny Christ died, and of those who denied Him many served to swell the ranks of the Islamic forces. Across Spain and into France swept the apparently invincible tide, to be met at last by the determined forces of Charles Martel at Tours in 732. In one of the most important battles of all history, the invaders suffered a crushing defeat.

In less than a hundred years from Muhammad's death, the dominion of Islam stretched from India to Spain, and its conquests were by no means over. That such a catastrophe should have overtaken the Church almost defies the imagination, yet it was not the spiritual movement of the church that suffered near extermination, but the proud ecclesiasticism which claimed dominion over the souls of men and offered to sacraments and idols the reverence that was due to God alone. Islam was a judgement upon pagan idolatry. It was a judgement upon Christian idolatry as well.

So far had the Church departed from the teachings of Scripture, and so blatantly was idolatry practised, that in 726 Leo III, Emperor of the east, sought to deal with these abuses. He forbade that reverence be given to images and to pictures. His son Constantine V pursued the same policy, but it was strongly resisted by many, both common people and clerics. The dispute resulted in shameful violence on both sides, for neither had any appeal to spiritual motives.

Paulicians

But there was not lacking a spiritual resistance to these evils, a resistance which had its origins much earlier than the clumsy, if sincere efforts of Leo, an unspiritual man, to order the matter on a purely human level. There were groups of believers who, among themselves owning only the name of 'Christians' or 'brethren', stood out strongly against the idolatry, sacramentalism, and other prevailing errors of the Catholic Church. They appear on the historical scene in the middle of the seventh century as 'Paulicians' in the region of Mesopotamia. Why they were named 'Paulicians' is not exactly known, but it may simply have been because of their respect for the apostle Paul and his writings. The Catholic Church ascribed to them all sorts of erroneous doctrines, if we can believe those whose lives denied the truths they professed, for to them practical holiness was of little account, and truth was turned into error. It is a sad commentary on the perversity of man's nature that ever a Churchly system could emerge calling itself the Church of Jesus Christ in which was practised every conceivable type of abomination, yet which believed itself supremely to enjoy the favour of a holy God because of an orthodox form of words to which it gave lip assent, and utterly repudiated in daily living. This same Church scorned the manifestly holy lives of men and women who sought to order their ways in humble obedience to Christ through His Word, and branded them heretics. Little did they realise that the great Judge, in that last day when we shall all stand before Him, will not ask for the recitation of a creed, but look for an obedient and submissive heart. " By their fruits ye shall know them," said our Lord, but the clerics of these dark ages could not be expected to understand the Scriptures.

Whatever opinions may be held about the Paulicians, it is generally conceded that they had a particular respect for the authority of the Bible, advocated a life of simplicity, were a devout and earnest people, and bore a strong witness against the unsavoury practices of the Catholic Church. Their enemies testified against them, but their lives testified of Christ. They claimed simply that they were in the succession of those people who still held to the teaching of the apostles, and with every Scriptural justification, they denied the right of the ecclesiastical systems of Christendom to own the name of churches because of their degeneracy.

In assessing the character of the Paulicians and other groups which have appeared down through the centuries, historians have tended too readily to accept uncritically what has been said and written against them by their enemies. The history of the Roman Church in its dealings with those who refused to bow to its dominion is a sordid tale of pillage and persecution. Not only did it seek to destroy the persons of those who opposed it, but also to bring the very memory of their names into ignominy by the most gross accusations, and to obliterate what they themselves wrote or anything written about them in their favour. It is hardly surprising, therefore, that much more literature survives which condemns than commends them. The great struggle of later centuries to produce the Scriptures in the lan-

110

guages of ordinary people illustrates most aptly the methods which Rome employed to maintain her authority over the souls of men. Copies of the Scriptures were hunted out and consigned to the flames, and along with them those who were responsible for their publication and dissemination, if they refused to recant from the 'sin' of having sought to spread the Word of God. These same methods were generously employed in the days of the Paulicians.

The Paulicians accepted no central authority to rule over the scattered assemblies. The local churches looked to God as their Head, and they were built up and strengthened spiritually by teachers who moved from place to place to minister in their midst in a manner similar to that of Paul and others in New Testament times. They did not draw up any code of doctrine to which they had commonly to subscribe as a basis of unity, and since different groups came into being through the ministry of different people, they no doubt differed somewhat one from another, both in form and in emphasis. Their spiritual unity lay in the life which they had in Christ, a life which manifested itself in their daily walk and witness. They owned a profound respect for the Word of God, which they accepted as their guide and basis of spiritual growth.

An Armenian book written somewhere between the 7th and 9th centuries with the title of 'The Key of Truth' gives an account of foundational belief and practice as it existed widely among the Paulicians of that time. The author was himself one of the brethren, but his name is unknown. Two things are particularly emphasized in regard to various practices which are enumerated; first, the reading of the Scriptures and prayer, and secondly, holiness of life in consistence with God's Word. Paulicians and others were charged by the Roman Church with being Manichaeans, but it is extremely difficult to understand how any could hold Manichaean views who so honoured the Word of God. To uphold the teachings of Mani, much of the Scripture would either have to be repudiated or changed.

The 'Key of Truth' repudiates the practice of infant baptism, but holds that the church has a responsibility to pray for the children of believers, and the elders to exhort parents to their solemn duty to bring them up in holiness to know the Lord and His Word. Baptism should be given only to those who requested it, as a testimony of their repentance and faith. This again was opposed to the false, Romish idea that baptism was the means of redemptive grace being bestowed. To the Paulicians it was a witness to a work that God had already accomplished. They also laid stress on the holy character not only of the person who was being baptized, but also on the baptizer. On the question of setting apart elders, the writer emphasized the conditions laid down in Scripture and exhorts that great care be taken to see that these conditions are observed. A brother accepting the office of an elder had to be willing to brave the dangers which his position invited, and to be ready to suffer for his Lord.

The Paulicians attracted men who had a passionate devotion to Christ. In the few facts concerning them already mentioned we can see the simple order and holy life of the earliest churches. Of those of their number whose lives were dedicated to the ministry of the Word of God in their midst we find men of humility and apostolic spirit who poured out their lives in the proclamation of the truth and died rather than deny their Lord.

Constantine Silvanus

Prominent among these men was Constantine Silvanus. He has been suggested as the founder of the Paulicians, but according to the testimony of the Paulicians themselves, they existed long before Constantine Silvanus' time, and the arbitrary association of his name with the foundation of these groups is likely little more than a demonstration of the human tendency to assign the beginnings of every movement of the Spirit to man rather than to God.

Constantine, a man of distinctive ability, was influenced by the Gospel about the year 653 through an Armenian traveller whom he had graciously entertained at his home. This man was a true believer in Christ, and recognising that God had led him to someone of more than ordinary capacity, he left with his host what must have been a very valuable gift, a manuscript containing the four Gospels and Paul's epistles. Never was such a gift put to better use. Constantine was enthralled by what he read, the entrance of the Word brought light into his soul, and through the working of the eternal Spirit he was made a new creature in Christ. Testifying to new life he had received, he soon found fellowship with groups of people of a like experience who rejected the idolatry and superstition of the organized Church, and met together in accordance with what he himself had learned from his study of the Scriptures. Constantine changed his name to Silvanus, the name of the companion of the apostle Paul, and embarked upon a life given over to preaching the Gospel and confirming the churches. His ministry was brought to a close only by his death in 684. He made his home near Kibossa in Armenia, and from there travelled in the ministry of the Word along the Euphrates valley in the east, and into Asia Minor in the west. God used him to the conversion of great numbers of Catholics and heathen alike.

In 684 the Byzantine Emperor, alarmed by the success of Silvanus and the increase of the Paulicians, issued a decree against them. To enforce it, he sent from Constantinople one of his officers named Simeon into Armenia, and Silvanus was stoned to death. Simeon, however, had been closely observing the Paulicians in their trials, and was greatly impressed by their calm fortitude in persecution, so much so, indeed, that he himself began to enquire about their way of life, was convinced of the truth and, yielding to Christ, became united with those he had been sent to destroy. He returned to Constantinople, but could find peace no longer in the service of the Emperor. Escaping to Kibossa, he entered the service of a greater King and took up the work of the man he had been instrumental in putting to death. It was not long, however, before he too joined the army of martyrs, for he was burnt together with a large number of other believers two years later in an all-out attempt by the Emperor to coerce the Paulicians into submission to the organized Church. In this he was completely unsuccessful. The fires of persecution but served to strengthen the faith, courage and devotion of the believers. Preachers and teachers were raised up to take the place of those who had given their lives for their Lord, and the congregations increased.

Sergius

Another notable servant of God among the groups of Christians known as Paulicians was Sergius, who ministered in Asia Minor during the first thirty-five years of the ninth century. Like Silvanus, he was brought to faith in Christ through reading the Scriptures. Asked by a godly sister why he did not read the Gospels, he realised that the Word of God was not only for the Romish priests, but for all alike. He received new life and a burning call to minister the Word of truth which had so transformed him. Maintaining himself by working as a carpenter, he nevertheless travelled extensively, and ministered

113

through letters which were widely circulated among the churches. His ministry was with peculiar authority, and he was used to instruct the believers and heal differences such as will always, unfortunately, exist in the churches of God while man has not yet reached to 'the measure of the stature of the fulness of Christ'. Sergius also met a martyr's end.

The middle of the ninth century saw the notorious persecution under the Empress Theodora. Within a space of five years it is said that a hundred thousand persons met their death in the wave of indescribable terror. But the Paulicians contained some whose spiritual strength was not equal to the rigors of the day. It may have been that the interval of tranquillity which had commenced over a century earlier and had continued during the reigns of more sympathetic Emperors had seen the addition to the groups of those whose devotion to Christ had not taken precedence over their devotion to their own rights. Such is an ever present danger to the churches of God. Where God's people can be persuaded to press their claims to their own rights in this unjust and sinful world as a matter of prime importance, soon fleshly means will be employed, and the churches will be rendered spiritually impotent. This is precisely what occurred with a section of the Paulicians. In sore despair, and oppressed beyond human endurance, they sought not the sufficiency of grace which comes from above and, following the indignant leadership of one of their outraged number, took to warfare against their oppressors. They allied themselves with the Muhammadans who were marching against the idolatrous, Catholic world in the name of liberty and pure worship of one God. It was a lost cause. It may well have seemed to these Paulicians that a heathen Christendom was farther away than Islam from the revelation given in Christ, but Muhammadanism denied the Scriptures, that through which alone God is able to bring spiritual quickening to the lives of men. The Paulicians were ultimately routed and scattered into the mountains. "All they that take the sword shall perish with the sword" (Matt. 26:52).

Bogomils

Yet a substantial remnant had remained, and these were to be the seeds of witness on the continent of Europe. Through the sympathy of the Emperor Constantine V, himself an inflexible opponent of image worship, some Paulicians had emigrated to

Constantinople and Thrace in the middle of the eighth century. There they preached the Gospel, and numerous churches were established in the area of the Balkan peninsula. These people came generally to be known as ' Bogomils ' which means simply ' friends of God '. It may be remarked here again how clearly the principle of life is manifested. Life reproduces itself. The church is the embodiment of the life of Christ, and is not dependent upon particular leaders or institutions for maintaining its existence. Where the vitality of the Spirit directed by God's Word exists in those who are part of that body, the churches will extend and grow. No power of earth or hell can overcome them. If they are stamped out in one place, it will only be to reappear in another, and the Scriptures alone will be proved sufficient to lead on and establish God's people in the way of truth.

The congregations of Christian brethren known as Bogomils were, in consonance with the spirit and tenor of the age, the subject of wild accusations by the adherents of the Roman Church. They were accused, naturally, of being heretics, and quite justifiably of denying much that was peculiar to Roman dogma, including the usefulness of the Church's sacraments and orders. To Mary they gave no special honour, nor to the figure of the cross or other relics; the Lord's supper was not celebrated in the Roman Church according to Scripture, they said, and her priesthood was corrupt. It is little wonder that they were accorded such malicious treatment. On the other hand, they were accused of evil and immoral conduct, something which is strangely reminiscent of the charges spread against the Christians in the early days of the Roman Empire's opposition to the advance of the faith. The heathenism of the Roman Empire which had loudly protested the moral corruption of the Christians was itself hopelessly degraded, and the Roman Church of a later century which denounced the ' heretic ' friends of God was itself riddled with graft and evil. It is surely not unreasonable to doubt whether the judgement of the latter was any more true than the judgement of the former.

Yet not all condemned the Bogomils in this manner, and the opposition of some influential if bigoted men took a form other than these crudities. These admitted their high standard of life and morals, that they preached love and grace from the Gospels, and exhibited the Christian virtues in their lives, but all, they alleged, from an evil motive, to lead people astray. The simple lives of self-denial lived by the brethren they

115

conceded, but attributed to their holding the Manichaean doctrine of the essential evil of the whole material creation. Whatever motive it was that lay behind these Christians' holy living, it was doubtless this uprightness of character which attracted to them many seeking souls who looked in vain for such humility and sobriety within the confines of the Roman fold.

Amidst trial and persecution, the work of God continued to expand for many years, to reach the peak of its development at the end of the twelfth century in Bosnia where the ruler and his family, along with some ten thousand others, joined the Bogomils. Catholicism lost its hold upon the country. Instead of ornate church buildings with all their attendant trappings, meeting places were plain and void of bells, images and altars, or the believers could meet equally well within their own homes. The Scriptural truth of the priesthood of all believers was recognised, the congregations were governed by a plurality of elders and edified through the teaching of ministering brethren. Those teachers, whose lives were devoted to an extra-local ministry of the Word, were supported by the tithes of the believers. The poor and needy among the churches were also helped according to the law of love in Christ.

The spread of these Friends of God constituted an increasing threat to the Roman Church, and Rome was not inactive in seeking to stem the tide of this meek and powerful opposition. Pope Innocent III sought the help of the king of Hungary, and in 1203 cowed the Bosnian leaders into subjection. They promised obedience to the Roman Church, the re-introduction of Romish practices into the churches of their own land, and the outlawing of all heretics. But great numbers of ordinary believers were not to be subjugated thus easily. They had found life in Christ, a satisfying rule in the Word of God, and had a faith in God which had not been dependent upon the conversion of their rulers. They refused to submit. This was the signal for recurring and violent persecution. The Pope first of all tried peaceable methods to win the brethren back to the ' mother Church ', but they increased the more. Finally, in desperation, he ordered the king of Hungary to invade Bosnia, and the country was ravaged by a war which went on for years. The devastation of war reduced the land to a shambles, but the churches continued to exist. In 1291 a new terror was added, the Inquisition, in which its officers vied together in the refinements of cruelty to exterminate the followers of Christ.

116

Throughout the fourteenth and into the fifteenth century this iniquitous persecution continued. Finally, the Turks, who had been harrassing the bastions of Europe and had already been beaten back, took possession of Bosnia in 1463 and the country settled down to four hundred years of Muslim rule. The Bosnians had made no resistance. After all, could the Turk be any worse than the Inquisition? But under the new rule, the bright witness of the Friends of God in Bosnia seemed to die out.

Cathars

Heretical churches, it was deplored, were spread from the Black Sea to the Atlantic Ocean. Companies of believers similar to those in the Balkans were particularly numerous in northern Italy and southern France. They were often called Cathars, that is ' Puritans ', a name which we have already found in earlier times. The policy of repression followed in the eastern Empire against ' heretics ' had driven numbers of Bogomils westwards, and the Crusades also fostered a new intercourse between the peoples of east and west. Wherever believers went, they found others of a like spirit, and these various groups, by whatever names they were known by the Roman clergy, were united in fellowship to their mutual edification.

As in the east, so in the west, teachers were raised up who fearlessly denounced the prevalent ecclesiastical errors of the day, and led people into new life through the preaching of the Scriptures. Among those were Peter of Brueys and Henry of Cluny, Peter's companion in labour during the later period of his ministry. Little is known of Peter's early life, but for almost two decades he travelled widely, fearlessly proclaiming the Gospel till he was finally arrested and burnt in St. Giles in 1226. Henry attracted many by his gift of oratory and fiery spirit. A man of ascetic temperament and piety, he commanded a large following, preaching with untiring endeavour from 1101 till his death in 1147. According to inveterate and age-long habit, those who, receiving the light of the Gospel through the preaching of these men, sought to return from the morass of dead formalism to the teaching of the Scriptures, were dubbed with sectarian names. Man never seems to have been able to learn that any movement of the Spirit can be greater than any particular person whom God, through His grace, has used in it. The preaching of Peter and Henry served to add to those groups who were called Cathars, or by a variety of other names which

117

I

they themselves never recognised. These believers in 1167 were able to hold a widely attended conference for teachers in St. Felix de Caramen near Toulouse. Elders came from as far east as Constantinople, a remarkable indication of the strengths and benefits of fellowship in the Spirit which is based upon something much more binding than organizational association.

One who laboured with great diligence for the conversion of these Christians to Rome was Bernard of Clairvaux. Born in 1090, he was to become one of the paramount religious forces of his age. Eloquent, ascetic, of a mystic turn of mind, and of a consistency of character which was not over-common in the Roman Church of his day, Bernard won later praise even from such men as Luther and Calvin. Even today we sing and treasure some of the hymns he wrote. But he was very intolerant. Bitterly and sarcastically he complains of the groups of believers who refused to recognize any man as their founder, saying that demon spirits were their originators. Bernard's efforts to win them back into the State Church met with practically no success. He died in 1153.

The Waldenses

' Waldenses' was the name given originally to congregations of believers who lived in the valleys of the southern Alps. One suggestion as to the origin of the name is that it is derived from Peter Waldo, a rich businessman of Lyons, born in the first half of the twelfth century. He was certainly not their founder, but became a preacher of note and indefatigable labour who was much respected amongst them. There is, in fact, no precise record of the origin of the Waldenses. They themselves traced their beginnings back to apostolic times, and claimed that the faith which they held had been passed down from father to son from the earliest ages of the church's existence. It may well be that these congregations were the spiritual progeny of Christians who fled northwards during the early Roman persecutions at the close of the apostolic era. Their antiquity was attested by their enemies, as was also their blameless life.

The Waldenses were characterised by their marked reverence for the Scriptures in which they found their rule of daily living and church order. Their congregations were, therefore, simple, void of the highly developed rituals and ordinances which marked the Roman Church. This was partly because, in the solitude of the mountains and valleys, they had been able to

118

continue their lives of devotion to Christ unaffected by the radical
and unscriptural changes that were taking place within the fold
of organized religion. In this sense, they were not reformers.
Living apart from Romanism, they had not rebelled against it,
and were not characterised, therefore, by the violent opposition
of reaction to the Church of those who had separated from Rome
because of its corruptions.

As we have already remarked, the Waldenses found in the
Scriptures a complete rule of daily life and church order. The
knowledge of Christ's dwelling within by the Spirit was to them
a truth of paramount importance, but in matters of Scripture
interpretation which did not deny the basic necessity of this
experience of Christ they allowed a generous liberty. Salvation
was through faith, and the Roman Church had authority neither
to open nor to close the door to God's grace. The proof of
salvation was holiness of life. Baptism was a testimony to faith
in Christ, and the Lord's supper was a remembrance of His
sacrifice. Elders ruled the local churches, and they were edified
also through the teaching of those who were set apart for an
itinerant ministry in their midst. While spiritual qualification
was of maximum importance in these teachers, education was
also valued as an aid to study and expound aright the Word of
God. The writings of some of the great, ' Church Fathers ' were
also profitably used, with discernment, for the Waldenses recognised the enlightenment of men of God, even although their
labours and thought, in some directions, had been constricted
by the limitations of ecclesiastical formalism. Their final court
of appeal was God's Word, and by that had all to be tested.

Peter Waldo, a rich merchant of Lyons, having procured a
translation of the New Testament, was touched by the Scripture
and felt the call to leave his business to serve Christ. He was
much impressed by the Lord's words, " If thou wouldest be perfect, go, sell that thou hast, and give to the poor, and thou
shalt have treasure in heaven: and come, follow me " (Matt.
19: 21). Waldo decided to obey literally and, making generous
provision for his wife and family, he gave what remained to the
poor and embarked upon a life of teaching God's Word.
Others joined him, and they went forth, two by two, as our
Lord sent forth His disciples, proclaiming the truth of Christ.
In 1179 they appealed to the third Lateran Council for permission to preach, but Pope Alexander III, not for reasons of
heresy, but considering them to be uninstructed laymen, refused
consent. Peter Waldo, enlightened by the Scriptures, felt that

man was raising his voice against that of God. He and his companions refused to stop preaching and, as a result, were ultimately excommunicated from the Church of Rome. Waldo was in the most intimate associations with the Waldenses, and his preaching brought much blessing and enlargement. The brethren had tended to become isolated in their remote valleys, but the influence of Peter Waldo and his associates was used, under God, to give a much needed impetus to the endeavours of the Waldenses to spread the Gospel over a much wider field. Peter Waldo died in Bohemia in 1217.

An interesting comparison with the ministry of Peter Waldo is found in Francis of Assisi. The son of a cloth merchant of Assisi in central Italy, Giovanni Bernadone was born about the year 1182. His nick-name, Francis, supplanted the name given by his parents, and by it he had been known down through the centuries. In 1209, as he was listening to the reading of Christ's words to the apostles from Matthew 10:7-14, he felt that same divine constraint that Peter Waldo had experienced over two decades earlier, and set out to preach repentance and the kingdom, having vowed himself to observe the utmost poverty and humility. As others were attracted to him, he drew up a 'rule' which was composed mainly of commands enjoined by our Lord, and in 1210 gained the reluctant approval of the Pope. It is here that the ways of Peter Waldo and Francis of Assisi divide.

Francis was a man of utmost zeal, devotion to the Lord and saintliness of character. Weak in body, his missionary vision yet took him as far afield as Egypt and Syria to preach Christ to the Muhammadans. But the 'rule' which he had established for his followers was soon modified and was ultimately transformed into a full monastic order. The emphasis on preaching gave way to an emphasis on begging, poverty gave place to riches, and the order degenerated into a worldly force which helped to keep people chained to the authority of Rome. The changes which took place in Francis' own lifetime were a deep grief to him, yet he seemed to accept them, however regrettable he might have felt them to be, with complete deference to the ecclesiastical power.

It is interesting to conjecture what Francis would have done had the initial request for the Pope's approval of his 'rule' met with the same rejection as Peter Waldo's application for permission to preach. It is doubtful whether Francis would have adopted Waldo's firm stand. There is an apt lesson to be learned from the different courses these two movements took, the associates of Peter Waldo to make a vital contribution to the strengthening of a spiritual church testimony, the Franciscans to become an instrument of Roman tyranny. We do not deny the devotion of Francis and his early followers, nor their desire to see a revival of true spiritual values within the Roman Church, but when any spiritual movement can be contained within the confines of a worldly, ecclesiastical system, it will soon be dragged down to the same level as the system that it tried to reform.

The reaction of the Roman Church to the Waldenses and Cathars (or Albigenses, another indefinite name by which some groups of believers were known) came to a head in a far-reaching decision which was made at the Council of Toulouse in 1229. The Cathars and the Waldenses had made great use of the Bible; it was their court of appeal in all matters of faith and practice. The clergy, therefore, recognising that Scripture was the basis of the main opposition to the Church of Rome, determined to remove this mischievous reading matter from the hands of the laity, who were henceforth forbidden the use of the Bible apart from the Latin Psalter and such other portions as were contained in the breviary. It was furthermore decreed that no part of the Scriptures should be translated into the tongues of the common people. This decree may have been, theoretically, local in its application, but it set a precedent for similar measures to be invoked elsewhere and, in practice, its strictures were widely and generally enforced. It was the Council of Trent, meeting from 1545 to 1563, which finally made these decrees absolute, declared the Latin Vulgate to be the only, authoritative version of the Bible, and ruled that every Catholic should accept only and unquestioningly the interpretation of Scripture given by the Church.

The fierce wrath provoked by the possession and reading of the Scriptures highlights for us the important place which the Word of God must occupy in the life of the local church. At this period in Church history we see more clearly than at any other that the struggle for the maintenance of a church testimony as it was known in apostolic days has largely been the struggle to give the Bible its rightful place in the midst of God's people. Rome sought to remove the Bible altogether from the hands of ordinary men and women. Protestantism has never made any pretence to follow such an example, but if the volume of the Bible has not been denied any who wish to have it, again and again the authority of the Bible has been removed by systems of Church order which have been superimposed upon it, or by the interpretations of blatant infidelity masquerading as enlightened religion. Wherever this has been the case, and it is a state of affairs all too common in the present age, the meaning, purpose and vitality of the church have been lost. But wherever the Scriptures have been restored to their rightful place, there has been a return to that simplicity of order, life and authority which, in the Acts of the Apostles, marked the companies of them that believed.

The Waldenses and like groups of brethren exercised a wide and enduring influence through which the truth of Scripture spread rapidly, and the number of assemblies of believers increased remarkably. Particularly in the first half of the fourteenth century, they increased as never before, and the impact of their spiritual teaching had an influence upon many quite outside the immediate circle of the churches themselves. For a long time the cities of Strassburg and Cologne were centres of life and teaching. The exaggerated claims made by the Roman Church, and the opposition to these of some of the civil rulers, no doubt helped to open the eyes of many as to the direction in which the truth lay. Where the secular authorities were sympathetic and stood their ground against the encroachments of Catholicism upon their liberty, the churches were able to develop and spread the Word of life in an era of comparative peace.

The authority of the Roman Church found its complete, logical expression in the theology of Thomas Aquinas, whose influence has continued right up to the present day, and whose works are used as the basis of theological instruction in the Roman communion. Aquinas began work on his great theological treatise about 1265 and died in 1274 before it was fully completed. A simple, prayerful man, he was, nevertheless, a prey to the grossest of error. It was he, probably more than any other, who lent sanction to the use of indulgences, a practice which led to such corruption and moral evil as to be one of the immediate factors which brought about the upheaval of the Reformation. According to Aquinas, the merit of Christ and the saints formed a pool of good works whose benefits could be transferred by the good offices of the Church to penitent sinners in order to mitigate, in this life or in purgatory, the penalties due to their evil deeds. It was not long before the sale of indulgences was a shameful, commercial racket which plundered rich and poor alike, and filled the coffers of the Church and the pockets of unscrupulous clerics. Aquinas taught that to be subject to the Roman Pontiff is necessary for salvation. This was further given official sanction in a bull issued by Pope Boniface VIII in 1302. It is little wonder that honest seekers after the truth rebelled, and that the assemblies of brethren found their numbers increasing rapidly as men and women found true peace in Christ, through the preaching of the Word.

The Council of Toulouse in 1229 had systematized the procedure to be followed by the Inquisition, and when the time was ripe, all was ready for its being brought into operation against the 'heretics'. Circumstances turned in favour of the Roman Church in 1348 when Charles IV, a man ready to cater to every papal whim, became Emperor of the Holy Roman Empire. A determined effort was at once instituted to stamp out the Christian congregations, and the Inquisition was brought into effect with diabolical efficiency. Many were converted " to the Catholic Church. Others were tortured and burnt till, by the end of the fourteenth century, Rome thought she was victorious. There were, however, some places of refuge from the storm. The teaching of John Wycliffe in England and John Huss in Bohemia was exercising a powerful influence in these countries, and many believers sought freedom to worship God in these foreign lands. But that brings us to another chapter in our story.

CHAPTER ELEVEN

GATHERING CLOUDS

EVEN within the Roman Church there were voices raised to contend against its unwarranted use of authority and the flagrant evil practices which seemed to be the norm. One of the most outstanding of these was Marsilius of Padua, one time rector of the university of Paris, and a physician by profession. In 1324 he produced his *Defensor Pacis* in which he propounded his radical views, views which caused Pope Clement VI to say of his book that he had never read worse heresy. Marsilius showed that the supreme standard in faith and conduct is the Bible. The church is the company of those who trust in Christ, not the ecclesiastical organization with its Popes, Bishops and clergy. The latter, therefore, have no authority to define Christian truth and compel obedience to their decrees. These offices were, in fact, of human origin. Peter had no special place among the apostles, and clerical distinctions were foreign to the Word of God. Final authority in the church is the prerogative of the whole company of Christians represented in a General Council.

Marsilius would doubtless have paid for his views with his life had he not received the protection of the Emperor till his death in 1342.

John Wycliffe

John Wycliffe was born near Richmond in Yorkshire sometime during the third decade of the fourteenth century. He entered one of the colleges of Oxford where he greatly distinguished himself. His scholastic eminence was such that he probably had no equal in the England of his day. While still quite a young man, he was gripped by the power of Scripture, and was resolved to impart to others what he himself had received. As a lecturer on theology in the university he had ample opportunity to set forth the way of faith, and his courage and transparent saintliness of character greatly commended what he taught. Fearlessly he pointed out how the Roman clergy had

124

banished the Word of God, and urged that it be re-instated to its rightful place within the church.

In 1374 Wycliffe became rector of Lutterworth and was preaching the Word to an ever widening circle. The source of faith, he taught, is the Gospel of Jesus Christ. The Pope can claim no arbitrary authority, but must be subject to God through His Word as everyone else. Such teaching, which was spreading rapidly among the people, was threatening to undermine the whole position of the Roman Church which, understandably, grew alarmed. In 1377 Wycliffe was charged with heresy, but his respect with the government whose authority he had defended against the encroachment of Rome (Wycliffe was no mean politician) and his popularity with many ordinary folks, made it impossible to proceed with the charge.

Wycliffe renewed his ministry with increased endeavour. Tracts in Latin and in English flowed out from his pen. But more important by far than all his other writings was the production of the first English Bible, the fruit of his ardent desire to see the Word of God translated into the language of the common people. It is not certain how much of the translation which bears his name was the work of Wycliffe himself, but this matters little. He was certainly the inspiration, under God, behind this momentous undertaking, and it reflects in no little measure his great love of the Lord, his sound understanding, and his spiritual insight. Wycliffe was not conversant with Hebrew and Greek, but he was a good Latin scholar, and the translation, completed between 1382 and 1384 was from the Latin Vulgate. The work received glad and wide acceptance, and in a new way the Spirit of God began to work.

Wycliffe himself was to receive increasing enlightenment through his intimate contact with the Scriptures when, late in his life, he gave himself to more mature reflection upon God's Word. He had long been a firm advocate of the doctrine of transubstantiation, but being convinced of the truth from the Word of truth, he proclaimed this doctrine with tremendous vigour as a blasphemous deceit, contrary to Scripture, and published his denial of it in a tract written in 1381.

The most important aspect of Wycliffe's teaching, however, was his ultimate acknowledgement of the Bible's exclusive authority. Interpretation of Scripture is not the sole prerogative of any man or organization; the meaning of Scripture is made clear by the Holy Spirit to those who are enlightened of Christ and approach God's Word in a spirit of humility and teachableness.

Salvation, Wycliffe held, is through faith, but the proof of faith is the sanctified walk. He did not divorce faith from works, but showed, as did the apostle James, that the latter is the inevitable outcome of the former. Although a priest of the Roman Catholic Church till the day he died, Wycliffe did not view the church as the outward ecclesiastical organization whose head was the Pope. The church, he believed, consisted of the whole company of the elect, and its only Head is Christ. In the visible expression of that church upon the earth Scripture recognised only two orders, elders and deacons, and every believer had a right to immediate access to God through grace in Christ. All believers are priests.

The greatest privilege to which any man could attain, said Wycliffe, was to preach the Word, and to carry the preaching of the Gospel to the remotest villages he sent out his 'poor preachers', simply clad, living on simple fare, to proclaim the new life in Christ, and to demonstrate it in their own lives. 'Lollards' they came to be called later, probably a name of derision meaning 'babblers' given by their enemies. The measure of the Lollards' popularity was the measure of the hunger begotten in the hearts of rich and poor, learned and unlearned alike by the Holy Spirit for the truth contained in the divine Word. Their preaching was no mere condemnation of Rome, but the positive setting forth of the Gospel of grace which brought liberation and life. They recognised a ministry which was dependent only upon the Bible for its authority and through which God would bring edification to all who cared to listen and obey. Congregations came into existence centred upon allegiance to the Scriptures, and some of these continued to exist for a considerable time, although the preachers were scattered through persecution, and it became a capital offence to read the Scriptures in English.

Wycliffe died on the last day of 1384 still rector of Lutterworth. That he died a natural death was due, in part at least, to the determination of Edward III that the king of England should be master in his own realm, and to the instability of the Roman Church at the time, for many of Wycliffe's ecclesiastical enemies would willingly have had him led to the stake for heresy.

The year 1378 saw the beginning of one of the most farcical scandals in the history of the Roman Church. On the death of Pope Gregory XI, what has come to be known as the Great Schism saw two Popes, Urban VI in Rome, and Clement VII in Avignon each claiming to be the true successor of Peter. For

126

nearly forty years the rift continued with the rival Pontiffs hurling anathemas at one another from their respective seats. Some nations supported the Pope at Rome, others the Pope at Avignon. The Catholic world was sorely perplexed, and till the first numbness of the shock wore off the ' heretics ' were spared the avid attention the Church was wont to lavish on them. In the brief interval, the true Lord of the church took His servant, John Wycliffe peacefully to be with Himself.

The importance of Wycliffe in the history of the spiritual movement of the church lay not primarily in his attitude to Rome, for, although he fearlessly condemned the abuses that abounded, yet he never cut himself off from the Catholic organization. His importance lies in the fact that his emphasis on the supreme authority of the Word demanded the re-establishment of that which alone is the basis of the church, and the rescue, therefore, of the Scriptural concept of the church from the morass of superfluous rite and superstition to which Romanism had degenerated. The existence of the church in its local aspect is based wholly and solely on the living Word. Where the Word of God does not occupy its rightful place, the church, as God meant it to be, will fall into decay and die. In Wycliffe's day the clergy were notoriously ignorant of Scripture, and not without cause, for the free access of the Bible to the common man would have spelt the ruin of the Roman system.

Why was there such violent opposition to the translation of the Scriptures into the vernacular languages? One of the main reasons was the threat this would have posed to Catholic ecclesiasticism. On the continent of Europe, for example, vernacular versions of the Bible were in use among the Waldenses and others, and wherever the authority of the Word was recognised, the Pope protested his own assumed authority in vain. The monochratic principle upon which the organization of the mediaeval Church was built was dependent upon the status of the Latin language, for it kept the mass of its adherents, to whom Latin was an unknown tongue, in complete religious dependence upon the will and the interpretations of the Roman hierarchy. To allow them the freedom to read the Scriptures in their own language and to trust directly upon the Spirit of God for its interpretation would be to foster a spirit of spiritual independence which would cut at the root of Roman authority. The Catholic system cannot be based upon a free subservience to the Word of God, and is, therefore, something completely other than what the Scripture calls the church of Jesus Christ.

Conversely, the true testimony of the church is based upon the glad acknowledgement of the authority of the Bible. When John Wycliffe gave the Bible to the English people in their own tongue, he was laying the foundation for the emergence once more of the testimony of the church of apostolic times.

John Huss

Through the marriage of Richard II of England to a Bohemian Princess, Anna, in 1383, new avenues of contact were opened up between Bohemia and England. Students from Bohemia were attracted to the university of Oxford, and one of these was Jerome of Prague. Jerome came under the influence of Wycliffe's teaching and returned to his own country to preach the ' new ' doctrines with great boldness. His faithfulness in witnessing to the power of the Gospel was the means of bringing spiritual life and enlightenment to John Huss who was destined to become such a remarkable power both in the religious and political spheres of Bohemian life.

John Huss was born of a peasant family, and rose through sheer merit to become rector of the university of Prague, one of the foremost universities in Europe. A man of transparent faith, his Bohemian eloquence made a tremendous spiritual impact upon the nation, but also roused nationalistic sentiments which gave expression to the age-long rivalry between the Germans and Czechs. Along with the spiritual power of those who followed John Huss, there was a political aspect to the movement which was much less spiritually healthy, and which was to be the cause of the regrettable developments of later days.

Huss' fiery eloquence and his fearless rebuke of the vices of the clergy inevitably brought him into conflict with the Roman Church. He was excommunicated by the Pope, and the writings of Wycliffe which were the root of his ' heresy ' were publicly burnt, but he was supported by the king of Bohemia and a great majority of the people. Bohemia was in confusion. The Council of Constance which convened in 1414 was approaching, and the situation in Bohemia affected by the teaching of Wycliffe and Huss demanded its attention. Huss, invited to attend, was given a promise of safe conduct by the Emperor of the Holy Roman Empire, Sigismund. He felt it his duty to bear witness to the truth before what was one of the most extraordinary companies of rulers and ecclesiastical dignitaries ever to assemble in one place. But he was basely betrayed. His safe conduct was only to a foul dungeon on one of beautiful Lake Constance's islets. The council, meanwhile, received a very convenient 'revelation from the Holy Spirit' that the Church is not bound by any promise made to a heretic.

Huss was cruelly treated, but nothing could induce him to retract what he had taught according to the Word of God. With great steadfastness and heroism he stood firm by his concession in loyalty to his Lord. In 1415, after a service in which he was publicly and shamefully degraded, John Huss died a martyr's death, burnt at the stake. Jerome of Prague, the man through whom Huss had been brought to the light, was soon to follow the same way.

The treatment meted out to Huss and Jerome roused the strongest resentment in Bohemia, and led to rapid developments amongst their followers. Various parties emerged, the two largest of which were known as the Utraquists and the Taborites. In both of these parties there was a mixture of spiritual principles and trust in fleshly means. The Utraquists were the more inclined to compromise with Rome, and ultimately received recognition from the Pope as the national Church, certain concessions being made to them such as the right of all to receive both the bread and the cup in the celebration of the Lord's supper, a practice which, of course, was foreign to the Catholic communion. Everything virtually passed back into the hands of Rome. The Taborites received their name from the little town of Tabor which was their centre. Much more than the Utraquists could it be said that they embodied the principles expounded by Wycliffe and Huss. They were in no way disposed towards compromise with Rome, but in their battle for the faith, they forsook spiritual weapons alone to resort to the sword. Under the able generalship of John Zizka they drove back the army of the Pope, raised to subdue them. In 1434, however, in a struggle with the compromising, Utraquist party, they were defeated.

Apart from these lamentable conflicts which were so foreign to the spirit of Christ, there were others who chose to walk the pathway of suffering, and refused to try to fight their spiritual battles with carnal weapons. These people were drawn generally from the most spiritual within the Hussite movement, both Utraquists and Taborites, and also from the Waldenses. They continued to seek their guidance for Gospel witness, church order, and daily living in the Scriptures. An outstanding teacher from their midst was Peter Cheltschizki. His understanding of the nature of the church was Scriptural and clear, and he sought that there should be a return to the simple practice of apostolic days where believers gathered together purely on the ground of their relationship with Christ, to be strengthened in their fellowship with God and one another for carrying out their commission of representing Christ in the world. About the middle of the fifteenth century these various congregations were known as the Unitas Fratrum (United Brethren). They had no desire to form any new party or sect, for they recognised their complete oneness of spirit with Christian brethren in every country where they might be found. They did, however, declare themselves separated from the Church of Rome.

The communities of brethren flourished not only spiritually, but in other respects as well. Among their number were people of intellectual capacity, and others of position and wealth. Learning was cultivated and, closely connected with these brethren, schools, widely respected for their standard of teaching, were established throughout north-west Germany and the Netherlands. Their aim was an education based upon the Gospel of Christ. Erasmus was a pupil of one of those schools at Deventer in Holland, and Martin Luther greatly respected the writings of some of the brethren which they published.

Early in the sixteenth century Pope Alexander VI persuaded the king of Bohemia that the growing influence of the brethren posed a threat to his throne, and they once more became the objects of persecution, not only by the Roman Church, but also by the Utraquists. The brethren were not immune from the rot of spiritual declension. Many became involved in the war between the Protestant and Roman Catholic powers of Central Europe in which the Protestants were defeated in 1547. In fact it was the apparent inability of so many of John Huss' spiritual descendents to maintain their allegiance to Christ free from political entanglements that spelt the ultimate disaster of what one might call the 'Hussite religion' in Bohemia. "For all that take the sword shall perish with the sword" (Matt. 26:52).

But there is another side to the story. Down through the ages God has prepared a remnant through which a testimony to Him has been maintained and His purposes worked out. The effects of war and persecution scattered some of the faithful believers into areas where they had a fresh opportunity of witnessing to Christ. Some settled in Poland and commenced a work which spread throughout the country. Another remnant of the brethren was also to be the spiritual ancestor of the Moravian movement of a later age.

The work which centred round Wycliffe and Huss was but the continuance of a testimony to the Gospel that had never died out, but the widespread sympathy it invoked among high and low alike was also symptomatic of the growing disgust that was engendered by the corruption of the papacy. It did not require a prophet to foresee that this increasing discontent must one day come to a head. The inevitable Reformation was drawing nearer. Meanwhile, another force of a more secular nature was helping to prepare the way.

The Renaissance

The Renaissance, which means ' rebirth ', is the name given to that revival of interest in Art and Classical literature which swept across Europe during the fourteenth century. There were numerous factors which gave rise to this new spirit, but it gained a decided impetus when, in 1453, Constantinople was captured by the Turks and many scholars fled to the west bring ing with them the influence of their own learning and many, priceless Greek manuscripts. Europe had become parochial in its interests and outlook, but suddenly the vistas of a new world broke through the darkness. A new age was dawning, an age of enquiry, adventure and a thirst for learning. This was the era which produced artists of such incomparable distinction as Michael Angelo, Raphael and Leonardo da Vinci. At the same time, the discovery of printing provided a means for disseminat- ing the new learning to an extent which, at an earlier time. would have been inconceivable. In the production of the Bible. whereas the copies of Wycliffe's translation had to be written out laboriously by hand, it was now possible to produce them in thousands.

The revival of interest in Art and the Greek and Latin classics was by no means wholly productive of good. It led some to an abandonment of Christian restraints and an occupation with pagan ideals, with the resultant collapse of moral standards which has made the Renaissance age noteworthy both for its culture and its licentiousness. But we are more concerned here with another result of the ' new learning '. It broke men loose from the fetters with which the Roman Church had bound their minds, and there was kindled a new spirit of investigation into the meaning of the Word of God which was carried back beyond

131

the imperfections of the Latin Vulgate to the original sources. Some of the best effects of the Renaissance found expression in the schools of the ' brethren ' which we have already noticed. There the new love of beauty was allied to the teachings of Christ and found, therefore, something of its truer meaning. It requires more than culture to make a saint; culture devoid of Christ, leads only to a polished paganism.

Erasmus

One of the most outstanding of the Christian ' humanists ' (as devotees of the New Learning were called) was Desiderius Erasmus. Born in Rotterdam about 1467, Erasmus was greatly influenced in his love of learning by his early schooling at Deventer. At the end of the century he was in England, and there came under the influence of the brilliant John Colet whose exposition of the Pauline Epistles at the university of Oxford made such a profound impact. Colet denounced the infamous lives of the clergy and stressed the authority of the Scriptures. Through his influence, Erasmus embarked upon his greatest work, the production of a Greek New Testament, freely annotated, with an accompanying new translation in Latin. The study of the Scriptures was now lifted on to a completely different plane. People could read the actual words that had given birth to the church, and could compare them with the great ecclesiastical system which held them in such a tyrannical grip.

Erasmus advocated the translation of the Scriptures into the common tongues. He also freely used his wit and gift of expression to criticise and satirise the superstition and error of the Church. Yet a stronger than he was needed to usher in a Reformation. Erasmus was too clear sighted a man not to be aware of the evils of Rome, and many of his writings were directed towards a change from within, but he was too much the passive scholar to go the length of breaking with the Church that he criticised. His contribution to the reformation, however, was unequivocal, although he may not have intended it to be such. The Greek New Testament renewed the emphasis made by Wycliffe and others on the pre-eminence of the authority of the Word of God, and at the same time opened the way to a clearer understanding of its contents. The Word of God made plain opened the way for a fresh expression of the life of Christ in His people gathered together in His name.

Erasmus' desire for reform within the Catholic Church, and the steadfastness with which he maintained his attitude has had many counterparts both before his time and since. If history teaches us anything, surely one of the clearest lessons is that great institutions are not easily changed, unless one considers the inevitable change wrought by time which, just as inevitably, is a change for the worse, where that which may at one time have held something of the divine, degenerates to the purely human. Rome has certainly changed with the times, but the direction of its move has not been towards the simplicity of the early churches. And the same is true of the great communions of that section of Christendom that is now called Protestant. Change there has been, but always it has been towards the dominance of man, not of God. The churches which stemmed from the preaching of John Huss became embroiled in the political strife of their times and lost out in the effectiveness of their witness. In every age God has had afresh to gather out a people unto Himself. He is still doing it.

William Tyndale

William Tyndale was a fellow student of Erasmus at Oxford. He was probably born in the valley of the lower Severn in the early part of the last decade of the fifteenth century, but neither the exact place of his birth nor the exact time are known for certain. It was Oxford, where Erasmus was so well known, that received his Greek Testament most warmly, and it was there that Tyndale, in his study of this much discussed book, felt the full impact of the Word of God upon his life, an impact which was to determine his life's work and lay the solid foundation of the Reformation in England. Soon he had a circle of friends gathering round him to read the Greek New Testament. The clergy began to grow alarmed at the threat to their authority posed by those who were beginning to recognise the authority of God revealed directly through His Word, and Tyndale left Oxford for Cambridge. There too he found some who had been touched by the power of the Scriptures, and others who were eager to learn. In Cambridge also the light of witness began to glow.

The alarm of the clergy increased, and efforts were renewed to destroy the influence of Erasmus' celebrated work. The most formidable adversary was no less a personage than Cardinal

J

Wolsey, papal legate and Lord Chancellor of England whose famous, *Ego et meus rex* (I and my king), gives some indication of the power he enjoyed in the country. Wolsey also had a seething ambition to occupy the chair of St. Peter, so it well suited his purpose to become the great champion of Catholic orthodoxy and the Church's stalwart defender against the 'pernicious heresy' of the Bible.

Tyndale left Cambridge and returned to his own part of the country where he occupied a position in the household of Sir John Walsh at Sodbury Hall for a period of about eighteen months. Sir John and Lady Walsh had engaged him to be tutor to their children. The Walsh household was devoted to hospitality, and Sir John's position, interest in learning and generosity brought to his home and to his table the noble and learned of the land. There the conversation would centre round the burning questions of the day, the New Learning, Luther, Erasmus and the Scriptures. Tyndale took his full share in the animated repartee, and substantiated his points by reference to the Greek New Testament, a copy of which he always kept at hand. Sir John and Lady Walsh themselves were by no means unsympathetic towards the views of their children's tutor. It is not surprising, however, that Tyndale succeeded in rousing the ire of prelates and clerics who gathered round the table in the great dining room of Sodbury Hall, and the fact that their own ignorance of the Scriptures was being constantly exposed made them little more well-disposed to this lowly scholar with the agile mind and ever-ready reply from the Word of God to priestly superstitions. Tyndale was shocked to realise how ignorant the clergy were of the Bible, but it spurred him on to the momentous decision that his life would be devoted to giving to the people of England God's Word in their own language. It was at Sodbury Hall that the full extent of priestly ignorance began to dawn upon him, and it was there, in answer to some outrageous remark spoken by a 'learned' theologian sent to convert him that he uttered his immortal words, "If God spares my life, ere many years I will take care that a plough-boy shall know more of the Scriptures than you do."

To pursue his God given task, Tyndale had to flee his own country when only about thirty years of age. During the remainer of his life he lived in exile, pursuing his purpose with dogged determination against incredible difficulties and disappointments. He lived his life as a hunted man, moving from place to place to avoid discovery and the confiscation of his precious manuscripts and books. In 1526 the first edition of his English New Testament was produced, and the books were smuggled into England to be distributed by friends, many of whom paid with their lives for their desire to allow God to speak to people through His Word. In an injunction issued by Tunstall, Bishop of London, prohibiting possession of these English New Testaments, he warns people against 'that pestiferous and most pernicious poison'. The scholar and statesman Sir Thomas More who, urged by Tunstall to come to the defence of the Church, spent the final years of his life vainly exercising all his literary skill to refute Tyndale's work, claimed that the translation of the New Testament was full of errors. To look for errors in it, he said, was like looking for water in the sea. The unprejudiced judgement of future years, however, was amply to vindicate Tyndale's version both from the Greek of the New Testament and the Hebrew of the Old. Tyndale himself was the first to recognise the imperfections that were bound to exist in a fallible, human translation, and he urged that corrections should be made wherever words could be found more accurately to represent the meaning of the original, but no other version has, in fact, had a greater influence upon our Authorised Version. In it the great bulk of Tyndale's renderings remain unchanged.

William Tyndale met the end he had long expected. Betrayed by a fellow countryman, he was charged and condemned for heresy. In 1536 at Vilvorde near Brussels he was led from his prison to the place of execution. Chained to a massive wooden cross with a noose around his neck, the faggots were piled around his body. At a given signal, the executioner tightened the rope, and William Tyndale entered into his glorious reward. Fire was struck to the dry tinder, and the unassuming body that had housed so great a soul was reduced to ashes.

While Tyndale was living out the last years of his life on the Continent of Europe, the tide of events was moving swiftly in England. Henry VIII, furious with the Pope's duplicity in failing to order affairs to suit his amorous designs, finally severed the connection of England with the Roman Church by the passing, in 1534, of the Supremacy Act which declared the king to be the 'Supreme Head of the Church of England'. The ban on the English Bible was relaxed, for a little while at least, and Miles Coverdale produced in 1535 the first, complete printed version of the Scriptures in English, basing his translation on Tyndale's great work on the New Testament and part of the Old. Coverdale's Bible was the first to circulate freely in England, and was doing so while Tyndale was dying a martyr's death at Vilvorde. In 1538, by royal proclamation, a copy of the Bible was placed in every church in the realm for the edification of all who desired to read. Tyndale was not here to rejoice on earth, but no doubt rejoiced in heaven that the labour to which he had given his life had at last borne fruit.

Henry VIII has been called the 'father of the English Reformation'. That may be so if what is meant by the Reformation is simply the severing of the religious tie between England and Rome, but the fat, licentious monarch who so readily sacrificed his wives and subjects, Protestants and Catholics alike, to gratify his every regal whim, was certainly not the father of that spiritual movement whereby men and women, regenerated by the power of a risen Christ, were free to meet around their Lord and display to the world the testimony of a glorified Saviour in the church. Spiritual reformation is based upon much more solid ground, the ground of the Word of God which liveth and abideth for ever. It was Tyndale whom God used to re-establish in the English speaking world of the sixteenth century the solid foundation upon which He could build, but this foundation and the church built upon it, as we have seen, has never been absent from the world since the church was first established at Pentecost, in spite of all the attempts of the arch-enemy to overthrow it. And the advent of the Reformation era was to bring with it its own subtle attacks upon the testimony of a living church.

CHAPTER TWELVE

THE WELCOME RAIN OF REFORM

WE now come to the events of the Reformation itself, if indeed we have not been dealing with one of these, for the centre of everything meaningful about the Reformation is a Book, not a man or men. What we generally mean by the Reformation is that great cleavage which split a major section of Christendom into two camps, Catholic and Protestant. Our history, however, is mainly concerned with something else, the tracing of the spiritual history of the spiritual church down through the ages, a church which has continued to witness while controversies and scandals have rent the ecclesiastical world, and mighty religious systems have risen and collapsed. There is a sense in which much of the change of the Reformation remains external to our purpose, yet the Reformation was productive of a completely new set of circumstances and a new religious attitude in many parts of the Christian world. To leave this out of consideration would be to leave ourselves without any knowledge of the background against which the spiritual movement of the church had to advance, and of the fresh problems it had to face from Reformation times.

It is also important to recognise fully the different forms which the Reformation took in different countries. In some places, much of the old and superfluous remained, although Rome with all her grosser abuses was vanquished. In others, however, there was a return to certain principles of Scripture which allowed not only the individual free access to the benefits of grace, but also a return, in part at least, to the corporate life of fellowship which was a distinctive mark of the early churches. To understand these various elements which made up the Reformation we must look at the lives of some of the great Reformers themselves.

Martin Luther

Martin Luther was born in 1483 the son of a miner. His father, though poor, was determined to educate him for a career in law, so his preliminary education completed, he entered the university of Erfurt in 1501. From his early years, Luther seems to have been possessed of a deep sense of the reality of things spiritual. His profound sense of sin and longing for inward peace ultimately led him to abandon the career planned for him, and he entered the monastery of the Augustinian Eremites in Erfurt where he applied himself diligently to the salvation of his soul through penances, fastings and prayers. The German Augustinians represented the better side of monasticism, were widely respected, laid emphasis on preaching, and contained some men of profound spiritual experience. Such a one was John Staupitz, Vicar General of the Order who, on a tour of inspection of the monasteries, found Martin Luther in deep exercise of spirit concerning the matter of his salvation. Staupitz counselled him to read the Bible, and pointed him directly to Christ through whom alone there is salvation and fellowship with God. Through reading Paul's epistle to the Romans, the light shone into Luther's heart, and he found peace with God. Justification was through faith alone.

Luther's profound experience was strengthened through his study of the Scriptures, and preaching was an art at which he displayed the most outstanding gifts. It was inevitable that the divine impact he had experienced in his own life should be used to measure his traditional beliefs and the worth of the religious institutions and paraphernalia which were all around him. It was inevitable too that he should find them sadly wanting. By this time he was lecturing on the Bible at the university of Wittenberg, and found not inconsiderable support.

In 1517 Luther found an excellent opportunity of giving practical expression to his faith. Pope Leo X needed money, a lot of money. He was building the church of St. Peter, and pocket money for his own, personal, rather extravagant tastes was also becoming somewhat short. The sale of indulgences had proved to be a remunerative occupation, so it was decided to extend the scope of this source of papal income. In furtherance of this design, a Dominican monk named Tetzel, a salesman of proven ability, was hawking his wares in the neighbourhood of Wittenberg with eloquent patter and ribald buffoonery.

No sooner will the pennies clink in the box
Than the keys will clink in purgatory's locks.

It was the last straw. Nothing was better calculated to expose the whole thing as a gigantic fraud. The spirit of Luther, filled with his experience of divine grace, was outraged by these blasphemous pretensions. Failing to stir the Elector of Saxony into action, he nailed on the door of the church at Wittenberg his Ninety-five Theses to unlock the sluice gates from which was to pour forth the flood of pent-up feeling that for generations had been built up by papal oppression. Indulgences, Luther said, can remit neither guilt nor divine punishment. True repentance alone brings pardon, and for the pardoned sinner indulgences are valueless. Friends printed copies of the Theses and they were distributed throughout Germany. At last someone had been found to express what so many knew, but dared not say.

Luther was summoned to appear in Rome in 1518, but the wise counsel of friends prevented his going to what would have been certain condemnation. The Pope referred the matter to his legate in Germany, and Luther appeared before him in Augsburg where he was asked to retract statements made in his Theses to the effect that the Pope can exercise no power in indulgences, the merits of Christ alone being sufficient for salvation. Refusing to do this, he fled back to Wittenberg. The supremacy of the Pope had not been a matter to which Luther had objected, but when he came to study the basis of the papal claim, he soon found that it rested on a very insecure foundation. About the middle of the ninth century, a collection of Decretals was put into circulation ascribed to the renowned seventh century ecclesiastic, Isidore of Seville. These included supposed decisions of Popes and Councils from as far back as the first century. Also included in this amazing collection was the Donation of Constantine in which, it was alleged, Constantine commanded the subjection of all ecclesiastics to Pope Sylvester and his successors, and also granted Sylvester overlordship over the whole of the western Roman Empire. The whole thing was a most skilful forgery, and obviously the work of a learned man, but the age was uncritical, and all was generally accepted as genuine till the fifteenth century when the Renaissance awakened the spirit of investigation, and the gigantic deceit was exposed. Yet it was upon these false decretals that much of the mighty power of Rome, both in Church and State, and the exaggerated pretensions of the clergy, were built.

Meanwhile, Luther was to be strengthened through the support of a man who was to become his lifelong friend and wield

139

a mighty influence in the furtherance of the cause. Philip Melanchthon came to Wittenberg in 1518 as Professor of Greek. Of an extremely shy and retiring disposition, he was, however, a most outstanding scholar. Almost from the beginning of his association with Wittenberg his remarkable gifts were at the disposal of the Lutheran cause. It would be difficult to imagine two men of more opposite characteristics than Luther and Melanchthon, but the drive and fiery personality of Luther coupled with the intellectual prowess and calm determination of Melanchthon formed a combination of immense strength and effectiveness.

In 1519 a great debate was arranged in Leipzig between John Eck, a most able champion of the Catholic cause, and Andrew Karlstadt, a supporter and colleague of Luther at Wittenberg. Luther attended the debate, accompanied by a bodyguard of his students and Melanchthon. The quick-minded Eck proved himself almost a match for the not too well prepared Karlstadt. The patent sincerity of Luther, however, dominated the proceedings, but the skilful Eck drove him relentlessly into a statement of his position from which there could be no return.

Luther denied the final authority of the Pope?
Yes.
He was in agreement, therefore, with the view of John Huss whom the Council of Constance had condemned and executed as a heretic?
Yes.
The Council, therefore, in Luther's view, had erred in its treatment of Huss, so the Councils of the Church are fallible?
There could be no other than an affirmative answer unless Luther were hopelessly to compromise the position for which he had taken his stand. He had been skilfully manoeuvered into an outright denial of the authority of the Popes and Church Councils. The irrevocable declaration had been made. He would now stand free from the bondage of ecclesiastical tyranny. He would bow to the direct Lordship of Christ, and His Word would be his sole authority and guide.

While the outraged Catholics bellowed, " Heresy," and a bull of excommunication was being prepared in Rome, Luther's fervid mind was giving expression to its convictions in a stream of publications which were to shake Europe. His three most famous treatises were, " An Address to the Nobility of the Ger-

140

man Nation," "On Christian Liberty," and, "The Babylonish Captivity of the Church." In these he unsparingly criticised the abuses and doctrines of Rome, demanded radical reform, and upheld the authority of the Scriptures, justification by faith and the priesthood of all believers. The papal bull of condemnation arrived, but here was one ' heretic ' who was not going to be led so easily to the stake. Something else was to suffer the ordeal of fire. A bonfire was arranged outside Wittenberg, stoked, we can well imagine, with a will. Luther, amidst a crowd of sympathisers and arrayed in the robes of his Order, approached the fire holding copies of the Pope's bull, the False Decretals and the Canon Law, and flung them defiantly into the flames. Citizens of Wittenberg and students of the university looked on with avid approval. The civil authorities made no move of protest. It was evident that not only Luther, but a considerable part of Germany was in a state of ecclesiastical rebellion.

While the debate at Leipzig was in progress, Charles V was elected as Emperor of the Holy Roman Empire. A loyal Roman Catholic and the most powerful monarch on earth at the time, his authority was yet limited in Germany by the power of the local Princes. One of these was Frederick the Wise, Elector of Saxony, of whom Luther was a subject, a master diplomat, and one who believed that a man should rule his own household. Charles was in a quandary. On the one hand, he held no brief for Luther or his followers, and he was constantly urged from Rome that, since Luther had already been condemned by the Pope, it was his plain duty to put the sentence into effect. On the other hand, there was an imminent threat of war with his neighbour, France, and Charles did not want to hazard his chances of success by alienating the powerful section of Germany which gave Luther support. The result was that, in 1521, Luther was called to present his case before the Diet of Worms. There he was rudely dealt with and called upon to retract what he had written. His reply was the same as John Huss had given over a century ago, that he would retract nothing unless it could be shown as contrary to the Word of God. Since he had been guaranteed a safe conduct, he was allowed to go free, but he was put under the ban of the Empire to be arrested for punishment, and his works were to be confiscated. It was due to the limitations of Charles' power and the strength of Frederick the Wise that the Imperial edict could not be put into execution. On his way home, Luther found himself ' arrested ' by the friendly agents of Frederick, and was carried off to the safety of Wartburg Castle. There, during nearly a year's confinement, he translated the New Testament into German. A translation of the Old Testament was to follow later.

While Luther was in Wartburg, the leadership of the reform movement in Wittenberg passed into the hands of Karlstadt. The new broom, with ready helpers, began to sweep out everything that savoured of Rome with such a frenzy of excitement that the whole community was in a state of uproar. The city fathers pleaded for Luther to return, which he did. Such was the power of his preaching that, in eight days, order was restored, and Luther was master of the situation. He was to further, within the next few years, some of the changes that Karlstadt had made, but for the moment there was a reversal to much of the old order.

Turmoil of another kind was soon to do great harm to the Reforming cause. The Peasants' Revolt of 1524-25 had little directly to do with Luther, but the Reformer and his followers were blamed. Luther was first of all disposed to mediate in the dispute but, fired by later excesses, in a fierce pamphlet he urged the Princes to crush the revolt unmercifully. The rising was drowned in a frightful bath of blood, and Luther's awful foolishness cost him the allegiance of many of the common folk.

In 1526 Charles called the first Diet of Speier to deal with Luther and his followers. The Diet, however, promulgated an edict of tolerance, allowing the ruling Prince of each German State to order the religious affairs of his own domain. At the second Diet of Speier in 1529 the Catholic majority ordered that no further religious changes be made in the States. Those which had been established as Lutheran might remain so, but Roman worship should be permitted within these territories, and Catholic States should not be permitted to change. Against this finding, an evangelical minority in the Diet lodged a protest, and it is from this protest that the name Protestant has been derived. Thus Germany was divided into two camps. The Protestant Princes formed a league, and likewise the Catholics, each ready to advance or defend its cause by recourse to the sword.

From this background of the Lutheran movement, it is evident with what vigour and courage Luther brought into full view the Scriptural revelation which had made such a mighty impact upon his own life, the revelation that each individual is saved through faith in Christ alone. At the same time, it is clear that many obstacles would have to be overcome if this emphasis upon personal relationship with Christ was to form the basis of a return to the Scriptural concept of the church. Did Luther see the implications of an acceptance of the authority of Scripture upon the foundation and life of the church as well as upon the individual's salvation? If he did, would he have the courage to pursue the Scriptural path to its ultimate goal?

The mounting feeling against the Roman Catholic Church which Luther's action had brought to open rebellion was not due only to spiritual causes. Rome had been guilty of the grossest exploitation of ordinary people for material gain, as well as theological error. The revolt of the reformation in Germany had, therefore, underlying social and political causes as well as the religious one. The vast majority of Luther's followers may have been convinced that the Roman Church had deceived them on the spiritual issues, and that Luther was right, but that does not go to prove that a large proportion of that majority had entered into Luther's spiritual experience. In fact it is very certain they had not. Luther himself said later, " The number of those who began with us and had pleasure in our teaching was ten times greater, now not a tenth part of them remains steadfast."

We have already seen how Luther, in his early search after spiritual truth, was greatly drawn to the Brethren. The many influences which later pressed themselves upon him, however, were to bring about a profound change. In the ruggedness of the conflict with Rome in what was a very rugged age, Luther's humility soon gave place to a boisterous dogmatism which was in no way mellower than the dogmatism of those he opposed. It may well be said that the Reformation could have taken place in no other way. Certainly more was required than a cultured Erasmus saying that there should be change and improvements, but let everyone keep calm and do things in moderation. Yet the boldness which was so essential to the cause also drew Luther into political affiliations and a realm of popular loyalties which were to divert his energies far from the pursuance of a purely spiritual aim. The Lutheran Church which he established was a compromise between his Scriptural ideals and his earthly loyalties. At the same time it carried over much that was extraneous and wrong from Rome itself. It developed into something far from the churches of the New Testament, a fact which the Reformer himself recognised, a vast mixture of the godly and the ungodly, tied to the State, an ecclesiastical system stamped by the same intolerance of those who differed from it as Rome.

It is of great interest to note what Luther had written in 1526, " The right kind of evangelical order cannot be exhibited among all sorts of people, but those who are seriously determined to be Christians and confess the Gospel with hand and mouth, must enrol themselves by name and meet apart, in one house, for prayer, for reading, to baptize, to take the Sacrament, and exercise other Christian works. With such order it would be possible for those who did not behave in a Christian manner to be known, reproved, restored, or excluded, according to the rule of Christ (Matt. 18:15). Here also they could, in common, subscribe alms, which would be willingly given and distributed among the poor, according to the example of Paul (2 Cor. 9:1-12). Here it would not be necessary to have much or fine singing. Here a short and simple way of baptism and the Sacrament could be practised, and all would be according to the Word and in love. But I cannot yet order and establish such an assembly, for I have not yet the right people for it. If, however, it should come about that I must do it, and am driven to it, I will willingly do my part. In the meantime I will call, excite, preach, help forward it, until the Christians take the Word so in earnest, that they will themselves find how to do it and continue in it." * Luther had a much deeper understanding of the nature of the church than he was willing to see put practically into operation. It may be pointless to wonder what would have happened had Luther pursued a different path, but his State Church, dominated by the civil power was destined to be a source of great spiritual weakness.

Ulrich Zwingli

Switzerland was, nominally, a part of the Holy Roman Empire, but was one of the freest parts of Europe and was virtually independent. In its free air the Reformation thrived, and the Swiss Reformation was to produce the undoubted leadership of the whole Protestant cause.

Ulrich Zwingli was born in the Swiss village of Wildhaus in 1484. After distinguishing himself brilliantly at the universities of Vienna and Basel, he was appointed first as parish priest of Glarus, and then to the Cathedral church of Zurich. In his earlier years he had some contact with congregations of brethren or Anabaptists, as they were often misleadingly called. Konrad Grebel, one of their most noted leaders, was a one time intimate

* Quoted by E. H. Broadbent in *The Pilgrim Church*.

144

friend of Zwingli, and was well known for his ministry in Zurich where the brethren were numerous. Zwingli had, therefore, considerable touch with those who sought to order their lives and gatherings directly according to the Scriptures, and at one period he was much exercised over the question of baptism. It is interesting to notice how the cornerstone of his reformation teaching in later years was his expressed conviction that the Scriptures contain the final rule for Christian living. Whether he fully accepted all the implications of all he taught is another matter, but to the extent to which Zwingli did carry out reform according to God's Word, he went much farther than Luther. Luther's respect for the Bible is not to be questioned, but, in a sense, it was overshadowed by the great fact of his radical experience of conversion. Subjective experience dominated an objective allegiance to the Word of God. He was willing, therefore, to allow practices which were not explicitly forbidden in Scripture, while Zwingli held that only those things that are laid down in Scripture should be accepted in practice.

Zwingli's real work of reformation began in Zurich in 1522. He vigorously denounced the superstitions of the Roman Church, and carried the battle into public debate. He was strongly supported by the Cantonal government which actually put into effect the principles which he enunciated, and set up an independent Church under the control of the civil power. Zwingli's insistence that church practice should be in accordance with Scriptural precedent meant that the Reformation in Switzerland was much more radical than that carried on under Luther. Vestments, images, relics, the mass, the celibacy of the priesthood, episcopal control were all swept away, and the preaching of the Word was made central.

There was, however, a much less happy side to these changes. Zwingli, as well as being a reformer, was also a patriot and a politician. He preached vehemently against the enlistment of his fellow-countrymen in the mercenary armies of foreign powers. The allying of his religious convictions with the politics of his country ultimately led to the warfare between the Protestant and Catholic cantons in which he lost his life in 1531. If, as seems probable, Zwingli's earliest associations with the congregations of brethren had shed some light on the true nature of the church, his extra-spiritual interests were to lead him irrevocably to advocate a State Church system in which the Scriptural functioning of the church was to be lost. When membership of a church is a matter of nationality and of civil law, can it really be said that the resulting congregation of 'Christians' is a church in the New Testament sense? The whole conception of a State Church is opposed to the very basis of the local church which is, that it is a company of people who are united because of their spiritual relationship with Christ.

Zwingli's theory of the Christian community as represented by its civil administrators acting in accordance with Scripture being the final authority in all matters respecting the Church is fallacious, because the Christian community is not synonymous with the church. The church of Scripture is but a remnant called from the world into fellowship with Christ to be a witness unto Him. That the church should ever be synonymous with the Christian community of a Christianized country we have no Biblical authority to believe, nor has it any historical precedent in over nineteen centuries of the church's life. Zwingli's view, and that of Calvin, has given rise to the widely held distinction among Christians of a church visible and a church invisible, the latter being the real church which, however, has no concrete expression upon the earth, and the former that great conglomeration of good and bad, truth and error, which is found in the great Churches of Christendom. Such a distinction has served to relegate the church to the realm of things theoretical and impractical, and will be looked for in vain in the Word of God. It is, however, necessary, in order to maintain the theory of a State Church such as Zwingli introduced.

We will have cause later on to remark upon the treatment which independent groups of believers received from the Reformed Churches. The inevitable outcome of Zwingli's theory was that the power of the State should be used against all who would not conform with the Church system which the State itself supported. The Reformation, therefore, was to bring but a continuance of the persecution, albeit from a different source, of Christians who sought freedom to worship God and witness for Him simply according to the Word.

A distressing indication of the intolerant spirit of the day was the great controversy between Luther and Zwingli on the meaning of the Lord's supper. Luther held that the words, "This is my body," must be accepted literally, and although he disagreed with the Roman view of transubstantiation, he held that Christ was physically present in the elements, or the doctrine of consubstantiation as it has come to be known. Zwingli held to the now commonly accepted evangelical view, that the bread and wine are purely symbolic. The controversy was pursued in a spirit of great bitterness, and the Catholics smiled with pleasure as they witnessed a split in the Protestant ranks.

John Calvin

John Calvin was born in Noyon, Picardy, in 1509, the son of a respected and influential family. His father originally intended that he should enter the priesthood, and with that in view Calvin was sent to the university of Paris. Later, however, he went to Orleans to study law. At both places he distinguished himself as a brilliant student. His classical and legal education were the means of developing his great natural talent which was to be so signally used in later years when he turned his interests to the realm of theology.

Somewhere during the years 1532-33 Calvin had an experience of conversion which radically altered the tenor of his life. He had a great sense of the authority of the Scriptures, and the study of the Word of God became his foremost thought. Back again in Paris, he sought the fellowship of a group of believers who were meeting for the study of the Bible and prayer, and their influence had an important and formative effect upon his spiritual career. The group contained a number of outstanding men, and was attended also by Margaret, Queen of Navarre. Its origin went back some forty years when the learned Jacques Le Fevre came to lecture in divinity at the Sorbonne. Le Fevre had been brought to a place of peace in Christ through the reading of the Scriptures, and began to gather others around him to listen to his fervent and able exposition of the Word. He taught plainly that salvation unto eternal life is through faith, before such doctrine had been proclaimed either in Germany or Zurich by Luther or Zwingli. It was but the teaching of the apostles, but so long had it been obscured by the teaching of salvation through the sacraments of the Church, that it seemed new to many of the hearers and caused no little stir. Among those who found salvation through Le Fevre's ministry was William Farel, later to become a renowned preacher of the Gospel and the person who, in 1536, persuaded John Calvin to stay in Geneva. Opposition to the little group in Paris became so violent that a number of the more prominent brethren, including Le Fevre and Farel, had to flee from the city in 1521. The gatherings, however, continued, and when Calvin joined their company one of the leading brethren was Nicolas Cop, rector of the Paris university. Late in 1533 Cop delivered

147

an address in which he propounded evangelical views and strongly advocated reform. Calvin was accused of having written the address and was forced to leave the city. He found refuge in Protestant Basel.

It so happened that Francis I, wishing, for political reasons, to justify his persecution of the French Protestants, issued a statement accusing them of anarchy such as, of course, would demand the intervention of the civil power in the interests of law and order. Calvin felt that he had to defend his slandered, fellow-countrymen, and, to this end, published in 1536 his Institutes of the Christian Religion. In this work he made a systematized presentation of the theology of the Reformation, demonstrating that it contained no new or heretical doctrines, but was simply a return to the beliefs and practices of the early church. The first edition of the Institutes was published when he was only twenty-six years old. It was later enlarged to the extensive treatise which we know today and which Calvin completed in 1559. The Reformation produced no other work of comparable greatness, and Calvin's Institutes still remain unrivalled in many respects. This masterly work gave him an influence which extended throughout Protestantism in many lands, and Calvin has emerged as the outstanding figure of the Reformation era.

In 1536 Calvin was passing through Geneva where he met William Farel. Farel implored him to remain, and after an inward struggle, Calvin consented to do so, believing that it was the will of God. Apart from a period of three years' banishment, he lived in Geneva for the rest of his life.

Geneva had become formally Protestant much more for political reasons than because of the spiritual hunger of the people, who were notorious for their loose living. Calvin sought to institute reform in a Church that was already under the control of the civil government. He believed that the civil government was a divine institution, but also that the Church should be independent within its own sphere, and stood out strongly for the right of the Church to excommunicate those of its members who failed to comply with its discipline. Calvin also drew up a creed to which each citizen should subscribe. These proposed measures aroused bitter resentment, with the result that both Farel and Calvin were expelled from the city. Calvin went to Strassburg where he spent three years. Meanwhile, matters deteriorated in Geneva itself, and Calvin was besought to return. He was loath to do so, but finally consented. This time he was in a much stronger position to carry through his reforms. In 1541 the 'Ecclesiastical Ordinances' were adopted whereby Church affairs were governed. The elders, who were the centre of Calvin's system, were appointed by the civil government as representative of the community. These elders, along with the pastors, formed the Consistory which was responsible for ecclesiastical affairs, and could go the length of excommunication. Wherever it felt necessary, the Consistory could appeal to the civil power for the imposition of other penalties.

Doubtless the Ordinances were not all that Calvin might have desired. His principle that church members should choose their own officers may conceivably be taken to mean that he would have wished less authority to have remained in the hands of the civil government. On the other hand, with Calvin's confusion of the church and the Christian community, it is not altogether easy to understand where, in his estimation, the influence of one should end and the other begin. It is certain that he allowed, and indeed encouraged, the civil authorities to interfere in religious questions to an extent which was in no way their right. The cruel case of Servetus is an apt illustration of this fact. Servetus was a Spanish physician who became an ardent opponent of Calvin's theology. In 1553 he was arrested in Geneva, and in a trial which was really a test of strength between Calvin and himself, was condemned as a heretic and burnt. Calvin felt it quite in order that the civil authority should adjudicate in matters of doctrine. Excommunication from the church, therefore, was not the final penalty. Disagreement could be punished even with death, and the State Church system inevitably became a means of tyrannising and persecuting those who would not conform.

On the positive side of what Calvin taught there is much to be commended, and the effects of his genius were to be carried far afield. Geneva became a haven of refuge for the persecuted from many other countries. Men such as John Knox of Scotland were profoundly influenced by the insight which God had given to Calvin. Knox, a man of unyielding strength of character and a spiritual giant, moulded the thought of an entire nation probably as no other man has ever done. Scotland, however, was well prepared for reformation. On the negative side there was the debauchery of the Catholic clergy which was a public shame and cried out for change in the name of common decency. But, on the positive side, there was the precious heritage of the old Celtic church (see pages 105-7)

149

K

which had never died out, and there was also the influence of Wycliffe which Scottish students had brought back from Oxford. These factors, coupled with John Knox's own peculiar genius in applying what he had learned of the Scriptures to the life of the church, were of incalculable benefit to the spread of the pure word of the Gospel.

One of the most potent emphases in Calvin's theology was the place he accorded to the law in the life of the believer. Salvation, he solidly maintained, is not by works, as the Romanists taught, but by faith through which the life of Christ is appropriated by the believer. Yet salvation, though not by works, is unto works. That a believer lives a life of righteousness is a proof that he has entered into a vital relationship with Christ, and the standard of that righteousness is the law of God contained in the Scriptures, the guide to the Christian's daily walk. Calvin, therefore, was strongly insistent upon character. He also realised the value of sound education, a conviction that Knox carried over into Scotland to make the Scottish peasantry and ministry among the best educated in the world. This emphasis upon a sound character and a sound mind dominated by the authority of the Word of God has, without doubt, moulded some of the most powerful lives the world has known in the service of Christ, and has produced a wealth of Scripture exegesis to which, under God, believers everywhere owe a profound debt.

The weakness of the Calvinistic system was the link which existed between Church and State. Membership in a State Church must inevitably degenerate to being based upon the formal acceptance of a creed, and when that is so the whole Scriptural foundation of the church is destroyed. Unity is sought and maintained merely on the basis of understanding, instead of the possession of spiritual life. Calvin sought the power of the State to uphold the purity of the doctrine of the Church, but it is extremely unlikely that a sub-Christian authority will for long be content to uphold an institution in whose life it has no say, and yet grant it full authority to mould the life of the whole community. The reciprocal influence of the State within the Church is bound to take place, and that influence will be to the State's convenience and the Church's spiritual detriment. It must, of course, be remembered that the idea of a secular State was largely foreign to the period of the Reformation, and, human nature being what it is, it is not at all surprising that the great Reformers' interpretation of the Scriptures should be coloured

150

by their allegiance to and conflict with the civil powers with which they were driven into such close proximity. Yet there were others, as we shall see, who continued to hold their faith in complete freedom from political entanglements.

The great heritage of the Reformation has been the freedom of access to the Word of God and the recognition that the Bible must occupy the place of pre-eminence in Christian thought and living. If Luther, Zwingli, Calvin and others failed in the application of Scriptural principles to the life of the Church, there was yet engendered a profound respect for the Bible and a freedom to seek God's mind and ways through its pages which has laid the way for others to follow more precisely in its path.

CHAPTER THIRTEEN

THE CHURCHES CONTINUING

WHILE the struggles of the Reformation were making their mark upon Christendom, other groups of believers, quite apart from this great movement of change, were pursuing their life of witness and devotion to Christ. They were not connected with Rome, nor ever had been, but were the spiritual progeny of those who, from earliest times, have maintained a simple testimony according to the Word of God. The centuries of fierce, Roman oppression and cruel persecution of 'heretics' had, to a great extent, driven these congregations of faithful believers away from the public eye, but the apparently propitious circumstances of the Reformation made it possible for them to emerge once again into the open. Thus we find coming into prominence, in the first half of the sixteenth century, groups of Christians who formed a third and increasingly powerful stream of religious life, totally independent of Catholics and Protestants alike. Being free from political association or violent, organized conflict with the civil power, they were in the privileged position of being able to view the Word of God with much greater detachment of mind, free from the subconscious thought that their interpretation of Scripture must harmonise with the conveniences of social and political affiliations. These groups of believers generally called themselves simply by the name of Christians or brethren, but administered baptism only to those who had an experience of regeneration through faith in Christ, and were stigmatised by the name Anabaptists, meaning ' those who baptize again '. This referred, of course, to the fact that the brethren did not recognise the baptism of children as valid, and in the eyes of both Catholic and Reformed parties were, therefore, guilty of baptizing a second time those who came into an experience of salvation through faith.

Conrad Grebel and Felix Manz

Congregations of brethren were particularly numerous and active in Zurich. Two men who played a prominent part in ministry among them were Conrad Grebel and Felix Manz. Both Grebel and Manz belonged to prominent families in the city, and were scholars of considerable distinction. Grebel was, as we have already noted, at one time a close friend of Ulrich Zwingli, but in Zurich, which was the centre of Zwingli's work, they came into serious conflict with one another. Grebel and Manz felt that Zwingli was much too conservative in his seeking a return to Scriptural practice. His conception of a State Church they held to be unscriptural, and they also felt that he denied clear spiritual light in respect to baptism. By 1525 both these men were convinced that Scripture allowed only the baptism of believers, and this gave rise to a public debate with Zwingli which was ordered by the civil authorities. The result was a foregone conclusion. The Council issued an order requiring that all parents who had not already had their children baptized should do so, and forbidding the practice of baptism by the brethren themselves. To Grebel and Manz this order was nothing short of man setting himself up in defiance against the Word of God. They refused to submit, continuing to teach the Scriptures with great boldness. People flocked to hear them, and many were baptized despite the severe penalties with which they were threatened. The following year the Zurich government ordered that any who baptized, or themselves accepted baptism, should be drowned, and a relentless persecution was instituted which spread far beyond the boundaries of the Zurich canton. Still the churches continued to grow. Grebel, however, died of plague in 1526, and Manz was arrested and drowned, a martyr to the faith.

It is sad to find that this effort to exterminate those faithful people who sought to order their lives according to God's Word found a willing party in Zwingli, himself ostensibly a champion of the authority of Scripture. He opposed the brethren with great bitterness, but had little success in winning them over to his cause.

Balthasar Hubmaier

Balthasar Hubmaier, a one-time friend of John Eck, the Roman champion and opponent of Martin Luther, was both a scholar and an able preacher. In 1519 he took up ministry at Waldshut in the north of Switzerland, and it was while he was there that his life underwent a great, spiritual change. He was much influenced through the writings of Luther, and threw in

153

his lot with the Reformers. In 1523 we find him in Zurich participating in the second, great, public debate which discussed measures of reform. There Zwingli and his party condemned the use of images and the doctrine of the mass. Hubmaier also ably upheld the need of change. Although the cantonal authorities favoured the Reformers, yet they felt it necessary to move with caution. To this Zwingli agreed. Hubmaier and others, however, felt that such a dilatory application of Scriptural principles bordered on compromise, and as their views developed they came to hold in general that the outlook of the Zwinglian party was much too conservative and accommodating to the traditional position. Shortly after this, through his study of the Scriptures, Hubmaier began to entertain doubts about infant baptism. These he discussed with Zwingli who, according to Hubmaier's testimony, agreed with him, yet later Zwingli was to denounce those who practised the baptism of believers and be party to the strenuous persecution initiated against them.

In Waldshut, many believers gathered in Hubmaier's own home to study the Bible. Soon he was ministering to a very large congregation. He showed that supreme authority rests in the Word of God, and the church, in its local aspect, is the company of those who, through profession of faith and consistency of life, demonstrate that they are partakers of the life of Christ. He repudiated any association with the State. He held that the principle of earthly government is allowed of God and that believers should, therefore, submit to the powers that be in the fear of God. The rule of God in the church, however, cannot be entangled with civil administration in the State, which is man's rule in an imperfect world. Hubmaier was not alone in his ability to minister the Word. There were other men of outstanding, spiritual gift who were used to the edification of the increasing number of believers' gatherings.

Hubmaier travelled far afield. Waldshut was implicated in the Peasants' Revolt, and the spiritual work suffered as a result, the city coming under Catholic domination, but Basel was an influential centre of spiritual activity, and the movement soon began to assume great proportions throughout Germany.

The sordid history of the Peasants' Revolt certainly supplies us with certain factors which, from the human point of view, contributed to the enlargement of the believing congregations. We have already seen how Luther flung moderation to the winds and urged the territorial Princes to quell the rising with the sword, which they did with the most terrible loss of life. The

154

result was a deep distrust of Lutheranism in the hearts of the mass of common folk, whether they had participated in the revolt or not. From now on, the Lutheran movement became associated, in the eyes of many, with the aristocracy and the power-mongering Princes. People who had spiritual needs turned to those who seemed to spend more of their time occupied with spiritual things than with the shady activities of political manoeuvering. Many found the spiritual guidance they sought in the companies of Christians who were often called Anabaptists.

Hubmaier, constantly forced to flee from one place to another, preached the Word of God wherever he went, and was the means of great spiritual blessing. In all, thousands were baptized, believers began to meet together in the simple manner they had learned from the Scriptures. At one point, in Zurich, Hubmaier was discovered by Zwingli's party and cast into prison. There, under torture, he retracted some of what he had taught, only to repent bitterly later and seek the Lord's forgiveness and restoration. He was able to reach Moravia, and there again brought light to many through his powerful preaching, and also through his writings. The spread of the Gospel, however, and the growth of Christian congregations, alarmed both Catholics and Protestants alike, and stringent measures were employed to deal with them. In 1527 Hubmaier was arrested and taken to Vienna where he was publicly burnt. A few days later, his wife was thrown from a bridge into the River Danube and drowned.

John Denck

The learned John Denck was another of the highly gifted men associated with the companies of brethren in the early part of the sixteenth century. In 1523, as a young man of about twenty-five, he was appointed to a responsible post in an important school in the city of Nuremberg. There the Lutheran movement already had a strong hold and was led by an accomplished man called Andrew Osiander. Denck was shocked to find that, although many of the abuses of Romanism had been abolished and Luther's emphasis on salvation by faith was firmly established, there was not a corresponding improvement in the morality of the people. Godliness of life seemed to be conspicuous by its absence. The problem which he faced was a concern to a number of men of influence within the Lutheran fold itself.

Martin Luther had made a necessary and uncompromising

emphasis upon faith in Christ as alone the basis of salvation, but he had not sufficiently balanced this glorious truth with the necessity of obedience to the will of God, and good works as the indispensable evidence of true faith. The result was that, although Luther commenced with a transparent evangelicalism, the movement which he initiated faded off into just as clear a formalism. Faith became no more than mental assent to particular articles of a creed. Philip Melanchthon, Luther's friend to the very last, came to recognise this clearly and departed radically from Luther's own views. That these differences did not cause the two friends to part company was due only to Luther's love for his younger brother, and Melanchthon's grace and tact. They were certainly to cause much difficulty within the Lutheran communion in later years. Andrew Osiander was another who was to recognise that an unholy life was a complete contradiction to salvation through faith, and towards the end of his ministry he gave clear expression to his convictions. But he had not reached this place of understanding during the time of his association with Denck, and when the latter tried to share the light that God had given him, he was roundly accused of error. So unbending was Osiander's position that he succeeded in having Denck expelled from Nuremberg.

Denck, like others who sought to follow Christ independently of the religious systems of the day, found that slander and persecution followed him wherever he went. His most fruitful work was probably in the city of Augsburg. Having found a haven there through the kindness of a friend, he discovered the city torn by religious strife, a three-cornered contest between Lutherans, Zwinglians and Catholics, and suffering from other forms of depravity. In the midst of this lamentable confusion, Denck was happy to meet some who were concerned not only to state their faith in Christ, but also to follow Him, and they began to gather together as a church. There were, however, already in Augsburg congregations of brethren, and in them Denck found a kindred spirit. Through a visit of Balthasar Hubmaier, he was convinced of the truth of baptism, and continued to be used in the city to the edification of the Lord's people. The congregation of believers grew rapidly, probably not least because of the anathemas and accusations that were being hurled to and fro between the three rival groups. The spirit of Christ and the Gospel obviously had little place in the sensitive sects which had grown up round the personalities of good men, and those who had experienced the grace of Christ

156

longed for the inward peace which comes from gathering round Him.

Denck was not allowed to remain in Augsburg indefinitely. Persecution drove him relentlessly from place to place, but everywhere he found faithful believers in Christ and was able to minister to them. Finally, worn out by the strenuousness of his life, he died in Basel in 1527, still a young man.

One thing of which Denck was much aware was his dependence upon the Holy Spirit in his understanding of the Scriptures. He was far from despising an intellectual appreciation of the Word of God, but at the same time he recognised that it is through total dependence upon Christ and submission to His will that the Word becomes a means of spiritual life and growth. The standard of the Scriptures was certainly reflected in his life. In his preaching and writings in defence of the truth, he never descended to that spirit of bitterness which is a denial of the truth and was so common in his day. Luther and Zwingli, avowing that they were standing up for the cause of Christ, may have been hurling imprecations at one another, but John Denck, while lamenting the difficulty with which, in his human weakness, he restrained himself from giving vent to resentment in reply to unjust provocation, determined that, as God granted him grace, he would never make an enemy of a brother in Christ.

Michael Sattler

Michael Sattler's name is associated with a conference of brethren held in Baden early in 1527 at which several articles of faith were drawn up. From what we have already seen, it is plain that the name 'brethren' or 'Anabaptists' as they were often called, did not refer to any organized system of Christian congregations. The different assemblies came into being in different ways through the ministry of different people, but had the one common bond of spiritual life which all alike had received through faith in Christ. It is obvious, therefore, that there would be differences within the various groups, although in the basic matters of fellowship with Christ and allegiance to His Word they were one, so it is not possible to produce a rigid formula of doctrine and ascribe it to the brethren generally. Nevertheless, the seven articles to which we have just referred serve as a good indication of the nature of their faith while, at the same time, they are not of such a restricted character that they brand those who held to them as a sect.

The seven articles held that

1. Only those should be baptized who had experienced the regenerating work of Christ.
2. The local expression of the church is a company of such regenerate people whose daily lives are lived in accordance with the faith they profess. Their fellowship is symbolised in their participation together of the Lord's supper, through which they remember the redeeming work of Christ.
3. Discipline must be exercised within the churches, and the final discipline is excommunication.
4. The Lord's people should live a life of separation from the sin of the world and from subservience to the flesh or anything that would compromise their faith. This included a separation from the rites of the Roman, Lutheran and Zwinglian parties.
5. The officers of a local church should be set apart by the church, and it is their duty to edify the believers through the teaching and preaching of the Word.
6. Believers should not resort to force, either in defence of themselves, or by participation in warfare at the command of the State.
7. Believers should not take any oath, nor should they go to law.

Here are ideas many of which are accepted as normal Christian practice today in widely separated groups of believers. Indeed, they embody principles which have never ceased to be practised wherever people have accepted the Scriptures as their sole standard and sought to live in conformity with their teaching. But in the general religious world of the sixteenth century, even with its militant Protestantism, such ideas were considered outrageous and heretical, and drew upon those who shared them the most violent abuse and cruel persecution.

Michael Sattler had formerly been a monk, but his entrance into a life of new fellowship with Christ made him an earnest preacher of the Word among the brethren in many parts, and was to mean also that he would share the same fate as others who had set out on the pathway of discipleship and service. Later in the same year as the conference in Baden he was arrested in Rottenburg and sentenced to a most cruel death of mutilation and burning for his beliefs. His wife was drowned shortly afterwards.

The leaders of the brethren did not suffer alone. Many others who dared to follow the truth shared the same fate. Altogether thousands were executed, and thousands more were beaten, branded, tortured, driven out of their homes. The edict of the Emperor Charles V, issued from Speier in 1529, commanded his officers to judge with all severity those of an age of understanding who received baptism again or who baptised others. Parents who refused to bring their children for baptism were treated in the same manner, and measures were also to be taken against those who tried to protect others from the legal punishment. It is to the credit of at least one Prince that he refused to obey the mandate, and to some judges that they refused to pass judgement on those who were accused of matters respecting their faith. There were not lacking people who, though disagreeing with the brethren, gave brave testimony in their favour, and asked why it was that those whose lives were blameless, and better than many among the Lutherans, should be made to suffer for holding beliefs on which the judges themselves were totally incompetent to pass judgement. Yet the slaughter went on, but the light of testimony continued to burn. It could not be put out.

The Munster Tragedy

It is not surprising that some extremists should have sought to attach themselves to the brethren, but it is unfortunate that the tendency has so often been to judge the whole of the so-called Anabaptist movement by the bad example of a few who were in no way representative of the believers in general. It should be remembered that the early church attracted men such as Simon the sorcerer (Acts 8), but it is not to be condemned on that account. The cruelty which was being meted out to innocent people roused fierce indignation in the hearts of many quite outside the assemblies. Some of these, not having the spiritual experience of the brethren, were ready to take up the sword in the cause of justice. To others, the billows of suffering which threatened to engulf the churches seemed to indicate that the end of all things was at hand, and this gave rise to the wild prophecyings of unstable spirits who, in the frenzy of fanaticism, bore crowds along on a wave of excitement that was destined only to plunge them into a welter of confusion. Whether or not

159

these people really had any connection with the brethren did not matter. They were all together dubbed Anabaptists, cursed as heretics, consigned to the flames of public execution, and from there to the eternal flames of hell. If any could have checked the tragic influence of fanatical preachers, they were the godly leaders of the brethren, but the greatest of these had already paid the supreme price for their faith when their saintly counsel was so sorely needed.

Melchior Hoffmann was an earnest, fiery preacher who claimed a divine revelation that the New Jerusalem would be set up at Strassburg. Going to Strassburg on the strength of his prophetic vision, he was thrown into prison and remained there till his death. But revelations of this nature are not so easily disposed of, even when they are proved wrong. Hoffmann's preaching had attracted a number of disciples, particularly in the Netherlands. Two of these were Jan Matthys, a baker, and Jan Bockelson, known more familiarly as John of Leyden, a tailor. Like Hoffmann, Matthys claimed to be a prophet, but was little content to wait till God should usher in the new age by peaceful means.

In 1534 Jan Matthys and John of Leyden went to Munster. God had rejected Strassburg because of its unbelief, they said, and the New Jerusalem would be set up in Munster instead. A preacher in Munster, Bernard Rothmann, had attracted a large following, and his forthright condemnation of Catholic error was the means of such public excitement against the Church that the Bishop resorted to force to quell the disturbance. The ruling Prince Philip, however, intervened and declared Munster an evangelical city. This was the signal for the influx of a great crowd of refugees. Some were sincere believers seeking a refuge from persecution, others were mere malcontents, still others were dangerous fanatics. Practically all were penniless and were a charge upon the liberality of the city. Rothmann led the way with his example of kindness and generosity. Among the crowd were Matthys and John of Leyden. It was not long before the extremists had deposed the magistrates and elected a Council of their own over which Matthys exercised control. Meanwhile, the Bishop of Munster had been collecting troops, and the city was in a state of seige.

One act of fanaticism rapidly followed another. There was a purge of ' unbelievers '. The choice was to be baptized, leave the city, or die. As a result of a further ' revelation ', Matthys with a few followers suddenly left Munster to engage the attack-

160

ing forces and was slain in battle. The confusion following Matthys' death quickly gave way to a new order as John of Leyden assumed absolute control. Through a series of further 'divine revelations' community of goods was enforced, polygamy was introduced, in spite of some stringent opposition in a city where the standard of morality was high. John of Leyden took the wife of the deceased Matthys, and they were crowned king and queen with great pomp. Still the struggle went on. The city was defended with great heroism, but the position was hopeless. The entry of the Bishop's troops was the signal for fresh slaughter. None was spared. The leaders were publicly tortured and put to death, John of Leyden in the very place where he had been crowned king.

The prophets of Munster may have had very little actually to do with the godly and peaceable groups of brethren whose lives were such a potent testimony to the power of the Gospel, but the name Anabaptist given to them all became a word of odium, aptly used by the three great Church systems to destroy all who dissented from them. The Munster tragedy, humanly speaking, was a tragedy for the churches of Christ.

What lessons may we learn from the events recounted in these last two chapters? We have seen three great movements rise and decline. The Lutherans and the Zwinglians maintained their numerical strength, but their spiritual power was rapidly dissipated. The companies of Christians called Anabaptists, if we consider them a movement which first appeared early in the sixteenth century and so spread in Germany as to cause alarm in the Lutheran camp, had in that country, within a quarter of a century, been reduced again to meagre proportions. Christ dwelling within human beings makes up the church, and however solid the beginning, the human element within the church allows for the dire possibility that what has begun in the Spirit may, after a very short time, end up in the flesh. Whatever remains is but a human organization, and not the church of Jesus Christ.

The tragedy of Lutheranism's early spiritual collapse throws into relief a lesson of vital importance, the necessity of balancing the preaching of faith by the preaching of works. Scripture gives no place to a faith which is simply a cold belief in a doctrinal statement with little or no effect upon daily living. The Epistle of James was written to emphasize the poignant fact that 'faith without works is dead'. The basis of the church is not faith; the basis of the church is spiritual life; and spiritual life is the result of the impact of faith upon the daily walk in relationship to God and man; spiritual life is the life of one who is inevitably made a new creation through faith in Christ.

In the Lutheran movement, faith divorced from works early resulted in a Christianity that was little more than a form. It is a salutary warning that those who reacted so strongly against the ritual of Rome to reinstate the truth of salvation by faith alone were so soon to return to the exact place whence they came, the place of dependence upon religious ceremony, because they did not give sufficient room to the corollary of faith which is holiness. The centuries have seen the spiritual collapse of many groups of Christians for this same reason, and the danger has never been more evident than it is among evangelicals in the present day and age. The urge to make people take the step of faith, to ' decide ', has its important place in the presentation of the Gospel, but a ' decision ' by no means always amounts to regenerating faith, and where the criterion of being a believer in Christ is only that a person has at one time made a ' decision ', then the church is heading fast in the way of formalism. Faith, if it means anything at all, means the reception of the indwelling Christ, and Christ dwelling in mortal bodies means holiness.

As we look back from the twentieth century, we are again and again shocked by the religious intolerance of a past age. We may understand its coming from those whose religion was but a veneer, and who never experienced the deep, spiritual change of regeneration, but it is indeed difficult to understand the burning bitterness towards those who disagreed with him of a man like Luther, whose life and thinking were so radically transformed by his experience of divine grace. The Scriptures themselves exhort us to ' contend earnestly for the faith ' (Jude 3), an exhortation which is largely ignored in these days of ' toleration ' and ecumenicalism where any kind of pious claptrap or religious superstition is acceptable as faith, and the end-all of everything would seem to be that we do not hurt anyone else's feelings. Yet there is no allowance in the Word of God whatever either for the physical violence or the carnal hatred which existed in the Reformation times among believers, people who were, without doubt, earnest children of God. It may seem that to accept as Christians those who exhibited such lamentable qualities is contradictory to all that has been said in the previous paragraph, but sad experience amply demonstrates the possibility of a regenerate man's falling a prey at times to the grossest, unspiritual thoughts and actions in what he considers to be the defence of the faith. It is a mark of spiritual immaturity from which, paradoxically, people who often have all the marks of being spiritually mature in other respects, suffer. It is not our present purpose to attempt a diagnosis of this malady, but let us take note of the fact, and learn to beware of it in our own lives.

One of the reasons for the spiritual degeneration of Lutheranism and Zwinglianism was a bitter intolerance which ruled out the possibility of either party's learning from the other, or from anyone else. Having each shut themselves up to their particular, rigid conceptions of truth, they banished true fellowship of the saints, and while they were busy anathematising the groups of brethren as 'sects', they themselves became slaves to the most bigoted sectarianism. Inasmuch as the hearts of the brethren were open to receive all who had experienced the power of new life in Christ, they were genuinely free from sectarianism. The root of sectarianism is intolerance, not of sin, but of brethren in Christ who, while holding fast to the Lord in faith and demonstrating their faith in holiness, yet diverge from us in understanding of such things as we can expect to see with final clarity only when we have together grown 'unto the measure of the stature of the fulness of Christ' (Eph. 4: 13). The intolerance of believers one towards another has been a mighty weapon in the hands of the Satanic power to divide and destroy the testimony of the church.

The brethren themselves were weakened through extremism, spurious pretensions to prophetic gift and divine revelation. Scripture shows clearly that revelation and spiritual insight are based squarely on knowledge of the Word. When the church loses those as ministers who, by the help of the Spirit, edify the body of Christ from consecrated minds diligently and prayerfully applied to the Word of God, then the door is opened wide for a 'revelation' which is purely carnal. It may be the product of the greatest sincerity, but its seat is the soul, and it is of the earth, not of heaven. Spurious revelation may be the ecstatic excitement which can transport people into a frenzy of 'worship', or the monotonous quackery of spiritual indolence which can transport people to the depths of sleep, (The ecstatics will accuse the quacks of being spiritually lifeless, and the quacks will accuse the ecstatics of emotionalism,) but it means ultimate death to the true witness of the church which is sustained only by the living Word of God. The brethren or Anabaptists were peculiarly open to this danger when persecution deprived them of their most able teachers, and there can be no doubt that many of them were deceived by the prophets of Munster and those who sympathised with them. It is profitable to note that the prophets were men of deep sincerity, convinced of the divine nature of their mission, and of boundless zeal, but of little intellect. This does not mean to say that God uses only the intellectual giants such as Origen, Tyndale or Calvin. History affords most striking examples of men of very little formal education who were outstandingly used in the hands of the Spirit, but it is also true to say that they were used in proportion to their allegiance to the Scriptures, and their minds were consecrated to the knowledge of God through His Word.

Pretension to revelation can be the outcome of an emotional spirit or of an unconscious desire to obviate the hard, mental exercise of understanding the Word of God. It is by no means strange to the twentieth century, and is an understandable reaction to the cold lifelessness of professing Christianity and to an intellectual approach to the things of God that is devoid of the Spirit. But God's way is the way of balance, the Word and the Spirit, both essential, and each dependent upon the other. The Spirit reveals Himself through the Word. It is through our understanding of the Word that we discern the mind of Christ; it is through our dependence upon the Spirit that we understand the Word of God.

CHAPTER FOURTEEN

FROM THE MIDST OF TRAGEDY

TRAGEDY has always dogged the steps of the church, but the church, built aright upon the foundation of the Rock Christ Jesus, was designed for catastrophe. In England, tragedy was called down upon the church by the gifted monarch Henry VIII who used his gifts to the furtherance of his own ends rather than God's. When the writings of Martin Luther were received in England there was consternation among the Roman prelates. Cardinal Wolsey, Lord Chancellor of the realm, saw that more than ordinary means would have to be employed if the authority of the Pope were not to be further weakened. With his encouragement, Henry VIII, renewed in zeal for the scholastic pursuits of his youth, cloistered himself in his library and, in 1521, produced the treatise against Luther which won for him from Pope Leo X the title of 'Defender of the Faith'. Having won such a title, he had to justify it, and set about ridding the kingdom of 'heretics'. Nine days after the receipt of the bull pronouncing him Defender of the Faith, he issued an order commanding all his subjects, on peril of dire punishment, to render every assistance to the Bishop of Lincoln to bring to judgement small groups of believers within his diocese who were meeting to encourage one another in the things of God and to read His Word. These were mostly remnants of the Lollard movement. Most of them were simple folk, and they were mercilessly treated. Many were terrorized by threat of death into informing against their own relatives and other Christian friends. They were then forced to do penance or shamefully punished. These humble believers may not have emerged from their sore trial as heroes, yet who can point the finger? A few of their number were selected for exemplary punishment, and died the death of martyrs.

Not many years later, about 1528, a working of the Spirit in Essex saw small companies of believers gathered in fellowship around the Scriptures. Some of these were from noble families, some were enlightened members of the clergy, but all met on the basis of their relationship with Christ. People called them

L

' brothers in Christ '. These groups were known and recognised by godly men such as Coverdale and Latimer, afterwards to be Bishops in the English Church, from whose ministry they profited. It was not long, however, before many were imprisoned and others scattered. But such was the testimony of the Lord's people. It was stamped out in one place only to emerge again in another.

The fortunes of believers who sought God through His Word varied with Henry's changeableness. In 1534 Parliament passed the famous Supremacy Act whereby papal dominion was finally thrown off, and the king became the supreme head of the Church of England. But this had little to do with Henry's religious scruples, if indeed he had any. Henry's severing of the connection between England and Rome was dictated by purely selfish motives. The change could hardly be called a Reformation. The Church remained practically the same, except that Henry was its head instead of the Pope. It did, however, offer respite for a time for the further spreading of the Scriptures. Meanwhile, the king was bringing to execution those who refused to accept his lordship over the Church, just as he had been persecuting those who had refused to accept the authority of Rome a little previously. Then again there was a change. Liberty was allowing too much of a departure from the accepted form. Henry had political reasons for wanting to appear a good Catholic apart from his allegiance to the Pope. The doctrine of transubstantiation was affirmed, with other Romish practices, as the creed of England, and departures from them were punished by sentences up to death by burning. The Bible, which had been open for all to read, was withdrawn from the public, and permission to read it was allowed only to certain limited classes of people. These iniquitous laws were still in force when Henry died in 1547.

Menno Symon

The tragedy of Munster was a shattering blow to the testimony of the brethren throughout Germany, but the Lord had His remnant who would carry forward the witness of the church, and His own chosen vessels through whom He would continue to minister life to His people. Menno Symon, who was born in Holland in 1492, lived through these times and was afterwards to become a teacher of note amongst companies of believers. At the age of twenty-four he was ordained a priest of

166

the Roman Church. As a priest, Menno knew nothing of the Scriptures, but in his celebration of the mass, questions would enter his mind as to whether the bread and wine had become the very body and blood of Christ. He decided to read through the New Testament, and at once came to see the truth regarding the Lord's table. Hearing of a man who had been executed for the crime of being 'sre-baptized', he became perplexed on this further question, and sought an answer in the Word of God where he failed to find any mention of infant baptism.

Menno Symon, not through the preaching of others, or the influence of the brethren of whom he knew practically nothing, but through the power of the Scriptures, began to find enlightenment for his soul, yet all this time he lived his own, careless, self-indulgent life. When the influence of the Munster sect began to penetrate into the Netherlands, he preached strongly against its error. He saw, however, that his preaching produced no deep effect. While he was applauded as an able champion of orthodoxy against the Munster evils, people continued to be led astray and to go to the wildest extremes. Those who complimented him were themselves careless about spiritual things. More than this, Menno recognised that his own life was spiritually powerless, and that he had nothing to offer the people in place of the Munster doctrine which he condemned. In great agony of soul he turned to Christ for grace and cleansing, and found both at the cross. His preaching henceforth took on a new urgency and authority. He proclaimed repentance and a new life to be found in Christ through faith, and courageously let it be known what convictions God had given him concerning baptism and the Lord's table, seeking also the fellowship of those who had experienced the regenerating work of the Spirit.

About a year after his great spiritual experience, Menno met a few godly men who were much burdened about the need of scattered believers, separated from the world and sectarianism, who were meeting according to the light they had received from God's Word. Among them, they told him, there was a hunger for the truth, and they pleaded with Menno to devote himself to this ministry. Menno felt the call to be from God, and in 1537 left the Roman Church and commenced his years of itinerant service in the midst of these congregations of believers. Leaving the shelter of Rome meant leaving the popularity which he once enjoyed and being called an Anabaptist or a heretic. Luxury and material security he had none. He was often in danger of arrest and imprisonment, but his ministry was to yield abundant fruit for the cause of Christ. He devoted himself to the strengthening of believers, gathering them together and building them up in the faith, for many had been scattered through the fierceness of persecution. Ultimately he was outlawed, a reward was offered for information which would lead to his capture, and death was the penalty for anyone who dared to give him shelter. In 1543 he fled from the Netherlands and found refuge in Fresenburg, the territory of a friendly German nobleman which was a haven for many persecuted believers. There Menno continued his ministry and gave himself also to writing. His works were widely circulated and were the means of combating much of the scandal which was being circulated against the brethren. In Fresenburg he passed away in 1559.

Some of the congregations who came under the influence of Menno Symon's preaching came to be called Mennonites, in common with the practice of calling churches by the name of some well-known person associated with them. It was, however, not a name that they either chose or wanted. From them have sprung the Mennonite communities of today, although the years have wrought changes from the simple principles which brought the believers together in the sixteenth century, and the spirit of freedom has given way to the all too common spirit of sectarianism.

Ignatius Loyola

Meanwhile, the forces of opposition to the resurgent power of the Word were doubly active. While God was raising up those who would stand firmly for the cause of the Gospel, one was also being prepared to win back to the fold of Rome the ground that had been lost.

However much we may lament the fruit of his labours, it cannot be denied that Ignatius of Loyola was one of the outstanding figures of the Reformation age. Born in 1491 in northern Spain of a noble Spanish family, he became a page at the court of King Ferdinand. Later he served his country as an officer in the Spanish army, and distinguished himself by outstanding bravery. When thirty years of age, he received a wound in battle which necessitated the abandonment of his military career. It was a happening that was to change the whole course of his life. During his slow recovery to health, he devoted himself to studying the lives of Christ, Francis of Assisi and the Mystics. Possessed of a longing to be rid of the sins of his old life, he cried to God to show him the way of salvation, and after a great inward struggle found deliverance. He determined that, as he had once been a soldier of the king of Spain, he would now be a soldier of the Virgin. Not waiting till his recovery was complete, he travelled to the monastery of Montserrat and there hung his weapons on the Virgin's altar, dedicating himself to her service and the service of Christ. From Montserrat he went in the rough garb of a pilgrim to the Dominican monastery of Manresa where he set himself to practise the disciplines which were to form the basis of his book 'Spiritual Exercises'. Loyola subjected himself to the most rigorous process of self-examination, observing with minute exactitude his postures, thoughts and reactions, and seeking to induce through them spiritual ecstasies. From these experiences, he evolved the rigid discipline which became the basis of the Jesuit order, and forged it into the formidable weapon of counter Reformation that it became.

The Jesuit discipline aimed at the complete subjection of the will of the individual to the purpose of the society, which was the extension of the Roman faith and the strengthening of the power of the 'mother Church'. Every member was assigned to a Confessor to whom he made a vow of absolute obedience in everything that did not involve sin. To his Confessor he was also bound to reveal his inmost thoughts, and was guided by him into the full rigours of spiritual discipline and warfare. The head of the order was a 'General' who was also subject to the discipline of his inferiors by assistants appointed to watch on him. At the same time, each member was appointed by his superiors to the work for which it was felt he was particularly suited, and was given extensive training. On the one hand, full scope was given for the development of an individual calling, yet all was implicitly subject to the aim of the order. The Order of Jesus, as Loyola called it, was a most remarkable institution.

Loyola's occupation with the Mystics at first brought him under suspicion from the clergy. The Mystics' quest for communion with God independent of priest or prelate was naturally not looked upon with favour by the Church. Loyola was, as a result, arrested on more than one occasion, but was always able to convince the religious authorities of his loyalty and to engineer his release. Actually, the system which he evolved was the complete antithesis of the Mystics' teaching, for each Jesuit came completely under the authority of his superior, and was in no

169

way encouraged to seek fellowship with God independently of those who were over him in the society.

The beginnings of the Society of Jesus go back to the year 1534 in the city of Paris. Loyola did not have a scholastic upbringing, but, convinced that if he were to do the work for which he felt a divine call he should have a good education, he returned to Spain and took up elementary schooling in Barcelona. He advanced rapidly, and in 1528, the year John Calvin was leaving the university of Paris, he entered it. There he gathered round him the six devoted friends who formed the nucleus of the new society. In 1534 they took a vow of service to the Church, and they received papal recognition six years later. Loyola himself was the first 'General', and held the office till he died in 1556. 'The Society of Jesus' was the name by which the society recognised itself. 'Jesuits' was the name given by Calvin and its opponents.

The work of the society spread rapidly, and not only was Protestantism held in check, but in certain areas territory which had been lost to the Roman Church was regained. Excellent schools, foreign missions, and preaching were all zealously used to advance the cause which was not a little aided by the most unscrupulous methods and intrigue. The Jesuit system of causistry minimized the nature of sin, and gave room to the most palpable falsehood and deception. When an act, it was held, is committed with the clear understanding of its sinfulness, and with the complete consent of the will, only then is it sin. The tactics of the Jesuits brought them into fierce disrepute even in Roman Catholic countries where, at times, their power threatened to dominate a whole nation, and in practically every Catholic country the society was, at one time or another, banned. Finally, late in the eighteenth century, the order was banned by the Pope himself. The Jesuits faded into the background for over forty years, but were returned to their former position in 1814 when the order of banishment was annulled by Pius VII.

One of the original six who met with Ignatius Loyola in Paris was Francis Xavier. Appointed as a missionary to the east, he deserves mention for the sheer energy with which he prosecuted his mission. In ten years of work between India and Japan he claimed 'converts' in hundreds of thousands. The work was entirely superficial, and so hopelessly compromised with heathen custom and traditions that it led to its complete downfall, but for zeal and self-sacrifice Francis Xavier put to

170

shame the efforts of many who had a much more worthy cause for which to strive.

In 1545 Pope Paul III was persuaded rather unwillingly to call the Council of Trent. There was a widespread desire for reform of the abuses within the Catholic Church, and the Emperor Charles V took the initiative in inducing the Pope to act, hoping at the same time that it might lead to a reconciliation with the Lutherans in his own realm. The Council of Trent met at intervals between 1545 and 1563 and was dominated, particularly in the later years, by the Jesuits. They rigidly opposed any leniency towards the Protestant view and, although certain reforms were advocated, the doctrinal position of the Roman Church in many important points was unmistakably outlined. The only authoritative version of the Scriptures was the Latin Vulgate, and its interpretation was the sole right of the Church. Tradition, along with Scripture, was to be regarded as an equal source of truth, but what exactly was meant by Tradition was not clearly defined. The position of the Pope as holding supreme authority over the Church was reiterated. While, on the one hand, God was, through His own chosen instruments, fostering the faith of those who were meeting in simple faithfulness to His Word, on the other hand a weapon was being designed with consummate care to bring the Scriptural expression of the church to destruction.

In England, after the death of Henry VIII, there followed six years of official favour for the Reformation cause. Repressive laws were repealed, and many earnest believers who had fled to the continent because of persecution returned again to their homeland. An illuminating commentary on the condition of the Church is given in a new set of 'injunctions' which were distributed during this period to the clergy. Among other things, they were instructed to preach at least four times a year, an indication of the place that had been given to preaching under the old order. The clergy were also asked not to occupy their time with such pursuits as drinking, gambling and general merry-making. It would seem that reformation, even on a purely ethical level, was none too soon in arriving.

But the progress of Protestantism was arrested with a shock on the accession of Mary to the throne in 1553. A fanatical Roman Catholic, she set about at once to scheme the destruction of everything that tended towards reform. Preaching and printing without her consent were forbidden, and the great Protestant Bishops, Ridley, Latimer, Coverdale, Cranmer and others were

171

thrown into gaol. The final humiliation was when the queen and her husband, the Lords and the Commons knelt before the papal legate to receive absolution from heresy on behalf of the nation. Rome had once more triumphed. Then began the welter of persecution which earned for the queen the title of Bloody Mary. It continued till her death in 1558. The world has never forgotten the martyrs Ridley and Latimer who died at the stake for denying the doctrine of transubstantiation, and Latimer's prophetic words to Ridley as, together, they faced the flames, " Be of good cheer, Master Ridley, and play the man; we shall this day, by God's grace, light such a torch in England as will never be put out."

Mary's cruelty probably did more to turn the minds of ordinary people against Rome than all the pro-Reformation propaganda of the previous reign. That great and good men should be butchered and burnt in the name of alleged truth brought a revulsion of feeling to the mind of the whole nation. It was well that Elizabeth who ascended the throne was of a more tolerant disposition.

Elizabeth was a Protestant more by force of circumstances than by conviction. In the reckoning of Rome she was illegitimate, as Rome had never recognised the divorce of her father, Henry VIII, from his first wife, Catherine of Aragon, so it was inevitable that she should throw in her lot with the Reforming party, although whether she had any deep religious convictions at all is doubtful. During the danger of the reign of her half sister, Elizabeth had been outwardly a Romanist. Nevertheless, her accession to the throne was the cause of immense relief and joy. Persecution ceased, and exiles came home again. In 1559 two Acts were passed, the first, the Act of Supremacy, making the queen Supreme Governor of the Church of England, and the second, the Act of Uniformity, obliging all to worship in accordance with the pattern of the State Church, which had a distinctly Romish flavour fitting in with the queen's love of pomp and ceremony. This was a source of offence to many, particularly to the returning Puritan leaders who had been given a place in the reconstituted Church. ' Puritans ' was the name given to those who had been influenced by the Reformed faith as it was practised in Switzerland and in France by the French Protestants called Hugenots. They claimed that the church should be run in accordance with the New Testament pattern, and objected to anything which did not find Scriptural warrant such as vestments, and kneeling for the reception of the bread

172

and the wine at the Lord's table which they feared was akin to the Romish practice of adoring the elements. Puritans occupied some of the highest positions in the land, and many of their number were men of great learning.

The strength of Puritanism in the country, and particularly in places of influence, was such that Elizabeth found it difficult to have all her own way. She little enough realised that the Puritans were her most dependable subjects and her best friends. Fortunately, she had the counsel of wise advisers who urged the importance of assisting the Hugenots and the Reformers in Scotland, something Elizabeth did not at all find easy to do, for she had no liking for the Genevan theology, and heartily detested John Knox, the champion of the Bible in the northern kingdom of her Catholic cousin, Mary. These circumstances provided a new if not complete freedom for the gathering of the Lord's people according to the Scriptures, but also gave ground for a reaction against a further, if less bloodthirsty tyranny, the tyranny of an imposed episcopalianism.

It was at this time that, outside the authorised Church, meetings were begun where godly people, some Puritan ministers and others, gathered for preaching and the study of the Scriptures. They were generally called the 'prophecyings', and were the instrument of much blessing. Elizabeth set herself in determined opposition to such congregations, ordering Edmund Grindal, then Archbishop of Canterbury, to suppress them. Grindal, himself of Puritan sympathies, refused from reasons of conscience to carry out the queen's command, suffering deposition as a result. The queen, however, nothing daunted by the insubordination of her subordinates as the Governor of the Church of England, proceeded to carry out her will against the 'prophecyings' herself. The sentences imposed on some of the Puritan propagandists, who were hanged, roused bitter feeling against her. Was people's relationship to God for ever to be dictated by the State?

There were godly Puritans who opposed any idea of separation from the Church of England. They were those who had been more influenced by Calvin's ideal of a State Church. They were content to bide their time. The constitution of the State Church had been changed so many times within recent years that it could well be altered again to conform more favourably to Calvin's Church polity. Thus they reasoned. Others, however, felt that to wait indefinitely before seeking to obey God's

173

Word was unjustifiable and, in any case, the conception of a State Church was unscriptural.

Independents

Independent churches were known in London and elsewhere in England early in the latter half of the sixteenth century, but a conspicuous increase in the number of such congregations was associated with the name of Robert Browne. Browne was a student of Cambridge and became a Puritan loyal to the National Church. When he was about thirty years of age, his convictions underwent a change, and in 1581 he, with another friend, were the means of establishing a congregation of believers in the city of Norwich. It was not long before his preaching brought the censure of the law upon the church and he, together with a sizeable proportion of the congregation, found refuge in Middleburg, Holland. There Browne continued his ministry, producing a number of treatises in which he condemned those who refused to leave the Church of England, and set down the principles of the church as he understood them from the Scriptures. In England in 1583 two men were hanged for distributing his writings. Browne showed simply that a church consisted of a company of believers who are united through their relationship with Christ. Each congregation sets apart the officers through whom it should be governed and is completely independent, yet owning a vital, spiritual link with every other company of born again people. As a result of relentless persecution on his return to England, Robert Browne returned to the established Church in 1585 and remained within it till his death in 1633.

Two other distinguished figures among the independent churches were Henry Barrowe and John Greenwood. The former a lawyer, and the latter a clergyman, both were convinced that the only conscientious course open for those who did not believe in the Scripturalness of the established Church was to leave it. They associated themselves with a company of believers in London who gathered on the ground of oneness in Christ. These godly people were unceasingly harassed, many of them thrown into prison where they died in the foul conditions they had to endure. Barrowe and Greenwood were alike imprisoned and, in 1593, were hanged.

174

Smyth and Robinson

About the beginning of the seventeenth century a congregation of believers which was to have far-reaching influence was meeting in Gainsborough. Not long afterwards, through God's blessing upon the ministry, a second company was gathering at nearby Scrooby. These churches were led by John Smyth and John Robinson, both former clergymen of the Puritan party of the established Church who had come to the conviction that they should separate from it.

The latter part of Elizabeth's reign had witnessed a slackening of the efforts to enforce religious uniformity, but these efforts were renewed with increased vigour on the accession of James I in 1603. Consequent upon this threat to their liberty, the believers at both Gainsborough and Scrooby decided to emigrate to Holland which they were able to do in 1607 after much suffering. In Amsterdam the church soon became the centre of unfortunate controversy, resulting in division. Greatly distressed by these events John Robinson, with some others, left Amsterdam for Leyden where the gathering was much blessed. Robinson himself was a man of gracious character and great breadth of vision. It later became possible for some of the members from both Amsterdam and Leyden to return to England, and different independent congregations were established in London. From these were developed the denominations which were to be known as ' General Baptists ', holding an Arminian position (see pp. 178-9), and ' Particular Baptists ', holding a Calvinistic position. This highlights a newer development in the history of independent churches, that of churches gathering on specifically doctrinal ground, a subject to which we will presently have to give attention.

It was from the congregation at Leyden that there originated an event notable in the history of both England and America, the sailing of the Pilgrim Fathers aboard the Mayflower for the New World in 1620. It was the start of the great Puritan emigration across the Atlantic. The first small company, led by their elder, William Brewster, landed in Plymouth, New England, to establish a colony where men could worship God unhindered, and give full expression to what He taught them from His Word. John Robinson remained behind in Leyden, and charged the departing company with words which go right to the foundation of the life of the church.

" I charge you before God and His blessed angels, that you

175

follow me no further than you have seen me follow the Lord Jesus Christ. If God reveals anything to you by any other instrument of His, be as ready to receive it as you were to receive any truth by my ministry, for I am verily persuaded the Lord hath more truth yet to break forth out of His Holy Word. For my part, I cannot sufficiently bewail the condition of those reformed Churches which are come to a period in religion, and will go at present, no further than the instruments of their reformation. The Lutherans cannot be drawn to go beyond what Luther saw; whatever part of His will our God has revealed to Calvin, they will rather die than embrace it; and the Calvinists, you see, stick fast where they were left by that great man of God, who yet saw not all things. This is a misery much to be lamented."

John Robinson has aptly stated one of the most essential elements in the life of the church, namely, the ability and freedom to progress, to develop in the understanding of the Scriptures. At the same time, he has just as aptly pointed out the root of sectarianism or denominationalism, limitation to a particular aspect of Scriptural truth. In that a denomination propagates a facet of divine truth, its work may be good and useful, but its weakness lies in its limitation, because it neither sees the whole truth nor is it willing to go on to apprehend it, so occupied is it with the blessedness of the amount of truth it does understand. It cannot be said that any Scriptural expression of the church apprehends the whole of truth. Such fulness of knowledge will be ours only in eternity. But the church, fully recognising the limitations of its understanding, must be pressing forward with a divine urge to know more, unrestricted by bounds imposed by human understanding. That vital, spiritual growth is essential to the church's life.

The rise of nonconformity, that is of congregations of Christians in different countries who protested against the conception of an established State Church and separated from it, gave rise also to denominationalism as we know it today. It could be very plausibly argued that sectarianism is almost as old as the church itself, but it is also true that sectarianism takes on a completely new aspect from early in the seventeenth century, and that for easily understood reasons.

So far, in following through the history of the spiritual movement of the church, we have seen two things clearly emphasized. First, the basis of the church is the life of Christ imparted through the regenerative work of the Holy Spirit to those who repent and trust. Secondly, the order and development of that divine life, both personally and in the church, is by means of the Scriptures through which God speaks to man. The Word of God is the food by which the church lives and grows. It is also the means whereby God expresses His supremacy in the midst of His people. The life of Christ and the Lordship of Christ through His Word are, therefore, the two things which mark out the church of the New Testament. When these are supplanted by anything or anyone else, the result is a departure from the principle of Scripture and ultimate confusion.

One of the most common threats to the supremacy of Christ in the assembly is loyalty to a man, a great and spiritual man may be, but a man nevertheless who receives some at least of the submission and dependence which should be accorded directly to God. The violent persecution of the pre-Reformation era, firstly by the Roman Empire, and then by the Roman Church, served in a very large measure as a protection against this danger. The tremendous struggle of God's people to maintain their right of access to God's Word, and the equally fierce determination of the Catholic Church that it should be withheld from the people, emphasized the supreme value and importance of the Scriptures to the assembly. Not only did the great, spiritual leaders stress this, but their very exaltation of the Bible made them direct targets for the fiercest acts of repression. To teach the Scriptures one day was to be thrown into gaol the next and to be burned at the stake the day after. A church which was dependent upon human leadership would have rapidly disappeared. The measure of the church's existence through centuries of the most violent persecution was the measure in which it reposed directly upon Christ through His Word while learning of Him through every minister He sent. The spiritual downfall of movements such as those of Luther and Zwingli was that, in becoming sufficiently powerful to withstand persecution, they became open to the domination of a man, and loyalty to him and to what he said superseded direct loyalty to Christ through the Scriptures.

The invention of the printing press, the influences of the Renaissance and the Reformation, brought a new depth of theological awareness within the range of ordinary people. The Reformation ushered in an era of pamphleteering. Every new enquiry into some particular aspect of truth became the subject of a treatise, and these writings exercised a profound influence

177

upon spiritual thinking. Nor was this influence bad. It was healthy and invigorating, but brought with it also the dangers that are an inherent part of all progress and everything new. There is a sense in which anything new or convenient is dangerous, not because it is bad, but because it may be given a place of importance which should be occupied by something else. A child with a new toy may want neither to eat nor study. A person who owns a car may become so enslaved to it that he will never walk a hundred yards, and suffer physically as a result. In the spiritual realm it is very easy to substitute sight for faith, to put what we understand of the Lord's ways, be it little or much, in the place of the Lord Himself, in other words, to build the church around a doctrine instead of around Christ. This was the danger of the post-Reformation period, and it multiplied in proportion to the increased number of ways in which Christian truth was systematized, or in which particular emphases were brought to the fore.

At this point it may be convenient to mention Jacobus Arminius, the great Dutch theologian whose name has been given to the great school of thought which has stood in opposition to the system of John Calvin. Calvinism and Arminianism of various shades and strengths have been, and continue to be, the basis of innumerable dissensions and divisions. Arminius was born in 1560 and was educated at the university of Leyden where he ultimately became professor of theology. A man of great learning and universally acknowledged graciousness of character, he was not at all personally disposed towards controversy but was, through the expression of his convictions, drawn into a war of contention that was to him a means of the utmost distress.

The question which exercised the minds of Calvin and Arminius, the relationship between the sovereignty of God and the free-will and responsibility of man, was not new. Centuries before it had been the question over which Augustine and Pelagius (see pp. 67-8) had striven. Still it tests the ingenuity of the greatest minds. Arminius had himself been schooled under the influence of Calvin's teaching, and was asked to write in defence of the moderate Calvinistic position. In doing so, he had the opportunity of making a thorough re-examination of the Scriptures, and came to the conclusion that the teaching he had held was Biblically indefensible. As against Calvin's teaching that Christ died only for the elect, Arminius held that He died for all, but that those alone benefit who believe.

Absolute predestination was rejected in favour of the doctrine that God predestinates on the basis of His divine foreknowledge. Arminius denied the Calvinistic conception of irresistible grace and taught that, although the work of grace is necessary for salvation, since man is incapable of doing anything really good of himself, yet it is possible for man to reject it, and even if he does accept it, may fail to persevere to the end, losing what he once received. Arminius himself was not a man of extreme views, but the views he held, and those of Calvin, have been taken to extremes by those who profess to follow them. Maybe were they alive today neither Calvin would be a calvinist nor Arminius an arminian.

Persecution did not cease with the Reformation as we have seen, nor were the established Church systems of Protestantism much more willing to tolerate dissent. It was some years before religious freedom was to be permanently recognised as a basic human right. But if dissent was still punished, public resentment at such punishment was on the increase, and the atmosphere of public sympathy towards the establishing of independent congregations was more congenial than it had ever been before. Nonconformism did have room to develop, even though it meant hardship and it was officially outlawed. Coupled with this new freedom to gather outside the command of the State was a new freedom to enter into controversy on doctrinal matters which was well supplied with material from the works of Calvin, Arminius and others. That this should result in the formation of groups of Christians based upon their allegiance to one particular doctrinal emphasis was almost inevitable if none the less regrettable. The establishment of the earliest independent congregations was generally on a much more sure foundation. Their basic objection to a State Church was that it did not allow for the scriptural conception of a church based upon a purely spiritual unity. In this way they recognised that believers must gather only because of their relationship to Christ, and that matters of spiritual understanding are secondary to spiritual fellowship. It was not long, however, before the order was being changed. Churches were being formed because of doctrinal affinities, and others were being split because of doctrinal differences. In doing so, spiritual life began to fade. Sectarianism became the order of the day. The ground of the church was deserted by all but the remnant whom the Lord has always preserved from the earliest times.

179

CHAPTER FIFTEEN

REFORMERS OF THE
REFORMATION

IN 1642 Britain was plunged into the civil war which brought about the downfall of the monarchy and the institution of the Protectorate of Oliver Cromwell. Cromwell was vehemently opposed to Rome and to prelacy, or the imposition of any one form of worship upon the country. His rule ushered in an era of toleration and freedom to preach and propagate one's faith such as had never been known before. Until this freedom was again removed by the restoration of the monarchy in 1660, the Gospel had free course, and spiritual life was greatly quickened.

George Fox

One of the most remarkable Christian teachers of the seventeenth century was George Fox. Born in 1624 in the village of Drayton, Leicestershire, the son of godly parents, his father a weaver, he was, as a child, of unusual gravity of mind. At the age of nineteen he embarked upon a search for spiritual reality, having been much distressed by the great contrast he observed on every hand between Christian profession and Christian practice. In his quest he grew to detest the sham of religious observances and lofty church buildings which so ill concealed the worldliness and spiritual emptiness of people's lives. The clergy from whom he sought help had turned him away empty, nor did he find any more solace from the Dissenters whom he approached in his deep hunger for fellowship with God. At last, in 1646, he felt the voice of God speaking to him, telling him that in Christ alone would his every need be satisfied. From that time he entered into a new joy and relationship with Christ, and determined to give himself to the spreading abroad of the light of the Gospel.

Fox was a man of strong convictions moulded by his reaction to the empty formalism of his day. He completely rejected a professional ministry along with the observance of the sacraments. The true sacraments, he held, are inward and spiritual, and need not be dependent upon any outward form. A Christian should not take any form of oath, nor take part in war. Violence should be completely abjured. The Christian should both suffer and forgive. Many were attracted by Fox's preaching, and meetings of the 'Friends' as they were called were begun in many places. The manner in which Fox and his friends carried out their mission was completely fearless. Fox would interrupt the service in a 'steeple house', as he called the church buildings, and would sometimes end up by preaching to the congregation himself. It is not difficult to understand how such acts as these tried the Commonwealth government's policy of toleration to the very limit. The opposition to the Friends was so violent that it became a threat to the peace. Yet however much they were threatened, beaten, or committed to prison, nothing could stay the progress of the movement. They were undaunted by every danger, and their zeal for the spread of the Word took them over on to the continent of Europe, to North America, and to the West Indies.

When the monarchy was restored in Britain, the rigorous laws against dissenters came down with particular severity upon the Friends. Many independent congregations during this time met in secret, but the Friends openly defied authority, and made no effort to conceal their gatherings. As a result, many were arrested and were flung into gaol where they died. On others were imposed severe fines which ruined them financially. Friends had already crossed the Atlantic, but it was during this period of renewed persecution in Britain that they won the man who was to give his name to one of the American United States. Sir William Penn fully associated himself with the Friends, or Quakers' as they were also derisively known, in 1666, and championed their cause both through preaching and writing. He helped many Quakers cross the Atlantic in search of a freedom to worship God which they were denied in their own land. In 1681 he himself decided to follow them, having received from the king, Charles II, in lieu of an outstanding debt to his father, a grant of the land afterwards to be known as Pennsylvania. The following year the city of Philadelphia was founded.

The Quakers did not establish churches in the New Testament sense, but the power of their testimony lay in the limited extent to which they did, nevertheless, return to basic Scriptural principle. George Fox laid great stress upon the inward witness of the Spirit through which God speaks to man. Alone in the countryside with his Bible, he would hear the voice of the Lord, and some portion of His Word would be lightened up to him in a new way. He felt that the power of revelation was upon him as it had been experienced by the apostles, yet that it was in accordance with what was already revealed in the Word. Fox may have tended to draw too much of a differentiation between the revelation of the Word and the inner revelation of the Spirit, but his emphasis on the reality of the Spirit's indwelling was salutary. The power of the Word is not recognised alone through the intellect, but through the Spirit's quickening.

The testimony of the Quakers in their early days must be ascribed to their complete openness to the Word and work of God through the Spirit who witnesses of Christ and leads us into all truth (John 15:26; 16:13). Fox's concern for 'truth in the inward parts' (Psalms 51:6) was another factor in his teaching which constantly requires to be kept in mind. Fellowship with God is not a matter of outward conformity to a religious ceremony, but a matter of the heart. On the other hand, our Lord established the church as the means whereby that inward fellowship may have a full expression and be a witness to the world. Life in Christ touches not only our personal relationship with God and the relationship within the family circle, but our relationship in the world with the whole divine family, and it is only in the life of the church that that relationship can be fully developed. Fox, in his eagerness to do away with the sham of an empty religious form, practically did away with the church altogether, for meetings of the Friends were not based upon a common experience of regeneration. No doubt, in his day, baptism and the Lord's supper had degenerated into meaningless rites, but that does not mean to say they must always be so. The saving factor is the ministry of the Word in the power of the Spirit. Where that is absent, all religious meeting will be a sham, even if it is only to sit in silence awaiting the Word from the Spirit as is the pattern of Quaker 'worship'. But wherever the authority of the Word is recognised, baptism cannot be administered or accepted lightly; it must be a testimony to a new life. Likewise will the gathering round the table of the Lord be a testimony to the reality of a deep, inward fellowship with God and with one another.

Fox's society was founded upon reaction. No doubt that is partly true also of a church testimony inasmuch as the work of the Gospel is a reaction to the sin of the world. But the church is much more than a group of people united by a negative outlook on the world; it is a group of people who are united by a positive fellowship with Christ, a positive purpose to be the vessel of His glory. It is a consuming spiritual vision, and fellowship with its risen Lord that is the power of the church. Any group coming together on lesser ground must ultimately find itself ill equipped to fulfil the purpose that God has for His people.

John Bunyan

The period of dreadful persecution which followed the collapse of the Protectorate in Britain produced a number of outstanding men of God. The name of Isaac Watts will ever be remembered for the great legacy he has left the church in his hymns, and John Bunyan for his Pilgrim's Progress, a book which has probably been read by more people than any other apart from the Bible. The scene of Bunyan's most noted labours was Bedford, the place also where he spent twelve years of his life in imprisonment for the sake of the Gospel. The church in which he was an elder and then a pastor was one of the early Baptist churches, but Bunyan said that he wanted no other name than Christian. Water baptism was not to him a condition of fellowship, and he steadfastly refused to allow that differences of judgement were a legitimate ground for division between believer and believer.

Jean deLabadie

The continuity of the spiritual succession of the church as opposed to the outward organization can be traced right back to the times of the apostles. The line has never been broken. No age has been without some testimony of the Lord's dwelling in the midst of His people. On the other hand, there have been movements which have returned only in part to Scriptural principle. To the extent that they have preached and practised divine truth they have been good, and their ministry has been a means of rich blessing to others, but their spiritual life and effectiveness have been restricted by a misplaced loyalty to a traditional organization from which they have not been able to separate. Where such movements have affected succeeding generations for their spiritual good and there has thereby been an apprehension of more spiritual light, it will be found that the ultimate result has often been a separated church testimony free to worship and witness in direct dependence upon God. An example of this very thing can be seen in tracing some of the effects of the Pietist movement which we will shortly have cause to consider.

The same principle can be observed on a slightly different level in the life of Jean deLabadie. Throughout the years of his own Christian ministry he traversed practically the whole range of ecclesiastical systems, beginning under the influence of the Jesuits, and arriving ultimately at the position of an ' independent '. It was unfortunate that the final years of his life were marred by excesses which brought great harm not only to himself, but to the church testimony to which he had made such a marked contribution.

Jean deLabadie was born in the year 1610 in Bordeaux, France, destined to become a member of the Society of Jesus to which end his education was directed. His theological studies, however, did not bring him spiritual satisfaction, but the reading of the New Testament was a revelation to his soul. Ordained a priest of the Roman Catholic Church he was, nevertheless, greatly burdened by the corruption of Christendom, and was persuaded from his perusal of the Scriptures that the only answer was in a return to the principles of apostolic times. Thus he saw his commission within the Roman communion to be one of reform. To extricate himself from his association with the Jesuits was no easy matter, but a prolonged illness made it obviously impossible for him to become a full member of the society. In this he recognised God's working on his behalf. Leaving Bordeaux he began, with the archbishop's permission, to teach first in Paris, and later in Amiens, gathering great numbers to listen to his exposition of the Scriptures. These people he formed into ' brotherhoods ', still with official permission from the ecclesiastical hierarchy, and they met periodically in one another's homes to study the Bible. At these gatherings Labadie expressed his longing to see the church return to its original condition. It is not surprising that his teaching led to persistent persecution, and he found himself compelled to leave his more settled ministry.

During this period of trial he was brought into touch with the teaching of Calvin. Labadie's convictions had been the direct result of his study of the Scriptures, but on reading Calvin's works he found that on the great, basic doctrines of the faith, he had been led to the same conclusions. He saw that the reformed Church also left much to be desired in a return to Scriptural practice, but he was one with it in his general apprehension of truth and hoped that, in association with it, he might have the freedom to preach the pure Word of God that he so desired.

By this time he had come to the conclusion that reconciliation between himself and the Roman clergy was impossible, and that there was no hope for reform within the Roman Church itself. Labadie had not arrived at this conclusion hastily. He had been ordained a priest when twenty-five years of age and now, in 1650, he was forty, having laboured within the Church for no less than fifteen years. He, therefore, turned his attention to the reformed Church which he joined at Montauban with the conviction that he would work for Scriptural reform there.

Labadie ministered later in Geneva and in Middelburgh, Holland. His powerful preaching had great effect, but the most signal blessing was through his Bible readings when he would gather a group of people in his own house and expound the Scriptures to them. Through his Bible readings in Geneva one young man who was later to become one of the leading figures in the Pietist movement was greatly helped. His name was Philip Jakob Spener. Labadie had been invited to the post of preacher in the church at Middelburgh by some godly men who were well known for their earnest Christian testimony. He was deeply disappointed, however, at the state of the church which was very far removed from the understanding he had gained from the New Testament. He found, too, that there was a radical difference of outlook between himself and those who had invited him to Middelburgh. They viewed the Church as a sphere of evangelism in which the purpose of the leaders was to bring the people to a knowledge of salvation, and then lead them on into the practice of their faith, whereas he saw from Scripture that the church is a company of born again people united and led through the working of the Holy Spirit. Nevertheless, Labadie continued with his work of reform. He introduced *ex tempore* prayer which was new to the church, and also encouraged the practice of mutual edification through the Word. Many people responded to his ministry both in Middelburgh and further afield, but it was becoming increasingly obvious that, if his teaching were consistently followed out, it would lead to a complete change in the whole character of the Church system. Opposition to such drastic changes was inevitable. When it came it was bitter and unrelenting. In 1669 Labadie

185

and those who supported him were expelled from the Middel-burgh Church.

For fifteen years Labadie had laboured zealously for reform within the Roman Catholic Church; for a further twenty years he had poured his gifts and effort into an attempt to reform the reformed Church. In both cases he failed. It could hardly be said that he had allowed insufficient time for the task. He was now a man of sixty years of age. The conclusion to which he was again driven was that reform from within the established system was impossible, and that separation was the only means whereby apostolic principle could be restored.

In accordance with Labadie's conviction, about three hundred people, under the guidance of three pastors and a number of elders, formed a new gathering in Middelburgh. Only those whose lives showed evidence of their being truly born again were members. The church, however, was not to be allowed to continue its witness undisturbed. The differences which existed between it and the reformed Church led to the city authorities' ordering the separated congregation to leave. Invited to take refuge in a near-by town, they gladly did so, but the persecution followed them and threatened to cause civil strife when the towns-folk, out of a genuine but unspiritual desire, determined to protect the harried church by resort to force. Labadie said he would not become the cause of bloodshed, and saw God's leading through these circumstances to go to Amsterdam where he and his few friends were well received and found religious liberty. There the work started afresh with great blessing, and the movement to come together on simple, Scriptural ground, spread throughout the country, many leaving the ordinances of the reformed Church and many more being sympathetically affected. So serious was the threat to the reformed Church system that the leaders appealed to the government for help, but the separated congregations were allowed their freedom.

Those who would serve Christ enter upon a life of intense, spiritual conflict. There is a complete and infallible guide in the Word interpreted through the presence of the indwelling Spirit, but there are ever forces, be they of this world or of Satan, whose influences are subtly calculated to divert attention from the way which is straight and narrow. The history of the Church is also the history of man's innate belief that he can improve on God's order, and Labadie, in his latter years, became a prey, albeit unconsciously, to this delusion. The assembly is not the abode of Christian perfection; it is the abode of the

186

family of God, those who through regeneration have been made partakers of His life and are developing in that life, sometimes in much weakness and limitation. Labadie was zealous for the full maturity of the Lord's people, and thought that end could more easily be realised by forming a community where those who belonged to the church could live together, could get to know one another intimately, and build one another up into a deep knowledge of Christ. To this end a house was rented in Amsterdam.

The 'household church' early ran into difficulties. One of Labadie's most earnest supporters, recognising the dangers of such an enterprise, and doubting its Scriptural foundation, refused to become associated with it. Separating from Labadie, he wrote a book in explanation of his position, pointing out that the substitution for a church according to the New Testament standard of an exclusive community was most unwise and was apt to give rise to evil rumours. After publication of the book, an anonymous reply appeared attacking the author in a most scurrilous manner. When it was discovered that Labadie had written this, his reputation and ministry were sadly affected. In all this the household became more separate from the community, and more closed in upon itself. One calamity followed upon another. It was found that, in spite of all the precautions taken to form a perfect company, there were some members who held views that were completely at variance with the Scriptures. When attempt was made to exhort them on the matters, their reaction, far removed from the spirit of Christ, was a reaction of calumny and revenge. So intense was the feeling excited against the household in Amsterdam that it was felt better that they should leave the city. They found a refuge on the estate of a wealthy sympathiser in Herford, but the fierce resentment of the local Lutheran population at their presence cut them off from any wide ministry and isolated them to occupation with their own internal affairs.

If Labadie was hated outside the household, within he was venerated as an apostle. People hung upon his every word and felt that they had never experienced true communion with God till they were touched by his preaching. Such an attitude was bound to lead to excesses. Community of goods was introduced, and at times during the meetings there was speaking with tongues and other ecstatic exhibitions. Labadie died in 1674, but the household continued and, in fact, increased for some time. At one stage two missionary parties were sent out, but it seems they were more interested in winning others to their particular experience of community living than of winning them for the Gospel. The enterprise ended in failure. Practical difficulties led the household to abandon the system of community of goods, and the members began to disperse. The 'household church' eventually died out.

The life and experiences of Jean deLabadie teach us many valuable lessons. After thirty-five years of selfless labour, he came to the inescapable conclusion that to restore the great religious systems of Christendom to the principles and practices of New Testament times was an impossible task. Seeing from the Scriptures the truth of separation, he bent his energies to the end that God might raise up assemblies of believers as He had done in the times of the Acts. In this he was the means of great spiritual blessing and, over a wide area, churches were raised up the effect of whose life was carried on. Where Labadie failed was in thinking that absolute maturity and purity of testimony can be maintained in any circle upon this earth. He was right in separating from the organized Churches on the ground that the. true church should contain only those who are partakers of Christ's life through an experience of personal regeneration, but he was wrong in ultimately trying to restrict the church to a household of those who had 'arrived' spiritually, an effort which was signally doomed to failure. The fallacy of his concept was ironically portrayed in his own unspiritual reaction to the disagreement of his former co-worker where he demonstrated his inability to accept, in a spirit of humility, any challenge to the absolute authority which he assumed.

The restricted circle of the household then led to other unscriptural attitudes and practices. The veneration which Labadie enjoyed was more than an elder should claim, and more than a believer should accord even to a highly respected instrument of God's working. The witness to the world around was seriously hampered, not free as the witness of the church should be, and the members of the household were unable to think except in terms of a false pattern of living which further isolated them from those to whom they should have been a testimony. At the same time, the introspective nature of their community life created a favourable atmosphere for soulish extravagances which still more dissipated their spiritual energy and hindered their effectiveness. All is a salutary lesson on the importance of adhering precisely to the Scriptural order and to the spirit of humility in which alone the Scriptural order can be properly interpreted.

Philip Jakob Spener

The middle of the seventeenth century saw the Lutheran and reformed Churches in a low spiritual state. In Lutheranism particularly, the prevailing tendency was towards an intellectual orthodoxy which demanded outward conformity to sacraments and pure doctrine, but paid little heed to godliness of life. Lutheranism taught the priesthood of all believers, but it was a truth which, to all practical purposes, had been forgotten. The position of the laity was passive. They had to listen to the orthodox doctrine preached to them, give their assent to it, and take part in the sacraments of the Church. That was the sum total of their Christianity. The protest against these tendencies has come down to us in history with the label ' Pietism '.

We have already noticed how Philip Spener was one of a group of young men influenced through the Bible readings of Jean de Labadie in Geneva. He was also influenced by the writings of English Puritans such as Richard Baxter and John Bunyan. All served to impress upon him the value of sound, Biblical exegesis.

Spener was born in Alsace in 1635, and spent his earlier student years in Strassburg. When over thirty years of age, he was appointed chief pastor of the Lutheran Church in Frankfurt. Deeply burdened about the need for discipline and reform, he nevertheless found himself severely restricted in carrying out what he felt was necessary, since authority was in the hands of the civil government. In 1670 he began gatherings in his own house for study of the Bible, prayer and mutual edification, and proposed such meetings from other congregations as a ' church within the Church ' which would be able to return to the apostolic manner of gathering, and grow in holiness of life. He emphasized that true Christianity must manifest itself in daily life, and is entered into through a conscious experience of regeneration. Believers are not passive in spiritual matters, but have a responsibility for building one another up in the faith, and they live a life of moderation and separation from the grosser pleasures of the world. Spener minimized the importance of formal creeds and dogmas in order to return to the direct authority of the Scriptures. He stressed the vital importance of a spiritual experience, and said that where there was

189

true life in the Spirit, intellectual differences in interpretation would look after themselves. His work caused violent controversy, and he was accused of heresy. What he taught was indeed destructive of the lifeless intellectual orthodoxy which summed up the Lutheranism of his day.

In the groups which gathered under the inspiration of his life, Spener brought back the Bible to a place of familiar use where it fed and fostered the lives of those who sought guidance through its pages. The logical outcome was separation from the Lutheran Church and, following to its conclusion the light they had received, some of the members of Spener's church at Frankfurt withdrew from it. Spener, however, protested at this step. He was not prepared to follow to the ultimate limit what he himself had taught. In 1686 he moved to Dresden as Court Chaplain, and from there to Berlin where he continued his ministry till his death in 1705.

August Hermann Francke

August Francke was born in Lubeck in 1663. As a young instructor at Leipzig university, he was one of a small group who met to study the Scriptures. Though this was at first but an academic pursuit, it awakened within him a desire for deeper spiritual realities. In 1687 he experienced the radical change of the new birth while he was engaged in a study on the words of John 20: 31, " But these are written that ye may believe that Jesus is the Christ, the Son of God; and that believing, ye may have life in his name." Following this he spent a period in Dresden with Spener who greatly influenced his thinking. Francke's forthright preaching, insisting upon the necessity of conversion and a godly life, brought blessing to many, but also led to his being denounced as a Pietist and ousted from a number of positions. At length he was appointed to a professorship in the new university of Halle. From 1698 he was a member of the theological faculty, and his spiritual influence dominated the university which became a centre of Pietism. Francke died in 1727.

Two aspects of Francke's ministry during his stay at Halle are particularly noteworthy as they had an influence which extended far beyond his own lifetime and far beyond the bounds of Halle itself. First there was the sense of missionary vision and responsibility which he engendered. Roman Catholic ventures in the field of missions were well known, but the great

Protestant Churches had generally failed to recognise any obligation in this direction. It is a measure of Francke's own spiritual depth and insight that his devotion to the Lord burdened his mind with an aspect of Christian service which had been largely foreign to orthodox, Protestant thinking. From Halle went the first Protestant missionaries to India in 1705, Bartholomew Zeigenbalg and Henry Plutchau. During their twelve years of labour in South India they translated the New Testament into Tamil. But of the many missionaries who went out from Halle, the most famous was Christian Friedrich Schwartz who died still serving God in India in 1750. All of these men were deeply influenced by Pietism, and the fruit of their ministry lingers on. Schwartz was used to lead to Christ a man whose descendants have been the foundation of a strongly witnessing movement of assemblies in India today.

The second noteworthy aspect of Francke's ministry was in the schools he founded. On reaching Halle, he was distressed by the condition of the poor, and determined to start a school. This was the first of a number of Institutions which he founded, including his famous Orphan Home. All of these were commenced with but slender financial means at his disposal and were carried on without appeals for money, solely through dependence upon the faithfulness of God. At Francke's death his Orphan Home housed 134 children, and 2,200 children were being taught in his schools. One of them was Nicolas Ludwig, Count Zinzendorf, later leader of the Moravian brethren.

CHAPTER SIXTEEN

THE FRUIT OF REVIVAL

PROTESTANTISM, divided into innumerable parties, was the scene of the bitterest internal strife. Catholicism, while outwardly united in one monolithic system, had long cut off the direct access of man to God through the imposition of sacraments and a mediating priesthood. Protestantism denied fellowship with fellow-believers; Catholicism denied fellowship with God. Within the Roman Church there had long been people, called Mystics, whose yearning after communion with God had led them to develop a life of meditation and strict temperance. The reverence in which Rome held some of these people is evidenced in the number of them who have been canonized, but there were also periods when they were severely persecuted, particularly under the influence of the Jesuits. One of the best known of the Mystics of the late seventeenth and early eighteenth centuries was Madame Guyon whose life still remains a source of blessing and inspiration. Although finally imprisoned by the king of France in the Bastille, her influence continued to spread beyond the walls of her awful dungeon.

The divisions of Protestantism, and more so the un-Christian strife which accompanied them, increased the hunger in the hearts of many sincere believers for freedom of fellowship between all those who were truly the children of God. This hunger was well expressed in the work of Gottfried Arnold (1666-1714). A product of the Pietist movement, and a friend of Philip Spener, Arnold was for a short time professor of history at Giessen, but later gave up his appointment to live a quieter life in which he gave himself over largely to writing. Arnold was concerned over the dreadful intolerance of the orthodox, and the fiercely polemic approach to Church history which swept aside everything that did not conform to the dominant religious system of its time. He himself was a historian, and had also read much of the writings of the ancient ' heretics ', whom he felt had not been judged on their own merits, but had been mercilessly crushed in a partisan struggle. In 1700 he published his ' Impartial History of the Churches and Heretics ' in which he sought to trace the history of the spiritual movement of the church as opposed to the history of the ecclesiastical organization. His book became widely known and caused a great stir, being proclaimed by different people both one of the most profitable and one of the most mischievous books that had ever been written. Maybe Arnold did believe that there was more truth among some of the 'heretics' than among the orthodox (he held that the Lutheran Church was Babel and could not be reformed), but maybe, too, he was right, and his conception of the spiritual continuity of the church is something which still receives too little regard in this the twentieth century.

The Mystics were primarily concerned with their personal fellowship with God, and did not see the importance of fellowship expressed in the gathering together of believers. Their influence, however, stressing inward holiness, along with the desire aroused through such men as Arnold for a practical expression of fellowship with all who were truly born again, led to the beginning of meetings which spread widely throughout Germany, the low countries and England during the first half of the eighteenth century. They represented many and various elements, but all regarded the unity and perfecting of the saints more important than adherence to an outward ecclesiastical form. All did not separate from the Churches to which they had belonged, but many did, and they gave their gatherings the name 'Philadelphia' which means 'brotherly love'. This may have originated from the historical interpretation of the second and third chapters of the book of Revelation held by numbers of them, upon which they based a call to all true believers to unite in the faithfulness of the church at Philadelphia (Rev. 3 : 7-10). The witness of these groups was fruitful in winning others for Christ. One of their converts who will always be remembered for his beautiful hymns was Gerhard Tersteegen.

The Moravians

Count Zinzendorf was born in Dresden in 1700. Brought up by his godly grandmother, he was from very early years an earnest lover of the Lord Jesus Christ. At the school of August Francke in Halle he was brought under further Pietistic influence which greatly affected his life, and from Francke he imbibed something of the missionary vision and spirit with which he influenced the Moravian movement in later years. In 1722 he met Christian David, a former carpenter who was seeking a place of refuge for persecuted Moravian believers whom he had won to the Lord in his own land. Zinzendorf invited them to settle on his estates in Saxony, and there they founded their first village community which they called Herrnhut. It was some five years later that Zinzendorf took over the leadership of the community after intervening in a bitter dispute which had threatened its disruption. He was a man of great tact and grace, and had outstanding leadership abilities. Not only was the dispute settled, but God granted a touch of revival which brought reconciliation and a new spirit into the company. The Moravians were opposed to the idea of identifying themselves with the Lutheran Church, but Zinzendorf was himself a Lutheran and a disciple of Spener's idea of a ' church within the Church '. A compromise solution was found whereby Herrnhut was recognised as an independent community within the Lutheran fold, and one of the Moravians was consecrated Bishop, allowing the sacraments to be administered. In spite of this, Zinzendorf was later banished from Saxony, while the Moravians won out in their desire to receive recognition as a distinct denomination.

The most striking thing about the Moravian community was its missionary outreach. On a visit to Copenhagen to attend the coronation of king Christian VI, Zinzendorf came in contact with people from the West Indies and from Greenland. From them he learned of conditions in these parts of the world. He returned to Herrnhut afire with a passion to carry the Gospel to these and other foreign lands. The community was organized as a base from which the Word of God should be spread far and wide. In 1732 a party set out for the West Indies, and in 1733 another party for Greenland. Some missions were started in the East, in Africa and the Americas. Herrnhut became a centre associated with many parts of the globe. Wherever these missionaries went they preached the Gospel and sought to establish communities on the pattern of Herrnhut, from which the work was controlled. Centralization of control proved a hindrance to the work and the system had to be modified, but the community pattern itself made for further difficulties. The strength of Moravianism was its vital, spiritual life. The weakness of Moravianism lay in the fact that, disregarding the Scriptural concept of the church, there was no adequate vessel to contain the life of the Spirit. The simple manner of the churches of the New Testament is the only pattern spiritually

194

designed to be universally applied to meet many and varied needs. Zinzendorf died in Herrnhut in 1760.

The Methodists

It was on a ship bound for North America in 1735 that John Wesley met a company of Moravian missionaries. He himself was diligently trying to earn his own salvation through constant religious exercises, but observed in the Moravians a faith and quality of spiritual life to which he was a stranger. This was an important milestone along the path of John Wesley's quest for peace with God.

John and Charles Wesley were the sons of staunch, Anglican parents, their father being the rector of the country parish of Epworth. Both owed much to the early training given them by their godly mother, Susanna Wesley, a woman of outstanding character, as indeed she needed to be with a family of nineteen children, even if eight of them did die in infancy. John was the fifteenth and Charles was the eighteenth. During the not infrequent absences from the household of her husband in the course of fulfilling his pastoral obligations, Susannah felt it her duty to gather servants and children together around the Scriptures and to pray. So well known did these family prayers become through the recommendations of the servants that the house would be filled and at times people had to be turned away through lack of space. Yet in spite of the godly example of their mother, and the constant teaching they received from the Word of God, John and Charles, although growing up to be devoutly religious, did not in their early years come to an assurance of salvation.

Both distinguished themselves at their studies, and both were ordained into the ministry of the Anglican Church. An idea of their religious outlook can be gained from the little club which Charles started in Oxford in 1729 where the members gathered to read helpful books and also to take part in religious exercises with fasting and frequent communion. Their ideas were high Anglican, and they were diligently concerned about saving their own souls through their good works. The university called them the 'Holy Club' in mockery, or 'Methodists', a name later applied to the Wesleys' gatherings which were of an entirely different character.

Late in 1735 John and Charles went as missionaries to Georgia. It was on the voyage out that they met the Moravians. The

195

following year Charles had returned to England, ill and frustrated. John remained till the beginning of 1738 when he too returned, his missionary life a complete failure. Not long after John's arrival in England, the brothers again came into contact with a Moravian, Peter Boehler, who was delayed in London *en route* from Germany to Georgia. Boehler spoke to them of salvation instantaneously received through faith. The experience came to Charles while on a bed of sickness, and a few days later John, who had passed through great mental anguish, found peace with God at an evangelical society meeting in Aldersgate Street, London. He described his experience in these words, " I felt my heart strangely warmed. I felt I did trust in Christ for salvation; and an assurance was given me that He had taken away my sins, even mine, and saved me from the law of sin and death."

The spiritual state of England in the eighteenth century was at a low ebb. The wars and struggles of the century previous had left an aftermath of godlessness and moral destitution. Illiteracy, immorality, drunkenness and coarseness prevailed. The enforcement of law was barbarous, and the condition of the prisons vile beyond description. It was an age of mental adolescence, of men who knew all and rejected all. There was the Deism of Voltaire whose convictions were moulded in England, and he returned to France to mould the mind of a nation to bloody revolution. There was the superior scepticism of Edward Gibbon who wrote the History of the Decline and Fall of the Roman Empire. Late in the century there was the brutal blasphemy of Thomas Paine, a Quaker's son. Rationalism had invaded the realm of religious thinking, and preaching had become powerless, the colourless homily on morals that drew but few to listen and left untouched those who did. Assemblies of God's people were comparatively few, and there too spiritual life was tainted with spiritual lethargy. If a religion is to be judged by its effects, there can be no greater indictment of scepticism than the general debauchery of the eighteenth century. There was need of revival.

Such was the England in which John and Charles Wesley began their evangelistic ministry, with the only message that could raise the country from the sink into which it had collapsed, the message of sin, salvation through faith by the sacrifice of Christ and the regenerating work of the Holy Spirit. But one after the other the doors of the churches were closed to them. The Churches did not want their ' enthusiasm . In

1739 John Wesley was invited to Bristol by George Whitefield who, also finding the churches closed to him, had begun preaching in the open air to the miners of a colliery district with great resultant blessing. Wesley was at first hesitant. As a meticulously exact Churchman, it had never seemed proper to him that preaching should be conducted out of doors, but the vast opportunities enabled him to overcome his prejudice, and he embarked upon the type of ministry that was to occupy most of his subsequent fifty years of labour.

The ministry of John Wesley and George Whitefield took them far and wide throughout the British Isles, while Whitefield also visited America six times. They journeyed mostly on horseback, and Wesley is said to have travelled some 250,000 miles during his fifty years of indefatigable service. The dangers were considerable. The age was a violent one, and the preachers, with those who believed, were, in the course of their tours, often attacked by unruly mobs. At the same time they were bitterly opposed by the clergy. But Wesley was undaunted, and God was with him. The crowds who listened to the Gospel sometimes numbered tens of thousands, and thousands were genuinely born again. The roughest and most hardened of sinners found peace at the cross with tears of repentance. During the meetings many would be stricken with conviction and would find their way to Christ with cries of remorse.

Wesley organized those who were converted through his ministry into societies, the first to be established being in Bristol and the second in London. Being a determined adherent of the Church of England, he long desired that his societies should remain a part of the established Church, but that separation should come eventually was wellnigh inevitable. The rigidity of Anglicanism could ill contain the vitality of the Methodist societies which it so stringently opposed. Society members gathered on the ground of their desire for salvation. Beyond that they could hold their own views on various points, but were not allowed to make them subjects of contention. They were free to attend any place of worship they wished.

Wesley would have preferred that preaching should be done only by ordained men, but the clergy's lack of sympathy with the movement forced him to use others in developing its organization. He would not, however, allow an unordained man to administer the sacraments. When Methodism was taken to America where there were often no Episcopal churches where

N

the members could receive the sacraments, the question of their administration took on a new importance. Wesley could not persuade the Church of England to ordain ministers for American Methodism, so he resorted to the expedient of granting ordination himself. This made the break between his societies and the established Church complete. Ministers were then ordained in Britain where Methodism took the ground of a separate denomination.

The organization which Wesley developed was of an annual Conference of ministers which controlled the movement. The work itself was divided into 'circuits', each with a superintendent under whom there would be several travelling preachers. All who preached in the chapels had to receive the recognition of the Conference. The Conference was a clerical body and, as such, was much aware of its authority and jealously guarded its privilege. This led to divisions within the Methodist ranks and the spiritual degeneration of the whole movement. If John Wesley were to make an anonymous visit to Methodism today, it is doubtful whether many of its churches would welcome him. They would not want his 'enthusiasm'.

Charles Wesley shared the travels of his brother for many years, but the great legacy he left to the church was his hymns. During his lifetime he wrote over six thousand, and there are but few collections of English hymns today which do not contain some of them. Charles Wesley's hymns are not only expressive of the deepest emotions of worship, but contain a wealth of expository thought on some of the main doctrines of the Bible. Charles died in 1788 at the age of eighty. John lived till his eighty-eigth year and died in 1791.

George Whitefield

George Whitefield's early life was very different from that of the Wesleys. He was born in 1714 in Gloucester, the son of an inn-keeper who died while he was comparatively young. Brought up in poverty, it was with difficulty that he was able to continue his studies, but he entered Oxford in 1733. While there he passed through great anguish of soul in his search after salvation and joined the Wesley's 'Holy Club' to seek peace with God through fastings and other religious practices. In 1735, through reading the Scriptures, the light dawned, and he experienced the mighty transformation of regeneration. Receiving episcopal ordination the same year, he started out on his career as a preacher although only twenty-two years of age. From the very beginning his outstanding power as a preacher was obvious. His treatment of sin and forthright rejection of the doctrine of baptismal regeneration, widely held in Anglican circles, scandalized many and closed many pulpits to him, but people were soundly converted, and immense crowds flocked to hear him.

Although Whitefield was an Anglican himself, and lived in a day when sectarian loyalties were intense, denominational feeling meant nothing to him. In this respect he was notably different from the Wesleys who, throughout their lives, were never able to rid themselves completely of Anglican prejudices. Debarred from the Church of England, Whitefield would preach wherever there was a door open to him, and through his field preaching reached countless multitudes who were completely estranged from organized religion. It was his example among the miners near Bristol, as we have seen, that first induced John Wesley to preach the Gospel in the open air.

Whitefield travelled incessantly throughout the British Isles and paid six visits to North America where he died in 1770. On both sides of the Atlantic he left a lasting spiritual impression. He was a lifelong friend of Jonathan Edwards who was also remarkably used of the Lord. Whitefield's theology was strongly calvinistic, while Wesley's was just as strongly arminian. At one point this gave rise to a fervid interchange of correspondence between the two, but their personal relationship was always maintained, even if it did have to pass through some stormy patches. Both proclaimed justification by faith, and the preaching of each was equally effective. Many who listened to Wesley chose to follow the Lord, and many who listened to Whitefield found that the Lord had chosen them. Whitefield, unlike Wesley, organized no denomination, but many thousands brought in real subjection to the feet of Christ were the fruit of his ministry.

The main impact of the eighteenth century revivals under Wesley and Whitefield did not lie in the formation of any denomination, for the spiritual blessing had a profound effect which extended far beyond the confines of Methodism or the Anglican Church, influencing the whole character of the English speaking nations of Britain and America. On the social level, a new awareness of the gross abuses of the day was stimulated, and a vigorous determination aroused to deal with them, the slave trade, for example, and the deplorable condition of the

199

prisons. The impetus behind those reforms was a direct result of the regenerating work of Christ through which the love of God was shed abroad in the hearts of men and women. On the spiritual level, a new God-consciousness was diffused throughout the land which yielded fruit in missionary expansion and produced such great pioneers as William Carey of India, Robert Morrison of China and John Williams of the South Pacific. It also prepared the way for a return in much greater measure to the simple, Scriptural principles of Christian gathering. The revivals of the eighteenth century constituted a very much needed re-emphasis on the experience of salvation through faith, and laid again the foundation of personal, spiritual experience which is essential to any further revelation. That revelation was not to come in any significant measure through the encouragement of the established Church or even of the Methodist societies which were the direct result of Wesley's preaching, but it would have been altogether impossible apart from the respect for the Scriptures that had been engendered, and the regeneration which had been experienced by so many through Wesley and Whitefield.

Robert and James Haldane

Scotland had seen revival under the preaching of George Whitefield and others, but evangelical teaching was decried by the increasing Moderatism of the organized Church which denied the inspiration of the Scriptures, and rejected miracles and the divinity of the Lord Jesus Christ who was upheld simply as a great religious Teacher. Two men who were greatly used to bring further spiritual enlightenment in these depressing circumstances were the brothers Robert and James Haldane, sons of a wealthy Scottish family. Both had served in the navy and, upon conversion, became ardent students of the Bible. Neither of them had received any formal, theological education, and as unordained men it was not popularly considered that they should entertain the idea of a preaching career. But they longed to be able to proclaim the Gospel, and looked to God to open up the way, which He did. James Haldane with others of a like vision travelled as far north as the islands of Orkney proclaiming the Good News wherever opportunity afforded, in church buildings or in the open air. Crowds numbering thousands flocked to hear them, and a deep work of the Spirit was done in many hearts.

Opposition, however, was not lacking. Many resented that unordained men should dare to preach, and this dislike was encouraged by the action of the established Church which passed laws against preaching by those who were not properly licensed, threatening with excommunication any who allowed them to preach or listened to them. The work of God, however, went on. The Haldane brothers and their co-labourers in the Gospel saw in the low spiritual state of the Church an urgent reason why they, who knew Christ, should proclaim Him to others. The blessing with which God signally honoured their ministry brought with it a concern as to how they could best help those who had believed. They had already reaped the displeasure of the established Church for preaching at all without a licence. Now they were perplexed by the obvious mixture of believers and unbelievers that the Church was, and felt that God could not build up His people where spiritual life as the basis of fellowship was absent. Recognising this fact, they saw that one course alone was open to them, and separated from the established Chruch to meet with those whose lives gave real evidence of an experience of regeneration. The first of these churches was in Edinburgh, the company numbering initially about three hundred, and James was ordained as pastor.

Robert and James Haldane were completely open to the guidance of the Lord. They accepted the Scriptures as God's rule for the lives of His people and for the ordering of the assembly. As the Spirit gave them light they sought to walk in it, desiring that the affairs of the church should be directed as Scripture laid down. One by one changes were instituted as they came to recognise clearly some further spiritual principle. They began to meet round the Lord's table each week, offerings were accepted only from those who were true believers; ministry was accepted through any in the company as the Spirit directed.

The Haldanes had been brought up in the Presbyterian fold to observe the baptism of infants, but they began to entertain serious doubts as to the Scripturalness of this practice. Being convinced that the Bible taught otherwise, they felt they had to refuse to baptize any more children, and they themselves accepted baptism by immersion as believers. Others whose study of the Scriptures led them to the same conclusion were baptized also. Nevertheless, the Haldanes saw clearly that baptism was not the basis of fellowship, and resisted any thought that the church should be divided because some were baptized

201

and some were not. It was a matter of intense grief to them when a section of the congregation who held rigidly to the view of the established Church in this particular, separated from them. Nevertheless, the larger group which remained continued the testimony with the sustained blessing of the Lord. The ministry of Robert and James Haldane resulted in the establishing of congregations of believers not only in the city of Edinburgh, but in other centres where there had been a saving response to the preaching of the Gospel.

Of most far-reaching effect was the ministry of Robert Haldane in Geneva. He had long desired the opportunity of preaching the Gospel further afield, and in 1816 crossed to the Continent. In Geneva the way opened up to minister to twenty or thirty divinity students who met for Bible study in his house. Geneva, which had been the centre of so much spiritual light, had sadly departed from the truth that had been proclaimed by Calvin and the early Reformers. Unitarianism had brought a blight upon the life of the Church, and the students who studied divinity at the Geneva Academy were ignorant alike of the doctrines of grace and of the Word of God. Robert Haldane found them in dire need, and began to expound to the group which met in his home Paul's epistle to the Romans. His commentary on Romans can still be classed as one of the greatest expositions of that book. The students were struck by the graciousness of Haldane's character, and were astounded at his knowledge of the Scriptures and his implicit faith in them. It is not surprising that the Word of God spoke so clearly to their hearts. They both read it from the printed page, and from the life of the man of God who expounded it to them. The religious authorities were incensed at Haldane's ministry. They were powerless to stop him, but those who sought to be obedient to the faith they had found were harried and tyrannized. Some were forced out of the established Church and began to meet separately to remember the Lord. Of those to whom Haldane ministered in Geneva, a number were singularly used in different spheres of Christian service, particularly to the blessing of the French speaking world, but by no means exclusively so. One of these was Jean Henri Merle d'Aubigne, the great Church historian, whose lucid style and spiritual insight produced the work on the Reformation which gained such outstanding popularity during the last century.

The ministry of Robert and James Haldane also contributed indirectly to a wide movement of return to New Testament principles in North America. A young man called Alexander Campbell who was preparing himself for ordination into the Presbyterian ministry came into contact with their teaching in Glasgow at the beginning of the nineteenth century, and was constrained to rethink his theological position which he had accepted with little question. The result was that his convictions underwent a radical change.

Alexander Campbell's father, Thomas Campbell, had been a Presbyterian minister in Northern Ireland, but in 1807 had moved to North America where he settled in Pennsylvania. There, quite unknown to his son, he felt obliged to withdraw from the Secession Presbyterian body of which he was a member and sought, according to the convictions he had received from the Scriptures, that believers should gather without sectarian prejudices, accepting the Word of God alone as their rule of faith and conduct. Thomas Campbell had left his family in Britain to follow him at a later date. When they were re-united, it was a great strength to both father and son to find that they had each been led in a similar pathway by the Spirit of God. Together they continued the ministry, and a church was formed in 1811 at Bush Run in Pennsylvania.

Nor was this the only movement of its kind. Another Presbyterian minister from Kentucky, Burton Stone, was used in a similar manner, and congregations of believers gathered together over a wide area. The fruit of the labour of these and other devoted servants of God still remain, although the sectarian spirit against which Thomas and Alexander Campbell strove so unremittingly has re-asserted itself, and the large denomination today known as the Disciples of Christ is the descendent of the simple company of Christian believers which first met at Bush Run, Pennsylvania.

The ministry of the Haldane brothers shows very clearly that where Christians are ready to accept the Word of God with a completely open heart and mind, and in a spirit of obedience, they will be led back to the simplicity of New Testament times in the gathering of the church. It is true that Robert Haldane did not seek to do in Geneva what he had done in Scotland. His time in Geneva was given solely to the exposition of the Scriptures, but the result was, apart altogether from his instigation, a return to the Biblical basis of the church by some at least whose study of the inspired Word had brought them to the same conclusion as Robert and James Haldane had reached years previously in the city of Edinburgh.

CHAPTER SEVENTEEN

THE REMNANT

THE nineteenth century is outstanding for progress no less in the spiritual realm than in the realm of science and social and economic development. In this century we see the fruition of the evangelical movement which had begun in the century before, and, indeed, we see a more substantial recovery of some aspects of Scriptural truth than had been seen for a very long time. We all know how much more easy it is to lose spiritual ground than it is to gain it. The work of a lifetime can be shattered in a moment, and if it is recovered at all, it may take generations. In the early chapters we have seen how the early simplicity and spirituality of the church gave place to a great, ecclesiastical organization, largely bereft of spiritual vitality. True, the testimony of assemblies of believers seeking to order their lives and witness according to the Scriptures has never died out, and they have been far more numerous than conventional Church histories would often lead us to suppose, but the nineteenth century saw, in still greater measure, in certain circles, a return to the spirit of the early church.

Nowhere is this more evident than in the great surge of missionary endeavour which commenced with the departure for India of William Carey in 1793. It is from this year that the era of modern missions is generally dated. It is altogether remarkable to notice how slow the church has been to awaken to its missionary responsibility, and this is all the more apparent when we consider the fervent missionary activity of the church's earliest years.

From the great Nestorian missions to the missions of the Jesuits in the sixteenth century there lay a thousand years which saw little of any kind of planned missionary expansion, and it was longer still before the determination that Christ should be preached worldwide laid hold of the hearts of those who really knew the Gospel. The Nestorians, for all their outstanding courage and selfless zeal, carried with them a Gospel that was by no means unmixed with the religious evils of the day in which they lived, while the work of the Jesuits, although it extended right to Japan in the east, was almost wholly superficial, and had to do merely with the change of a few externals, not with a change of heart. Even the Reformation made little difference. Orthodox Lutheranism did little to develop missions, while the extreme emphasis of many calvinists practically forbade any initiative to reach others with the message of Christ. The stern words spoken to young William Carey, "If the Lord wants to convert the heathen, He can do it without your help," were typical of a large section of calvinistic thought which is by no means without expression even in the present day. It was left largely to such people as the Pietists and the 'Independents' to initiate the worldwide expansion of the Gospel which, in the nineteenth century, was to develop to such a great extent.

The Oxford Movement

God often uses the very grossness of the Church's departure from 'the faith which was once for all delivered unto the saints' to stimulate His own people to a fresh return to Scripture truth. The quickened spiritual discernment which brought this about in England was in some measure due to the condition of the established Church, a condition which is well illustrated by a religious institution which can harbour a movement such as the Oxford Movement or the Tractarians.

1828 saw the repeal of the obnoxious legislation which infringed the liberty of Roman Catholics and nonconformists, and they were now permitted to sit in the House of Commons. Non-Anglicans would thus have power to vote on matters affecting the established Church, a situation which caused great alarm among some Churchmen, and stimulated them to an examination of the nature of the Church itself with a view to preserving it from constant alteration by government enactment. Of these champions of the established Church a number were associated with Oxford, hence the name Oxford Movement which was given to their society. The most well known was John Henry Newman, later to become a Cardinal in the Roman Catholic Church. Others were Richard Hurrell Froude who died at the young age of thirty-three but, nevertheless, exercised a considerable influence, John Keble, and Edward Bouverie Pusey who joined them slightly later but was to become the leader of the movement when Newman joined Rome. These men sought to establish the unbroken succession of the Church of England from the ancient Catholic Church, and advertised their views in a series of papers which they called 'Tracts for the Times'. From these the name 'Tractarians' has been derived. They made much of the glorious tradition of the past, and held to a doctrine of Apostolic Succession whereby the authority of the apostles was transmitted to Bishops down through the centuries by the laying on of hands. (It is noteworthy that some of those who are supposed to have had this authority have been most conspicuously lacking in elementary Christian qualities.) Only those, they said, who are in the apostolic succession can validly administer the sacraments which are a means of saving grace. The doctrine of transubstantiation was held, and there was a return to many Romish practices, truths, they believed, which the Reformers had wrongly repudiated. It is evident that this movement in the Church of England was drifting strongly Romeward, yet to Pusey, a man of undoubted earnestness, it was a return to primitive Christianity.

The Anglo-Catholic Tractarians gained a large following from among the clergy. The laity, for the most part, placidly accepted whatever came their way. The differentiation between clergy and laity, and the disinterestedness of the latter on matters which basically affect spiritual life, is something which is completely foreign to the spirit of the New Testament churches. It is not to be expected that every believer should be versed in all the intricacies of theological debate, but wherever there is life in the Spirit and a respect for the Scriptures as the Word of God, there will be a healthy concern for eternal truth in the church as a whole. Indifference is symptomatic of spiritual death, and any religious system in which such unquestioning indifference can be the accepted norm is very far from the church as Christ meant it to be.

In 1839 Newman issued Tract XC. It roused tremendous controversy, and resulted in further tracts being forbidden. In Tract XC Newman dealt with the question of interpreting the thirty-nine articles which outlined the definitely Protestant faith of the Church of England. These he said, could be conscientiously signed, but intepreted from the standpoint of the Catholic Church, not interpreted only as their authors originally intended. The furious outcry which resulted charged the Tractarians with evasion and Jesuitry, and the Bishop of Oxford denounced a system of interpretation whereby the articles could be made to mean anything anyone wanted or nothing at all. A few years later, in 1845, Newman was formally received into the Roman Catholic Church. Some hundreds of clergymen and laymen followed him.

The departure of Newman and his followers did not mean the break up of the Anglo-Catholic party. It was seriously weakened, but, under the able leadership of Edward Pusey was, within a few years, stronger than it had ever been, and was continuing to grow. Up to the present day it has exercised a powerful influence in a large section of the Anglican Church, and has wrought almost unbelievable changes to restore ideas of the Middle Ages which great men like Ridley and Latimer opposed to the point of giving their lives at the stake. But the thirty-nine articles remain, in theory at least, the standard of faith of the Church of England. We see here again how impossible it is to guard the faith by the imposition of a credal statement. The Scripturalness of every creed is more than matched by man's ingenuity at interpreting it to mean precisely what he wants. There is but one way to preserve the purity of the church, and that is by preserving the flow of the life of the Spirit of God within it.

It is interesting, if somewhat perplexing, to note that John H. Newman's early training had been evangelical. His brother, Francis W. Newman, had a career which is no less difficult to understand. In 1832 he joined Anthony Norris Groves as a missionary in Baghdad, but later became a leading exponent of Rationalism.

Christian Brethren

We have seen how one of the fruits of the eighteenth century evangelical revival was an awakening of the Lord's people to a sense of their missionary responsibility. Another fruit was a further rediscovery of the ground of Christian unity and meeting. The many groups of Christians generally classed as 'Independents', and in some of which a simple gathering on the ground of relationship with Christ had been observed, had largely slipped into the denominational groove. This, with the return to mediaevalism instigated by the Oxford Movement, stimulated God's people in different places to make a more urgent enquiry into the real nature of the church.

In our recounting the history of God's working down through the ages, it has been inevitable that particular names should stand out as the names of men who were specially used to bring about a return to Scriptural principle. God's means of fulfilling

207

His purposes are His people, so it would be wellnigh impossible to give an adequate account of any spiritual work without mention of some of those who were involved. Yet in mentioning God's mighty men we always need to remember that they were but instruments in God's hands. A movement of the Spirit of God is greater by far than any single individual who may be concerned in it, and if any company of Christians is so completely dependent upon a man that it folds up when the man is taken away, it only goes to show the extent to which it was based on the human rather than on the divine. It is true that there have been many useful associations of Christians who have owed their strength to the organizing genius of some devoted man of God, but the church is of a completely different order. While accepting the ministry of all whom God sends with gift to edify it, the church is grounded solidly upon its relationship with Christ and looks to Him alone as its Head. It has been for this reason that the gatherings of regenerated people have never been completely destroyed, even in times of the most cruel persecution when anyone who seemed to have an acceptable gift of ministry among them was hurried to the flames.

The return to the ground of Christian unity and meeting which took place in the nineteenth century has been, without doubt, one of the most outstanding of modern times and has had a world-wide effect, the full extent of which it is impossible to calculate. As with practically every spiritual movement, it did not begin through one man or in one place, but was the meeting of elements of spiritual enquiry from widely scattered areas. Duncan Mathieson, Donald Ross, John Smith and Donald Munro are names associated with it in the north of Scotland. Dublin, Plymouth and Bristol were also centres of which we shall have more to say, and from as widely diverse parts of the world as New York, Rangoon, British Guiana and South India there arose stirring which further contributed to what God was doing. From about 1812 to 1820 there was a considerable correspondence between god-fearing men in these places who were concerned about the need of a demonstration of Scriptural fellowship among believers on the level of the local church.

In Dublin, a Roman Catholic doctor, Edward Cronin, came to a regenerating experience of Christ. From early in his Christian experience he was impressed by the truth of the essential oneness of God's people, and in order that he might give as full expression to this as possible, he made it his policy to attend various 'Independent' and nonconformist churches to partake of the Lord's table. He soon found, however, that these groups were unhappy with his attitude, and wanted that he should identify himself fully with one of them in order to preserve the privilege of breaking bread. This he felt he could not do as it was at once cutting him off from other believers and giving tacit approval to sectarianism. He confided his perplexity to a friend, and together they felt led to meet in one of their own houses for prayer and to remember the Lord. Others were added to their number, among them John G. Bellett and Anthony Norris Groves. The gathering was moved to a large room in the house of E. W. Hutchinson, a Dubliner. Anthony Norris Groves was a dentist by profession, and had come from Exeter. He had been led to Christ as a lad in his teens, but even before that had a great desire to become a missionary. After his conversion, and as he entered his professional career, the desire persisted, but his wife did not share his sense of commission. She was, however, a most devout Christian, and her husband and she were together completely given over to a life of witness for Christ. They were not without means, but they lived very simply and used the remainder in the service of the Lord. Groves had left his missionary call in the hands of God, and in a few years time his wife felt the constraint of the Spirit to yield her life also for the greater furtherance of the Gospel. Since they were attached to the Church of England, Groves felt that he should seek ordination and go abroad with the Church Missionary Society. With this end in view he went to Dublin for further studies at Trinity College. It was while there that his convictions underwent a change through the reading of the Scriptures, and John G. Bellett, who was a lawyer, and he joined themselves in fellowship with the group of believers meeting in the house of F. W. Hutchinson.

At the same time, in a different part of the city, another small company was meeting of a few people who had been constrained by like motive to come together. One of these was John V. Parnell who later became Lord Congleton. When, through the leading of God, these two groups became aware of each other's existence they united, gathering still in Francis' Hutchinson's home. God so blessed the witness that the gathering became too large to be accommodated in a private house, so a hall was rented in a convenient location and the meetings continued with the Lord adding unto them. One of their number who was to become widely known and exercise an extensive influence was

209

John Nelson Darby. J. N. Darby was a Londoner, but was serving in Ireland as an Anglican Curate. Like the others, his views underwent a radical change, so he left the established Church and from then on his considerable intellectual and spiritual gifts were at the disposal of the increasing number of assemblies which were coming into being in different parts. He eventually moved from Dublin and established himself in London where another assembly was formed. From there he moved widely amongst companies of believers in the ministry of the Word. One of the places Darby visited was Plymouth which was to occupy a role of considerable importance in this new moving of the Spirit.

The assembly of Plymouth was favoured with a number of teachers of the most outstanding ability, and under their ministry the gathering grew both in size and influence. At one time some eight hundred were in fellowship. It was here that the nickname 'Plymouth Brethren' originated, a name, of course, which was never recognised by the believers themselves. The best known of the Plymouth assembly's teachers was Benjamin Wills Newton, and J. N. Darby was widely known as being associated with the gathering. These two men were later embroiled in the dispute which was to be the beginning of the most regrettable division and dissipation of the testimony.

But we must turn our attention to Bristol where there was yet another rapidly developing fellowship of believers meeting in obedience to the Scriptures on the ground of their relationship with Christ. George Muller was born in Prussia in 1805 and was educated for the ministry although unconverted. It was through attendance at a Bible study group held in a private house in Halle, the great centre of Pietist activity, that the Spirit began to work in his heart. He found peace through faith in Christ, and grew quickly in the knowledge of the things of God through his diligent study of the Scriptures. His great desire came to be to work as a missionary among the Jews, and with this end in view he came to pursue further studies in England. It was while there that he was inspired by the example of Anthony Norris Groves who was abandoning a lucrative career to go to Mesopotamia without any earthly security. He also met Henry Craik who was to be his lifelong friend and was to share in the life of the assembly which ultimately grew up in Bristol. Muller's desire to work as a missionary among the Jews did not materialise, but through his fellowship with Craik he entered into a deeper understanding of the nature of the church.

210

As he sought the Lord, his understanding further increased. In 1830 Muller married A. N. Groves' sister, a godly woman who was to be a great help to him in later years.

The year 1832 saw the Mullers and Henry Craik in Bristol and the commencement of the testimony at 'Bethesda' which was to prove so fruitful. At first they numbered only eight, but with the Spirit's blessing the company grew and was increasingly active in work and witness. They met without any organization in simple dependence upon the Lord to lead them since they were one in Him.

As various questions arose, they searched the Scriptures for the answer, and God honoured their faith. Those who had formed the original company had all been baptized as believers, but the question soon arose as to whether they should accept into full fellowship those who had not been baptized yet were of undoubted godly character. At first there was some division of opinion on the matter, but as they sought the Lord they came to the conviction that they should receive all whom the Lord would receive irrespective of differences of understanding or measure of spiritual maturity. Never afterwards was the question of baptism a subject of dispute.

Eldership was another matter which urged them to a careful examination of God's Word. They saw that elders were not set apart by the formal vote of the church, or though the dictation of any man, but by the appointment of the Holy Spirit. The seal of their calling is the obvious mark of God's blessing upon their labours, their possession of the qualifications clearly laid down in Scripture, and their recognition by the church as divinely set apart. It is the duty of the church to submit to them in the Lord. Regarding ministry, it was understood that God endows some with special gifts and responsibility for the edifying of the church, but gift is not confined to these alone, and all must be given opportunity of expression that the church might benefit through whatever the Lord has given to each one. George Muller was possessed of a grace and sense of balance in holding spiritual convictions which is all too rare among God's people. He was fully aware that a truth given undue stress might cloud over a still more basic facet of the faith and bring irreparable loss to the whole church. Baptism, for example, if insisted upon as a condition of fellowship, immediately makes the practical expression of the unity of the body impossible and denies, therefore, the whole basis of the church.

Bethesda was greatly blessed by the mature and saintly counsel of Robert Cleaver Chapman, a not infrequent visitor to Bristol from Barnstaple from where he ministered the Word for about seventy years before his death in 1902 at the age of ninety-nine. Chapman's early training was in law, but he was led of God to give up his career and to devote himself entirely to teaching the Scriptures. His spiritual help and advice were sought by people from all over the world, and he himself travelled abroad in presenting the Gospel, exercising a ministry which was of lasting blessing.

George Muller was a great man of faith, and his name is most widely remembered through his Orphan Homes which he opened in Bristol. In this venture he was inspired by the example of August Francke of Halle who had developed a similar ministry over a hundred years previously, and had proved the faithfulness of the Lord to supply every need (see pp. 190-1). Muller opened his first Orphan House with twenty-six children in Bristol in 1836. From that small beginning the work grew in simple dependence upon God to meet every requirement, and the testimony to answered prayer has been a means of blessing right down to the present day.

Wherever God's people are, fellowship is soon established. There was a link of spiritual communion between the brethren in the north of Scotland and Bethesda and between brethren in many other places as well as Bristol, Plymouth and Dublin. Of organizational ties there were none, but spiritual relations in the family of God recognise one another wherever they go, and fellowship is at once established on the only true and lasting foundation, that of spiritual kinship.

Satanic powers are ever concerned to destroy the work of God. It is a significant fact that any attempt to return to a Scriptural conception of the church and the Scriptural ground of meeting is always fiercely assailed. This was true of the movement which we are at present considering. While one section continued to move on in the stream of blessing, another was the scene of the most lamentable controversy and division. It is almost impossible to calculate the number of divisions that have taken place through the years, to such an extent has the testimony been torn into fragments, and further divisions continue to occur. The first great split concerned the assembly at Plymouth which had known so much blessing, and two of the most gifted and devoted men were involved, B. W. Newton and J. N. Darby.

Darby and Newton had long held differences of opinion on

212

various matters of Scripture exegesis and church order which had given rise to a dangerous party spirit in Plymouth itself. No doubt Newton's dominance in the assembly was unsatisfactory, not because he did not deserve the respect of the able teacher he was, but because it limited the spiritual vision of those in the assembly whose loyalty to him tended to overshadow their loyalty to the Lord. Darby spent a considerable portion of his time on the continent, but returning from one of his tours in 1845 he went to Plymouth to deal with the disorder, as he felt it, existing in the church. It is hard to feel that his attitude was any less arbitrary than the attitude of Newton in ordering church affairs could have been. One Sunday morning, at the close of the meeting, Darby publicly announced that he was going to 'quit the assembly', and he left with those who supported him to gather separately. This, however, was but a prelude to the great issue of dispute that was raised some two years later.

During Bible readings which Newton had been giving on the Psalms, someone had taken notes which were then circulated among interested friends. It so happened that a copy of these notes came into the hands of one of Darby's sympathizers, and upon scrutinizing them, he found them to contain teaching respecting the sufferings of Christ which he felt was wrong, and so seriously wrong as to justify a charge of heresy. Newton was a man of undoubted ability, but he had a fault which is not altogether uncommon among able exponents of the Word. He could, at times, be so abstruse in his mode of expression that it was very difficult to understand exactly what he was driving at. That his comments on the Psalms were heretical was clear only to those who condemned him. The great controversy that was aroused showed that the notes, apart from being an unchecked account of what had been said, were so lacking in clarity that they could be interpreted in a variety of ways. Newton's critics had mingled bias with discernment and put the worst possible construction upon his teaching.

Newton's reaction to the charge was both humble and gracious. He affirmed the orthodoxy of his belief respecting the nature and work of Christ, while admitting that he had used expressions which were capable of an unorthodox interpretation. He did not, he said, hold to the doctrines that had been deduced from the notes of his addresses, and expressed profound sorrow that they should have caused spiritual injury to any of the Lord's people. Furthermore, he withdrew anything

213

written or spoken that might have been a cause of offence with a prayer for the Lord's forgiveness and that any evil effects might be counteracted. Newton's reply was published in a paper entitled, "A Statement and Acknowledgement respecting Certain Doctrinal Errors". It is a sad measure of the doggedness and lack of grace of his opponents that such a complete acknowledgement of anything that could be construed as error was absolutely rejected. The charge was pressed with untiring energy, and the reply was interpreted in the same spirit as the original notes. Darby 'excommunicated' Newton and the whole Plymouth assembly for condoning the teaching that Newton denied.

But matters did not rest there. The following year, 1848, two brethren from Newton's meeting in Plymouth visited Bristol and went to Bethesda where it was their custom to break bread while in the city. The brethren at Bethesda had remained strictly aloof from the Plymouth controversy, maintaining fellowship with both parties as fellow-believers, and in full consonance with this attitude welcomed the two brethren into fellowship since they were satisfied that they did not hold to the error that had been ascribed to Newton. In doing this, they maintained with Muller and Craik the principle of each assembly's independence and the assembly's right and responsibility to accept all whom they judge to belong to Christ. Darby, however, was dissatisfied. The two brethren, he held, came from an assembly where heresy was taught. They should not, therefore, be welcomed anywhere among the Lord's people since their fellowship with Newton in Plymouth showed that they condoned his error. Their presence in another assembly would introduce the same contamination there.

Darby demanded that Bethesda should judge the whole question of Plymouth. This they at first refused to do, since the dispute was not a matter in which they were involved, neither did they feel it right to sit in judgement on a whole assembly. Pressure, however, was insistent, and within Bethesda there were some who felt the question should be examined, so eventually they consented. In a letter detailing the results of their deliberations, signed by ten of the assembly's leading brethren, it was stated that no one would be received into fellowship who accepted the views attributed to Newton, but that even if Newton's doctrine were fundamentally wrong, no one coming from under his teaching could be rejected unless it was clear that he had understood and accepted the error. This reply was received by Darby with the utmost disapproval. Bethesda, he said, was being party to the error of Newton and must, therefore, be treated in the same manner. Now assemblies everywhere were urged to judge, not Plymouth, but Bethesda. Darby said that no one from Bethesda should be accepted, nor anyone who would have fellowship with them. Thus Darby excommunicated the church at Bethesda and all who would not hold them guilty of evil.

It was evident that this attitude would lead to wide dissension, for it was destructive of the very basis of the church. Believers were no longer to be united simply because of their relationship to Christ; another condition was added, condemnation of Bethesda. Even Darby's great personality could not win all over to such a position, but the measure in which he succeeded is wellnigh incredible. On the continent where Darby was widely known for his able ministry, and in other parts of the world as well, believers sat down to judge the 'Bethesda question', to condemn brethren they did not know, of heresy they did not hold, attributed to a man who did not teach it. And now, over a hundred years later, the 'Bethesda question' is still a live issue.

It was inevitable that such a spirit should lead to further divisions in later years, and their occurrence to the present day forms a sorrowful history of sometimes great spiritual insight and devotion sadly constricted by narrowness of mind and human prejudice. It is not within the scope of our present purpose to go into all the details of these seemingly endless disputes, but it is instructive to mention some of the reasons which have rent asunder assemblies of God's people. Differences on obscure points of doctrine have figured largely as causes of dissension. These are some of the doctrinal issues which have at various times led to division : the 'sealing of the Spirit', one party holding that the believer is 'sealed' at the new birth, the other that the believer is 'sealed' on 'seeing the risen Christ'; differentiation between a believer's 'standing' before God and his 'condition' before God; propitiation, as to whether made by Christ on the cross, or by Christ our High Priest in heaven; distinction between the new birth and receiving eternal life.

Another common cause of division has been disagreement on points of church order. A sadly outstanding example of the lengths to which some brethren have gone on an issue of church government occurred in 1881. In that year there was disorder in an assembly in Ryde in the south of England. The disorder was so persistent and so stultifying to spiritual life that some brethren, refusing to become involved in such harmful disputation, met together in Ryde as a separate assembly. During this time, Dr. Cronin, who was in London and in fellowship with the assembly at Kennington, visited Ryde and broke bread with the separated company of believers. Protest was raised in the Kennington assembly which went to considerable lengths to enquire into the matter and, having decided that Cronin had done wrong, and Cronin being unrepentant, excommunicated him. Meanwhile, the Ramsgate assembly was taking a close interest in matters. Some were not so much interested in what was happening at Ryde as in what they considered to be the tardiness of Kennington in taking action against Cronin for an obvious error, so part of Ramsgate assembly excommunicated the entire Kennington assembly for not excommunicating Dr. Cronin soon enough. This split the Ramsgate assembly, as those who did not agree with the action were forced to gather separately, and the question was referred to the assembly in Park Street, London, where Darby was in fellowship. There, some led by Darby judged in favour of the party which had censured Kennington, while others, led by Kelly, judged in favour of those who had not. Park Street assembly was split into two rival gatherings. So the process of destruction went on, dissipating the testimony and being fostered by some of the most able men of God.

The destructive principle which lay at the root of this lamentable state of affairs we shall examine a little later, yet these groups of brethren, given the odious name of 'Exclusives' which are today found in many parts of the world, have expounded aspects of Scripture truth which have been a blessing to many and are sadly lacking in the general life of the church today. They have produced a rich volume of exegetical literature which can be a source of immense spiritual profit, although, on the other hand, they have produced some works couched in so obscure and foreign a terminology that it is practically unintelligible to any who have not been nurtured in their own circle. We may legitimately lament the tragic divisions of the Exclusive brethren which have so limited the effect of their public testimony, but it would be entirely wrong to think that their testimony has been in vain. From their midst have come men of outstanding spiritual perception and godly character, and their writings have exercised an influence which has contributed substantially to the emergence in other parts of the world of churches meeting on the basis of life in Christ.

While the assembly at Plymouth saw the beginning of the stream of controversies and divisions we have just been considering, the assembly at Bethesda, Bristol, and others, such as the company at Barnstaple which came under the influence of Robert Chapman, continued on the ground of fellowship on which they had begun, accepting all who were accepted of Christ. These assemblies continued to grow in number, and their influence has extended to many parts of the world. Like the 'Exclusives' they have produced an extensive and valuable literature. As is amply demonstrated throughout the history of the church, the tendency of any movement of the Spirit to crystallize into a sect is never absent, and there are inevitably assemblies which have adopted the rigid ground of sectarianism, but there are others which have not.

There are certain particularly noteworthy factors about these companies of Christian believers. One is the consistent loyalty they have maintained to the inspiration of the Scriptures. The past hundred years has seen the penetration of rationalism into practically every major Christian denomination. Unbelief has been taught in theological colleges and preached from so-called Christian pulpits, but wherever there have been believers gathering on the simple principle of the New Testament churches, rationalism has been conspicuously absent. Not only has the Word of God been defended with spiritual and intellectual vigour, but it has been defended by the testimony of experience such as can be moulded only by God's unchanging truth. This surely is the greatest bulwark against error, the transforming experience of union with Christ. When a person knows that, whereas he was blind now he sees, all the arguments of unbelief fall to the ground as so much senseless clatter. As long as believers meet because they have been made partakers of the divine nature, the Bible will remain to them the Word of God, their spiritual food and drink.

It is also significant that familiarity with the Scriptures has not been confined to a few. The Bible has taken its place in the life of the family and the individual as an indispensable spiritual guide for daily living. Another important factor in the movement has been the witness it has produced in practically every stratum of social and business life. The emphasis that all believers are priests with the privilege of worship which issues in a responsibility of witness has not been confined to the

217

realm of theory, but has been given serious practical expression. This has resulted in incalculable spiritual blessing through the means of a quiet, consistent Christian testimony. An extension of this same factor has been a wide and vigorous missionary effort which has penetrated into most parts of the world. The movement which had its beginnings in Dublin, Plymouth and Bristol has been influential far beyond the meetings which might be specifically associated with it, and is but typical of similar movements which today can be found in many different countries.

The two different streams of development which issued from Plymouth and Bethesda can be more clearly examined by looking again at the experiences of two of the great men of God associated with them, J. N. Darby and A. N. Groves, so it is to them that we must turn in the next chapter.

CHAPTER EIGHTEEN

THE WITNESS SPREADS

J. N. Darby

JOHN NELSON DARBY's experience and teaching are of singular importance, not only because of the vital part he played in a return to the ground of Christian gathering, but also because of some of the misconceptions he later came to hold. A man of great devotion to the truth, spiritual insight and intellect, yet not without some of the limitations of which all mortal men are heirs, he was possessed of a logical consistency of purpose which demanded that whatever he saw of the truth should be put into effect and its implications honoured to the utmost possible degree. What he taught he practised, but when he set out upon a certain road he seemed unable to recognise the signs that were telling him he was going the wrong way. His experience demonstrates, on the one hand, the life of a man completely devoted to the Lord and, on the other, the spiritual havoc that can result when the mind is so fixed upon a principle that everything must give way before it, and the church itself can be sacrificed so long as the principle remains intact.

We have already mentioned J. N. Darby's early career, his association with the company of believers in Dublin, and his subsequent wider ministry elsewhere which took him for considerable periods to the continent. In 1838 he received an invitation from the French speaking part of Switzerland where he found wide scope for his great gifts. Rationalism, which had invaded most of organized religion, dominated the national Church, and there were many earnest children of God ready to welcome someone who preached the Word. The ground had also been prepared by the labours of others who had gone on before. Some twenty years previously, Robert Haldane had held his Bible readings in Geneva, and an assembly existed as a direct fruit of his labours, an assembly with which Darby maintained fellowship.

There were others who had received blessing through the ministry of Samuel Frohlich. Frohlich had studied theology

219

and had decided himself a Rationalist, but was brought to personal faith in Christ in 1825 at the age of twenty-two. He was ordained to the ministry of the State Church in Switzerland, but his evangelical beliefs and his enlightenment through the study of the Word of God led to his being deposed. He himself ministered the Word as far as Strassburg where he died in 1857, but his influence was felt over a much wider area. The companies of believers which came into being through his ministry or influence have been called Nazarenes, and can be found from the shores of the English Channel to the Black Sea. Frohlich's bitter experience at the hands of the great, organized Churches led him to fierce denunciations of the superficiality of nominal Christianity. The Nazarenes in eastern Europe and the Balkans have also been relentlessly persecuted which in some instances seems to have led to an excessively exclusive attitude where they feel that salvation is rare if not impossible outside their own circle, but their quiet faithfulness to the Lord under harsh conditions has been a testimony to those around them of the grace of God.

Darby, then, found a good foundation in Switzerland for the exercise of his gifts, but it was in Lausanne where a company of people gathered round him in an established meeting that he fully developed the line of teaching for which he is particularly known.

Darby's thought was ordered by his view that the dispensation and the church were in a ' state of ruin '. He saw the history of mankind divided into a series of dispensations in each of which God sought to establish a mode of relationship with man. Each of these dispensations, he pointed out, was ruined at the outset by man's sin or disobedience, and the aim of God in each particular dispensation was never, therefore, brought to fruition. One such example was the Israelites' worship of the golden calf when the dispensation of the law was being introduced. God's purpose had been that the whole nation should commune with Him as priests (Ex. 19 : 6), but their disobedience rendered this purpose impossible, and the priesthood was confined to the tribe of Levi, thus, according to Darby, bringing the whole dispensation into ruins. This same principle he applied to the dispensation of the church. At first, churches were established according to God's order, but in the time of the apostles themselves apostasy and decline had set in, shattering the church and frustrating what God had set out to do. Once this happened, said Darby, the dispensation was never restored.

220

One of the difficulties of Darby's view is that it practically leaves God in a position of permanent frustration, with but a few faithful left each time surveying the scene of desolation. That man is guilty of persistent disobedience to God is an obvious fact, but that God's purposes are thus so absolutely foiled is difficult to accept. If the bulk of the nation Israel rejected Him, yet there remained a remnant through whom He was able to work. It may be true that the world is in a state of apostasy hastening on to final judgement, but the divine purpose is not ruined. The pearl of great price, the church, has been found. The treasure, though hidden, is there. The cross has meant victory, not only in heaven, but wherever Christ is truly exalted here upon the earth.

Darby's misconception seems to have stemmed from a faulty idea of the nature of the church. He shows that the church originally was the gathering together of all believers in a particular locality, and that the sum of these congregations made up the church on earth. Although today we use the term 'church' in a variety of ways, Scripture does not call the sum of groups of believers living upon the earth the 'church'. The church, in its final sense, transcends the ages, and includes all who have been or who will be believers in Christ. Its earthly expression is composed of companies of believers each of which owns an immediate and direct relationship to the Lord, and which are related to one another simply by the bonds of the Spirit. Darby, however, interposed the conception of an earthly Church between the two, a Catholic Church system with a common order in which inclusion in or exclusion from one part of it was binding upon the whole. In this it would appear that he left the ground upon which he had first united with the believers in Dublin, and returned in principle to the ground of the Establishment from which he had separated.

But the church was, in Darby's view, a thing of the past. It was now in a 'state of ruin'. Indeed what he said is correct if we accept his basic assumption that the church of the New Testament and the professing Church in the world are one. That may have been so for a short time after Pentecost, but it did not long remain. Since, therefore, churches could not exist any more, what were believers to do? First of all, said Darby, they were not simply to imitate what the apostles did, but seek in the Word what God had to say regarding the present position. The fact of ruin had to be admitted, and believers should gather together in the unity of the body apart from the world.

The system of the church may have been destroyed but, Darby pointed out, there are 'certain unchangeable blessed principles from which all is derived'. Believers must return there, to the basic facts of the Lord's presence in the midst of His people exercising His authority and discipline. "For where two or three are gathered together in my name, there am I in the midst of them" (Matt. 18 : 20). The question naturally arises, if all is derived from these unchangeable principles, and they were the basis of the church in apostolic times, will not a return to these same principles today issue in the same result, namely, the formation of the church? Darby did not think so, and it was his refusal to recognize as the church that which in fact is the church, that led to the lamentable divisions which followed from his teaching. He felt he would have been committed to the church as to the body of Christ, but the fellowship of a company which did not have the status of the church could not be regarded as binding to the same extent, and liberty could be taken to separate from it on practically any pretext.

Yet although Darby condemned the formation of churches, the gatherings of the two or three which he advocated exercised a church's disciplinary powers. Those who were gifted of God to serve His people, he held, could be recognized, but not designated as elders, for where there was no church there could be no elders. These assemblies, therefore, possessed all the 'machinery' for maintaining order and exercising discipline, without the sense of responsibility and committal one to another which comes from the acknowledgement of God's having built His people together in the assembly. It was almost inevitable that widespread division should result. The unofficial 'machinery' of administration in the assemblies was also a denial of Darby's own wise counsel that what the apostles did was not to be blindly imitated. However much in theory he may have recognized the transient nature of the apostolic office at the beginning of the church era, in practice he really assumed an apostolic position. It was only the apostles or their representatives, he affirmed, who had the right to appoint elders, a position which cannot be supported from Scripture at all, and the apostle, therefore, emerged as the binding factor in a great, Catholic, church system. We have already seen the sad results of this in Darby's dealing with the Bethesda question, where he 'excommunicated' the whole assembly and set a precedent for the perpetuation of a practice which still continues. Darby's denial of Bethesda was purely and simply because he had departed from the ground of Christian gathering for which he originally left the established Church, and returned to an unscriptural, Catholic position.

To carry Darby's teaching to its logical conclusion would render much of the New Testament inapplicable to the circumstances of the present, since teaching given with reference to the churches can have little meaning if churches do not exist. Not that he or those who followed him ever denied the importance of Scripture. Just as they found a place for church order while refusing to accept the existence of churches, they found an application for New Testament teaching although refusing to accept the existence of the circumstances for which it was primarily meant. More serious than that was the result that was bound to accrue from such an intense occupation with 'apostasy' and 'ruin'. They became more concerned with what they were testifying against than what they were testifying for. Turned in upon themselves they have lost the power of vital growth.

Yet we must not detract from the very positive ministry that Darby exercised. His original mind penetrated into vital truths of Scripture, and set them forth with a spiritual power and conviction that resulted in great blessing. From France and the low countries, down into Italy, assemblies of believers came together occupied with the Word, the coming of the Lord and the witness and holy life that that great expectation encourages. Darby laid much emphasis on the liberty of the Holy Spirit to speak and work through God's people. If his teaching on the ruin of the church led to the constricted witness and thinking of some, his emphasis on the liberty of the Spirit led to the expanded witness and thinking of others. Where the Spirit is free to do His work of guiding into all truth, the thinking of one man cannot dominate indefinitely, and any unwise emphasis made by one will be corrected in what the Spirit reveals through another.

It is a great pity that J. N. Darby's experience should have been so characterized by the inflexibility with which he opposed other brethren in the Lord who disagreed with him. A kindly and gracious man by nature, all grace seemed to depart when engaged in a discussion on spiritual principles where minds differed. After the severing of his fellowship with Bethesda his relationship with George Muller was never restored, although attempts were made to bring them together. Muller, on his part, seemed to develop an answering spirit of distrust towards

Darby. It is a sad reflection on the subtlety of human nature that such an estrangement should exist between two great men of God. The breach had not been lessened when Darby died in 1882. Muller followed him to glory in 1898. We know that now they are united.

Anthony Norris Groves

When Groves left Dublin he still had in mind attaching himself to the Church Missionary Society, but as a layman. He found, however, that his ministry would be severely restricted, and that he would not be able to put into practice the convictions to which he had been led through the Scriptures regarding the nature of the church. Trusting wholly in the Lord to meet his needs, and upheld in prayer and fellowship by the assemblies of the Lord's people in Britain, he left for Baghdad in 1829 with his wife and family, travelling overland across the south of Russia. They were strengthened and blessed through the fellowship of companies of believers whom they met on the way. As the work in Baghdad got under way, opportunities of witness opened up in each of the various communities, but the missionary party was soon to undergo the severest trials.

In 1831 there were rumours of war, and plague broke out in Baghdad. Crowds fled in terror only to be confronted by the peril of an advancing army. Of the half of the population who remained in the city, hundreds were dying all around in the most awful conditions. All this time the waters of the Euphrates were rising, bringing devastation to the crops for miles in every direction. At length the water began to trickle into the city, and then poured in in a mighty flood sweeping thousands of houses away in the torrent. Food failed, and thousands of plague-ridden, famine-stricken people were huddled together for safety on what dry land remained. In the space of a mouth over thirty thousand people had perished. When the plague had passed its peak, Groves' wife was stricken down. All that could be done for her was of no avail, and she died shortly after. Then their youngest child, born to them in Baghdad, was taken away, leaving the father with the two elder boys.

As the waters assuaged and the plague abated, the advancing army laid seige to the city. Within, all law and order broke down. Robbery and violence prevailed, till relief came with the city's capture. The house in which the Groves were living was on somewhat higher ground and escaped the ravages of the floods, but all around was indescribable misery and desolation of which they had a full share. Yet the Lord had protected them from further physical harm in spite of the fact that their home had been attacked and plundered a number of times. One can imagine Groves' sore grief and trial yet, although he understood not what it all meant, the ministry in which they had laboured apparently shattered, and bereft of his wife and one child, his devotion and confidence in the Lord remained unshaken. "Notwithstanding all," Groves wrote, "He is a God of infinite love."

In 1832 the company in Baghdad was joined by Dr. Edward Cronin and John Parnell, both from the fellowship in Dublin, and Francis Newman. These were days of happy fellowship and activity in the preaching of the Word from which not a few were led to an experience of new life in Christ. The following year Groves went to India which was the scene of his most fruitful labours. He travelled in the company of Arthur Cotton, the great Christian engineer whose skill harnessed the waters of the mighty Godavari river to bring fertility to the Godavari delta.

Groves had a great desire to see a general return to the Scriptural ground of Christian gathering, and he felt this would be most easily accomplished in a country such as India where the roots of denominationalism had not as yet gone deep. Denominationalism he saw as a major hindrance to the effective spread of the Gospel. To counteract it he sought fellowship with all who were children of God, upholding a witness to the simple truth of Scripture regarding the church, and counselling obedience to the Word. His personal life and testimony were a widespread blessing. Groves' deep knowledge of the Scriptures both in mind and experience, his grace and unselfish devotion to the Lord had been matured in the school of affliction through which he passed in Mesopotamia, and his deep spiritual insight enabled him to see beyond the blessing of much outward activity. He was able to offer counsel which was wise and constructive. His friendship and counsel were valued, but only in so far as they did not impinge upon the spirit of sectarianism that was strengthening its hold upon those who professed faith in Christ. The preaching of the Gospel and the fellowship of the Lord's people in India had generally been uninhibited, but with the growth of the work, denominational organization was being strengthened, and each group was enclosing its adherents in an exclusive company after the

225

pattern of denominationalism in the West. Groves clearly saw the evil of this and earnestly sought to prevent it through his proclamation of the truth, but he found himself misunderstood, accused of adopting a superior attitude, and seeking to undermine the stability of the church organization. He was also deeply concerned by the failure of many missionaries to identify themselves with those whom they sought to reach with the Gospel. His determination that he would allow no distinction between himself and the people of the country to hinder the ministry to which he had been called bore fruit which is very much evident in the present day.

Groves, on a visit to England, married for the second time and, on returning to India, settled in Madras where he felt he should support himself for a time as Paul had done. He took up the practice of dentistry, at the same time continuing his ministry. Again he sought to help those in the various missionary societies, but was strongly criticized and found fruitful co-operation impossible. It was at this time that he left Madras for Chittoor. Groves encountered many difficulties, but neither was encouragement lacking. He possessed a happy knack of easy fellowship with all, an attitude which was free from any shadow of superiority, and his own example demonstrated the relationship between everyday work and Christian witness. He wanted to show that all who knew the Lord should serve the Lord. The influence which Groves' life exercised upon a few godly men was itself a justification of all the years he laboured in India, for from these few flowed out a tide of life and blessing which has contributed largely to what God is doing in the country today.

Probably the most outstanding of Groves' fellow-workers was Victor Aroolappen. Aroolappen's grandfather was a Roman Catholic, but was led to a saving knowledge of Jesus Christ through the ministry of the great Pietist missionary from Halle, Christian Schwartz. Aroolappen himself was nurtured in the Gospel, but his fellowship with Groves was the means of strengthening his faith and establishing his mind in the Scriptural truths respecting the church. A man of marked ability and spiritual gift, he consistently refused the offer to associate himself with any denominational group, and moved throughout the South of India ministering the Word to the lasting blessing of many. The fruit of his labours have been multiplied through the generations, and from the line of his own family God has raised up men of a like spirit whose service has been one of the main contributing factors to a further movement of the Spirit through which God has been calling together assemblies of His people throughout India within recent years.

Anthony Norris Groves died in 1853 while in England at the home of George Muller in Bristol. It is interesting to note the attitude of Groves to the teaching that was being developed by J. N. Darby. Throughout his life he regarded Darby with the greatest respect, but that did not prevent his recognizing the grave dangers implicit in what he taught. In a letter written to Darby in 1836 he frankly voiced his fears, expressing his conviction that he had departed from his original principle that the ground of fellowship is possession of the life of Christ, that the companies which had grown up around him would more and more gather on the ground of doctrine or man's opinion, and that they would soon find within themselves the same evils as existed in the systems from which they had separated. These were prophetic utterances, a further indication of Grove's own discernment and of the importance that the fellowship of the Lord's people should never be narrower than the fellowship that the Lord Himself owns.

The nineteenth century saw an impetus to significant development along two other lines, the increased dissemination of the Scriptures worldwide by means of Bible Societies, and the growth of undenominational 'faith' missions, also exercising a worldwide influence. The essential tool of all missionary activity is, of course, the Word of God, but the Bible made available in a constantly increasing number of languages, itself accomplished a spiritual work even apart from further organized missionary efforts. An outstanding example of the power of God's Word was its effect throughout the Russian Empire from about 1812 when the Czar Alexander I allowed the British and Foreign Bible Society freedom to open branches in some of the remotest corners of his domain. Opposition to the distribution of the Scriptures was sometimes extreme and came mainly from the ruling Orthodox Church, but, in spite of persecution, the opportunity to read and make available the Bible in Russian and the various languages of the Empire remained till the Bolsheviks came to power.

The word of the Gospel had penetrated Russia through some of the Mennonite colonists and others, but these communities remained largely separate, living their own lives with special privileges and religious freedom granted them by the government on condition that they did not attempt to proselytize among the Russians. The impact of godly lives and personal words of witness no doubt had an effect on many, but it was directly through the reading of the Word of God that groups of believers began to come into being and spread to the Empire's utmost corners. They accepted no sectarian name, and called one another 'brethren', but they were dubbed 'Stundists', that is 'meeting-goers' a word which originally came from the gatherings of the German colonists.

The reading of the Scriptures was to these Russians a revelation of spiritual truth and power such as they had never before conceived. The Orthodox Church in which they had been brought up with its deadening forms and traditions had left them in ignorance of God and the transforming power of personal faith in Christ. The Bible revealed Christ, and in seeing Him they knew the touch of regenerating grace. Since freedom to read the Word, much less liberty to obey it, was denied them in the Russian Church, they separated from it to meet around the Lord who dwells in the midst of the two or three. As the Spirit taught them they were eager to obey. Baptism and the Lord's table were observed. The old clerical system was abandoned, and elders were raised up from the midst of the churches according to the Scriptures. They found that God still gives to all some gift for the building up of the assembly, that the Gospel be spread abroad, discipline be maintained, and the saints be edified.

The vast majority of Czarist Russia's population were peasants, but the work of the Spirit penetrated every section of society. The homes of some of the aristocracy were open to Lord Radstock for Bible readings. His able expositions of the Scriptures were the means of many conversions and the further spread of the Gospel through those whose lives had been changed by faith in Christ. Another well-known name associated particularly with the distribution of the Word of God is that of Dr. Baedeker of travel-guide fame. His journeys, however, were of much more than geographical interest. He had an eternal aim in view, and was active in distributing the Scriptures in Russia during a period of the severest oppression at the end of the last century.

The union of the Church and State in Russia had always been the means of imposing sanctions upon those who dissented from the official religion, but the assassination of the Czar Alexander II in 1881 brought a violent reaction determined to crush every protest against either the temporal autocracy of the State or against the spiritual autocracy of the Orthodox Church. Believers were forbidden to gather together. When it was found that they continued to meet secretly, the meetings were broken up and they were punished by fine, imprisonment, or exile to the far corners of the Empire. But even this was a means of spreading the Gospel, for the Lord's people witnessed wherever they went, and the distribution of the Scriptures continued. In an all-out effort to stamp out the 'Stundists' as they were called, they were debarred from many occupations, forbidden to move from one place to another, and their children were taken from them to be brought up by those who were loyal to the Orthodox Church or placed under the guardianship of the clergy.

Yet the working of the Spirit continued. Its extent was only fully revealed in 1905 when religious liberty was at last proclaimed, and many hidden groups of believers came out into the open. But the freedom was of comparatively short duration. The companies of God's people were again being persecuted when the Great War broke out in 1914. 1917 saw the beginning of the Russian Revolution when a new terror swept throughout the land over the ruins of the old, Imperial Russia and the Orthodox Church. Atheism was forcibly imposed upon the country, but the eternal Gospel is not so easily destroyed by the temporal might of man. As religious persecution has been moderated over the years, there are indications that the great steppes and mountains which extend from the shores of the Baltic to the borders of China are not without a vital testimony to the regenerating power of a risen Christ.

The last hundred years have seen the formation of numerous undenominational missionary societies based mostly, but by no means exclusively, in Europe and North America. They have accepted the challenge of the Lord's final command to His disciples to take the Gospel into all the world, and have carried the message of salvation into some of the remotest corners of the globe. These 'undenominational faith missions' as they are generally called, form a development which is of wide significance. Although their aim has been to see churches established wherever they have gone, their own fellowships in the countries of their origin are something apart from the organized churches. That such societies should ever have come into being is itself an indictment of denominationalism, and shows the need felt by many men and women of God for something more than is to be found in general Church circles if the stated purpose of the Lord in the church is to be fulfilled. It is true that some

P

of these societies have built their efforts round a particular doctrinal emphasis such as, for example, the Wesleyan view of 'sanctification', but the great majority of them comprise men and women, maybe differing in doctrinal outlook, yet who are united with one another as born again of the Spirit into the family of Christ. In this respect, therefore, they have partly returned to the simple basis of the New Testament church, and have demonstrated that, apart from a common and firm acceptance of the basic, Biblical facts through which regeneration is experienced by those who believe, detailed doctrinal agreement is in no way necessary to spiritual unity, fellowship or service.

That multitudes of people all over the world have been brought to a vital experience of Christ through the devoted labours of those working in the fellowship of 'faith missions' is a fact for which all true children of God should be profoundly thankful. Their selfless service has had an effect which eternity alone will reveal. On the other hand, there have been weaknesses. The great failure of missions, as is commonly recognized today, has been that their ministry has not resulted in the establishment of churches of Biblical simplicity and authority. Too often, in fact mostly, they have produced but replicas of the denominational system of the West, with all their attendant shortcomings. This has been the case not only with the work of denominational missions. They, obviously, have set out to reproduce the same type of organization as that to which they belong. It has, unfortunately, been almost equally the case with missionary societies which have possessed a much more Scriptural basis of fellowship. To such an extent has the denominational complex laid hold upon Western Christianity, that even undenominational missions in foreign lands have built up denominations based upon their own particular societies.

These, however, are not the sole expressions of Christian testimony worldwide. Churches as they were in the times of the apostles have never ceased to exist, as we have seen, and wherever God works through the power of His unchangeable Word, people made partakers of the divine nature, anxious to obey the Word which has shed a flood of light into their souls, have gathered together and are gathering together as the disciples did in the Acts. In many countries of the world today such churches exist and continue to grow in number. They are not the direct result of organized missionary effort, but neither can they be divorced from it. The church is not 'indigenous' in the sense that it can be the product of a particular land or a particular race. The church is the product of the Word of God, whether it be preached by a person with a fair skin or a dark one, and wherever the church emerges founded upon Christ and dependent upon Christ, it is in answer to the faithful proclamation of the eternal truth, by whomsoever it has been proclaimed. To claim that it is due to the efforts of one nation is pride and a denial of the basic truth of the church that all human barriers are destroyed at the cross. The church transcends race. It has the quality of the eternal and the divine, and is the product of the divine Word through whomsoever it has pleased God to channel it.

As we have pursued the history of the spiritual movement of the church, one thing surely has been clear, that the working of the Spirit of God in any one age or in any one country cannot be viewed as an isolated outpouring of grace. Every movement could trace its vital beginnings back for centuries, and would find that God had contributed through people of different countries and races the elements of truth and light which ultimately led to the restoration of an outstanding church testimony. That it should be so is, in fact, part of church life itself, that the whole body is 'fitly framed and knit together through that which every joint supplieth, according to the working in due measure of each several part' (Eph. 4 : 16). Outstanding movements of the Spirit of God today could be cited in China, India and other countries. Their origin is not in a man, but in God, although God uses men to accomplish His purposes. Their basis is the life of the Spirit, their rule is the Word, and the breadth of their fellowship is not national, but the breadth of the church. If in any instances they have become constricted to a purely national outlook, to that extent they have become sectarian.

An instance of a spiritual movement of far-reaching importance and influence in Japan today is associated with the name of Kanzo Uchimura. Uchimura, the son of a Samurai scholar, born in Tokyo, had his first contact with the Gospel during his student days in Sapporo, Hokkaido. There he took a stand as a Christian, but it was to an experience years later in North America that he attributed his real conversion, when he entered into new life in Christ through faith. That experience changed the whole course of Uchimura's life, and he returned to Japan with a burning zeal to proclaim the simple word of the Gospel, uncluttered by sectarian accretions, to his own countrymen.

A man of forceful character, and a prolific writer, Uchimura

231

edited or contributed to a number of journals both in Japanese
and in English. But his outstanding work was the encouragement he gave to gatherings for the study of the Scriptures. He
held one such gathering in Tokyo till his death in 1930. Other
groups of a similar nature have sprung up throughout the
country and in other countries as well. They meet in homes
or in hired halls, in town and in country, some numbering
hundreds, others but two or three, but all seeking to enter into
a closer understanding of Christ through His Word. These
meetings became known as 'Mukyokai' which means 'non-
church', not signifying a denial of the Scriptural fact of the
church, but a denial of the organized systems of Christendom as
being what was meant in the Scriptures. Uchimura believed
that the complexities of denominationalism have covered over
the truth of what the church was meant to be which is simply
the unity of those who have received new life in Christ, not a
unity determined by creeds, forms or ceremonies.

Mukyokai groups are completely independent one of another
which was attested by the fact that, during the last war, the
Japanese government had to deal with each one of them separately, while they were able to amalgamate other churches into
a federation recognised by the State, which could be easily
controlled. After the prevalent fashion, Mukyokai has been
'denominationalised' by those who have viewed it from outside.
It was looked upon, during Uchimura's lifetime, as the work
of a brilliant man and dependent upon him. In an article entitled 'Non-Church Christian Work in Japan' in the Japan
Mission Year Book of 1931, F. W. Heckleman writes of ". . . the
work of Uchimura Kanzo, which was, up to his death unique
for Bible Study, personal experience, and the publishing of a
Bible Study Magazine. This work is now at a standstill, and
may end for want of a leader; but it is not possible now to state
what the future will be." It is interesting to view this statement well over thirty years after Uchimura's death. If Mukyokai
was at a standstill in 1931 it is certainly not at a standstill today,
but forms, without doubt, one of the most powerful Christian
influences in the country. It has survived the ravages of war
and continues to expand because it was based not on the experience of one man, but upon the unchanging Word of God.

While the twentieth century has seen materialistic forces
apparently win the allegiance of hundreds of millions, yet there
has also been a spread of the Gospel unparalleled in previous
years. These are days of rich, spiritual harvest in many parts

of the world, when the seed that has been sown in toil and tears is blossoming forth. There is also, in not a few countries, an unprecedented desire to return to the simplicity in Christ which was demonstrated by the early churches. A volume alone could be written about what God is at present doing in this respect, gathering together His people as He did in New Testament times. The day will no doubt come when that volume should be written, but, for the present, it is the path of wisdom to allow God to do His work without attempting to acclaim those whom He is using as His instruments. We are living in an age supremely conscious of technique and man's own skill, an age given over to hero worship. Unfortunately, this is not a tendency altogether foreign to the people of God, and it is but too easy to give to men, albeit unwittingly, a glory that should go to God alone. How easy it is to lay more emphasis on a 'Prophet' of God than on the word he bears. But the 'Prophet' will pass away, and the Word only remains. It is when the 'Prophet' has gone and the Word still abides with its same power and authority that we can most surely judge what has been of God and what has been of man.

CHAPTER NINETEEN

THE TORCH OF THE TESTIMONY

WHAT has been reviewed in the previous chapters of the history of the spiritual movement of the church comprises but a small part of the New Testament witness to Christ that has been owned of the Spirit down through the ages. Eternity alone will reveal the full extent of God's working through companies of faithful believers, the memory of whose testimony and very existence have been obliterated by the prejudice of an organized and carnal Christianity which saw in the spiritual authority of the subject twos and threes an indictment of its own spiritual impotence. But what is the relevance of the Spirit's activity in the past to the attitude and service of the Lord's people in this the twentieth century?

The whole subject of the church may appear fraught with complexities, and the term 'church' itself is used in so many ways that the inconclusiveness of its modern use often adds to the confusion. Yet Scripture is not confused. The perplexity which the subject arouses, arises not nearly so much in a failure to understand what the Bible says, as in a failure to apply what the Bible says to the general Church of Christendom. If we could but set the whole anomalous development of Christendom aside and begin with the Word of God alone and a mind to obey it, is it to be supposed that our problem would be just the same? "Of course not," would be the answer, "but that is just what we cannot do, set the whole anomalous development of Christendom aside. We must accept the situation as it exists, and begin there." Is that not the crux of the whole matter? Granted the chaotic fact of organized Christianity cannot be ignored, but in our seeking the mind of Christ, is that really where we must begin, in a prime occupation with what has been produced by an alliance of the ingenuity of man and perverted or limited truth? Should we not begin with the Word of God itself? Surely if the history of the church teaches us anything at all, it teaches us that the testimony, be it that of an individual or of an assembly, that has been honoured of God, has been the testimony established on His Word. All spiritual blessing and

234

advancement begins there, not in an attempt to accommodate certain Scriptural precepts to an existing religious system, but in an unconditional desire to honour the Word of God.

It is precisely here that the failure of so much Christian thought lies today. The great bulk of Christian service in these days is conditioned by a largely unquestioned acceptance of organized Christianity as the church. The Church is regarded as a field of evangelism in which the Gospel must be preached and which must be revitalized by the coming of revival. The establishment of churches according to the Word is of little concern, and the effort to promote revival takes its place. Thus the preaching of redemption becomes an end in itself, and the full message of the Gospel which is concerned not only with the salvation of the individual, but with his relationship in the church and all that entails, is left half proclaimed. We are not deluded into thinking that the preaching of personal salvation is no longer necessary, simply because the spiritually powerless and defeated lives of men and women all around us often happen to sport a 'Christian' label, yet the existence of no less spiritually powerless and defeated organized Christianity has terribly deluded us into thinking that the preaching of the church is no longer necessary. The church exists, so that part of the Gospel no longer applies, we reason, when in fact, according to the standard of Scripture, the church may not exist at all, but only a name. It is apt to note how full was the message preached by the apostle Paul. He was, he says, a minister both of the Gospel and of the church (Col. 1 : 23-25). By no means did he minimize the importance of personal redemption as basic to the whole of God's purpose, but he recognized that the consummation of God's purpose was in the church, and to leave it out of his message would be to be content with only half a Gospel.

If 'church' is one word that is commonly misused, 'revival' is another. In the Old Testament, revival signified the restoration of a devotion to the Lord that had grown cold. When we speak of revival today we generally refer to some outstanding response to the Gospel, a receiving of spiritual life where before there had been death, usually within the context of the organized Church. It is significant that the New Testament knows no parallel to the modern conception of revival. The instances of a spectacular working of the Spirit of God as, for example, at Pentecost, recorded in the book of Acts, were of a completely different nature, and were essentially of the same nature as the

Old Testament outpourings. To equate generally the spiritual experience of Jews and Gentile adherents of the synagogue with the conversion experience of those of a later age is misleading, as has already been pointed out in one of the early chapters of this book. The faithful who, in full trust and devotion to God, awaited the coming of the Messiah and joyfully accepted Christ as the fulfilment of that hope were not passing at that precise moment from estrangement into fellowship with God. The work of the cross was as effective before the historic event of Calvary as after it, and faith made it real in justification as the writer to the Hebrews reminds us. Furthermore, the revival of Pentecost led to the establishment of the church. We do not in the New Testament read of any such revival within a church already established. The point is not to decry or minimize the importance of any spiritual awakening God might vouchsafe to send. We thank God for every touch of genuine revival and pray for more, but it would seem from Scripture that it is something extra, as it were, to the purpose God has set out to fulfil in calling together the church. Revival may be a vital, contributing factor to God's purpose, but is not itself the fulfilment of His design.

The Old Testament revivals under Hezekiah and Josiah are interesting in this connection. Why is it that the prophets Isaiah and Jeremiah who were engaged in their prophetic ministries during the periods of these great outpourings, so completely ignore them? May the answer not be that the heart concern of the prophets was the continuance of the stream of God's purposes through a remnant prepared for the revelation of the Messiah? All that was basic to the plan of God lay there. The revivals were but a parenthesis, albeit a glorious one, in the divine plan, and their ultimate value would be determined by what they contributed to the stream of God's eternal purpose.

The history of the spiritual movement of the church aptly illustrates what has just been said, and the problem of modern missions further confirms the view. In many countries of the world, the cry is that a church has been produced which is not itself productive. Evangelism, or maybe revival, has begotten that which has not the strength to beget. Redemption has not been followed by the church, and the result is spiritual barrenness.

In our review of the great revival outpourings under Wesley and Whitefield, it has been suggested that their main significance lies in their preparation of the way for the outstanding return to the ground of Christian fellowship and gathering of the nineteenth century. That does not detract in the least from the mighty work that was accomplished through the ministry of these two great men of God, but it does indicate that the ministry of no one man is complete in itself. It is but contributory to what God is doing through others, and all finds its full expression in the church towards which all ministry must flow. The difficulty is that the gift of the evangelist is much more readily accepted than the gift of the teacher. The born again Christian views with no prejudice the preaching of redemption, but deep rooted prejudice and traditional loyalties may often be touched by the teaching of the Word, so we dismiss the teaching that offends, hold on to evangelism and our prejudices as well, making the manifestation of the church impossible. How many of us have really learned not to be offended in Christ?

Evangelism or revival must find its consummation in the church; the church must be founded upon the living Word, Christ; the organized Church of Christendom, therefore, cannot be accepted as a *fait accompli* in place of what the written Word so clearly reveals.

What then is to be our attitude to it, since it can be neither accepted nor ignored? In this the Scriptures do not leave us without an answer. No situation is foreign to the Word of God, and before the apostle Paul laid down his life for his faith the declension had already set in which still characterizes the Christian scene. It is dealing with this very question that Paul wrote his last letter, the second epistle to Timothy, a young servant of God who was, no doubt, as perplexed by the prevailing confusion of his time as many people of God are today. The second epistle of Paul to Timothy is of immense significance for the present age.

Paul's message is succinctly summed up in four verses, 2 Tim. 2 : 19-22. First of all, he says, " The foundation of God standeth, having this seal, The Lord knoweth them that are his : and, Let every one that nameth the name of the Lord depart from unrighteousness " (vs. 19). All around may be declension and confusion, but the Lord knows His own people, and His own people know Him. The proof of their knowledge is that they desire to obey Him and live lives separated from unrighteousness. This sums up God's personal relationship to each one of His own, and their individual responsibility towards Him.

Paul now turns to the scene of confusion, the structure of

professing Christendom. He likens it to a great house containing vessels of value and vessels that are worthless (vs. 20). Here it is, the mixture that is called the Church. Paul almost implies that such a mixture is inevitable, but is it to be accepted because of that? "If a man therefore purge himself from these," he goes on to explain, " he shall be a vessel unto honour, sanctified, meet for the master's use, prepared unto every good work " (vs. 21). From whomsoever or whatever it be interpreted that a man should ' purge himself ', this verse leaves the child of God standing solely in his relationship to the Lord outside any Church or organization. He is back precisely at the place where he was spiritually born, knowing only that he is alive in Christ, and has to rediscover his relationship in the divine family. He stands where alone he is free and usable.

What, finally, is his responsibility in such a situation? " Follow after righteousness, faith, love, peace, with them that call on the Lord out of a pure heart," says the apostle. From the ground of our individual relationship with Christ we have moved on to the ground of the church, where the two or three are gathered together in His name, and He is in the midst of them. There is no detailed description given whereby we may know God's people. Paul's words, " Them that call upon the Lord out of a pure heart," leaves the transparent sincerity of the believer to be discerned by the believer. " The Spirit himself beareth witness," Paul says in another place (Rom. 8 : 16). It may be difficult to explain in terms that would satisfy an unregenerate man how children of God recognise one another, but the witness of the Spirit is a reliable guide. Human judgement may becloud that witness and mistakes can be made, but as long as the Spirit's witness is the guide, the question of fellowship will never be a problem. It is when some test to satisfy man's mind is set as a qualification for fellowship, by-passing the witness of the Spirit, that difficulties arise.

The separated company of the church will be characterized by four things, righteousness, faith, love, peace, all matters of the heart, not of the head. They all leave much room for development, and development necessitates knowledge. A mind applied to know Christ is of vital importance for spiritual maturity, but only if it is directed by a heart already related to Him. Righteousness is the obvious outcome of regeneration; where there is the nature of Christ there will also be the character of Christ. Faith is the attitude of complete dependence upon God and subservience to Him which alone allows the Spirit to work.

Love is the outflow of the Spirit's life within us to one another. Peace is the satisfaction of knowing the Lord in the midst.

These are the simple elements of the church from which the people and purposes of God can grow to maturity. They are the elements of life, life which is reproductive, but to be reproductive it must remain free. The organization of Christianity has again and again, down through the centuries, led to barrenness. It has been when the life of the Spirit has burst the constricting bands of denominational organizations that the church has been revealed in its primitive power and authority.

The testimony of the church is positive, not merely reactionary. Doubtless, an element of reaction remains, inasmuch as the righteousness of Christ rightly reacts against the ungodliness of the world, but the separated church of 2 Timothy 2 : 22 is pre-eminently a testimony to the truth, not a testimony against error. It is a testimony to the truth that all who are born of the Spirit into the family of Christ are one, and must grow and witness together in the fellowship of the church where the Lord dwells in their midst. The church meets on that positive ground, neither adding anything to it, nor taking anything away. But it entails sacrifice. It means the taking up of the cross, the cross of misunderstanding, of shame, of being called ' separationists '. Yet every spiritual movement has begun in sacrifice. That is another of history's lessons.

The true church is the scene of a continual, spiritual struggle for its own existence. " Hold the pattern of sound words which thou hast heard from me," Paul exhorts Timothy (2 Tim. 1 : 13). If we do not hold firmly on to the fellowship of the church, it will slip from our grasp. It is of all things most vehemently assailed. It is tempted to compromise with organized Christianity. It is tempted to organize itself in order to conserve what it has gained. It is tempted to sectarianism by limiting its growth to a certain emphasis of Christian truth. When it succumbs to any of these temptations, declension follows, for progress has been limited, and when it has reached the end of its possible progress, it must fade out as a spiritual power. This is the picture that history so graphically portrays, the picture of spiritual power followed by declension, but from every scene of declension God calls out His remnant. The denominations of today are often the churches of yesterday. They each carried the torch of the testimony so far, then strayed from the path to rest content with what they had achieved. But the torch was taken up by others, and will be borne forward till the Lord Himself comes. The church, therefore, knows no organizational continuance. Its continuance lies in the spiritual life of the Lord's people wherever it has the opportunity of manifesting itself by their coming together in His name.

It is God's order today as much as it was in New Testament times that His people should gather simply on the ground of their relationship with Him, but we do well to look a little more closely at some of the temptations involved if we are to continue to be allowed to bear the torch of the testimony. In the many examples cited of God's working, it will be noted how often one or two gifted men have played a particularly prominent role. This has been of God's ordering, for God works through His people according to the gifts He gives them. Yet every spiritual movement is much greater than any man. To understand this is easy in retrospect, but not always so easy in fact, where people live so much by sight while protesting that they live by faith alone. It is much easier to gather round a man than round the Lord, and the church will always face this temptation where the Lord finds a vessel particularly meet for His use. The world and organized religion will ever be ready to help them, to call them followers of a Priscillian or a Wycliffe or a Haldane, anything but followers of Christ. It was this danger to which the assembly at Corinth had nearly succumbed when Paul wrote his first letter to them.

The assembly based on the sure ground of Scripture faces a most subtle peril, the peril not of willingly accepting a denominational or sectarian position, but of allowing itself to be pushed into it. 'Exclusivism', among those who are truly children of God, is an odious word. The assembly is separate from worldly and ecclesiastical organizations not to be exclusive, but to be inclusive, for it is only outside the camp of denominationalism and sectarianism that a welcome for all who are regenerate can be maintained whatever their own religious background. What are more exclusive than the great systems of organized Christianity? Witness, for example, the feverish concern of modern ecumenicalism for 'unity', and the difficulties of agreeing on a basis of inter-communion simply because it is 'against the rules' in so many denominations. In other words, denominationalism is basically exclusive. It is so because it is based upon limitation, the acceptance of one aspect of divine truth, the acceptance of a particular rule or form, the acceptance of one man's interpretation of Scripture. When an assembly allows itself to be forced into that position of limitation, it becomes denominational.

Throughout the centuries, God's people who have sought fellowship only around Christ have struggled for namelessness. Consistently they have denied the name of some man or other label which has been attached to them, desiring only that they should be known as Christians, or brethren, or by such other simple designation as might find warrant in Scripture. It has always appeared to be a losing battle, and to some it may appear unimportant, yet when a company of believers has been willing to accept a name, it has also accepted the limitations that have gone with it. The struggle for namelessness is not an insignificant factor in the struggle of the church for its existence.

A little more may be said on doctrine and pattern in the church. The history of the spiritual movement of the church is the history of spiritual life. The fellowship of the church must be based squarely on the fact of spiritual life. What then is the relevance of doctrine and pattern? The latter part of the nineteenth century saw a widespread revolt against dogma. The widest liberties were allowed in the acceptance of the credal statements of the large denominations, with the result that they could mean anything or nothing, and it is today quite common to find within one denomination leaders who hold views that are poles apart, and some views that are quite incompatible with personal faith in Christ. It is often stated that the lack of unambiguous doctrinal statements with an insistence on a strict mode of interpretation is responsible for this state of affairs. But is this so? Rather does it seem that confusion and powerlessness exist, not because doctrine does not matter, but because nothing matters. Doctrine does matter, but the understanding of the things of Christ is the outflow of the life of Christ. The development of the great doctrines of grace in Scripture by the apostles was the result of their passionate devotion to the Saviour. Apart from that relationship of devotion born through regeneration, the most orthodox doctrinal statement or no doctrinal statement at all will equally mean spiritual death.

Spiritual life, where it is the sole basis of the fellowship of the church, is not unconcerned about doctrinal matters. On the contrary, it is vitally concerned, and always concerned, so that doctrine is not something learned out of a text book and finished with, but a progressive entering into more and more of the fulness of the Word of Truth. The Bible starts with experi-

241

ence, and from there moves on to fuller understanding. The dynamic experience of union with Christ cannot but determine our attitude towards Him. Which person, who has been truly regenerated, could believe that the Lord Jesus Christ was only a fallible human being? Those who belong to the family of God will develop a doctrine that is honouring to Him. History teaches us that dogma alone can never protect the spiritual life of the church, but the life of the Spirit is itself the surest protection of sound doctrine.

If, as has already been stated, the church knows no organizational continuance, it follows that pattern is not the prime mark of the New Testament assembly. Not that pattern is unimportant, but a church cannot be established by merely setting up what is thought to be a Scriptural form. It is not simply a matter of applying the correct technique.

The New Testament does not specifically set down rules and regulations whereby the fellowship of the church should be governed as, for example, instructions were given for the building of the tabernacle in the Old Testament. What may be deduced as details of a church pattern in the Acts or the Epistles were but the natural means whereby the outflow of the life of the Spirit manifested itself. Scripture always commences there, with life, and where spiritual life is truly uninhibited, spiritual pattern follows. That does not mean that the churches will show wide diversity of pattern. Differences there will be from one place to another, just as there was not a rigid sameness about the assemblies in apostolic times, but we have seen amply demonstrated through the centuries that although churches may grow up in different countries completely independent of one another, yet the pattern of their fellowship is not greatly dissimilar. Just as spiritual life determines doctrine in the church, it also determines pattern. The principle of fellowship, for example, in the family of God where all believers are priests, immediately excludes the acceptance of a distinction between clergy and laity and the adoption of an episcopal form of government. Wherever people are willing to obey the implications of spiritual principles as found in the Word of God, they will find that assembly order does not leave a great deal to be determined by human choice, neither does it allow the application of a cold, mechanical form. The development of the highly organized systems of denominational Christianity as we know them today has no valid, spiritual reason, and has but served to preserve 'Churches' which could

fellowship

otherwise exist no longer since the life of the Spirit has departed from them.

The spiritual life and the Scriptural order of the church go together. The order is the outcome of life, but it is also conversely true that the continuance of life is dependent on the order. All believers are priests and all are witnesses. The assembly does not recognise any member of its fellowship as a non-participant. The assembly is the focal point of Christian service and responsibility. Its order must encourage the constant flow of spiritual life, otherwise the order itself will be destroyed. Neither can it attract to its fellowship those who are unregenerate. The life and work of the assembly can afford no lasting lure to the unconverted, for fellowship, worship, intercession, are things which are foreign to the life of this world.

In some countries today there is great concern among the large Christian bodies to make the Church popular. Every conceivable scheme is being brought into play in order to attract people to the Church. It is forgotten that the true church can never be attractive to the world, and was never meant to be. It is something which is completely beyond the world's understanding. People are brought into the church through the witness of the Lord's children who comprise the church. When the life of Christ is expressed through a spiritual order, believers will maintain a witness that is spiritually effective. Others will be regenerated, and they will be added to the church, not because they, as worldly people, were attracted to it, but because they have been subject to a divine change which enables them to enter into life on a higher plane. The church's mission is not to fit in to the world, but to see men changed so that they will fit in to the church.

unless their hearts are longing for the Spirit's life.

The church of the New Testament is no mere theory. It is a fact of this, the twentieth century, as it was of the first. The principles of the unchanging Word of God, having been demonstrated and tested for almost two thousand years, have proved themselves applicable to every age and every circumstance. The church authoritative, holy, witnessing, invincible has continued and will continue, not in outward show and ostentation, but wherever the Lord has found a people willing to gather round Him in submission and obedience. It is a church that is indissolubly one, bound by ties of the Spirit. Amid the bitter conflicts and tragedies of so-called Church history, the life of the spiritual movement of the church has flowed on through the ages. The splendid unity of a heavenly race, living a heavenly life passed down from spiritual generation to spiritual generation has never been broken. They are pilgrims and strangers still upon the earth, bearing the reproach of Christ outside the camp, pressing 'on toward the goal unto the prize of the high calling of God in Christ Jesus'. They gather round Christ their Head, owning His Word their guide, bearing the torch of the testimony.

BIBLIOGRAPHY

The Life and Epistles of St. Paul	W. J. Conybeare
A History of the Christian Church	Williston Walker
The Pilgrim Church	E. H. Broadbent
Great Leaders of the Christian Church	Elgin S. Moyer
The Spreading Flame	F. F. Bruce
The Ante-Nicene Christian Library	
Early Christianity outside the Roman Empire	F. C. Burkitt
The Columban Church	J. A. Duke
Nestorian Missionary Enterprise	John Stewart
Wycliffe and the Lollards	J. C. Carrick
William Tyndale	J. F. Mozley
William Tyndale—A Biography	Robert Demans
A History of the Reformation	T. M. Lindsay
The Reformation in England	J. Merle d'Aubigne
The Life and Times of Martin Luther	J. Merle d'Aubigne
Portrait of Calvin	T. H. L. Parker
The Oracles of God	T. H. L. Parker
Tracts and Treatises	John Calvin
The Anabaptist Story	W. R. Estep
A Popular History of the Free Churches	C. Silvester Horne
Journal of George Fox	
George Whitefield's Journals	
The Life of John Wesley	John Telford
John Wesley's Journal	
Lives of Robert and James Haldane	Alexander Haldane
The Tractarian Movement	E. A. Knox
A History of the Plymouth Brethren	W. Blair Neatby
A Narrative of some of the Lord's Dealings with George Muller	
Collected Writings of J. N. Darby	William Kelly
The Diary of an Indian Christian	G. H. Lang
Anthony Norris Groves	G. H. Lang
Edmund Hamer Broadbent, Saint and Pioneer	G. H. Lang
Mukyokai	John Kennedy

INDEX

John Kennedy is a missionary to India. Born in Great Britian he was educated in the University of London and the University of Glasgow. He came to India in 1951. He works largely among the more simple and indigenous groups of Christian believers scattered throughout India. Kennedy presently makes his home in Tamilnadu, India. He is also author of Mukyokai, and Secret of His Purpose.

 SeedSowers

COMFORT AND HEALING

OTHER BOOKS ON CHURCH LIFE

CHRISTIAN LIVING

Please write or call for our current catalog:

SeedSowers
P.O. Box 285
Sargent, GA 30275

800-228-2665
www.seedsower.com

The man who Jesus healed - the paralytic—
He told to pick up his mat and walk,
The very thing that he depended on,
after an encounter with Jesus, was
easily carried away by the one who depended on it